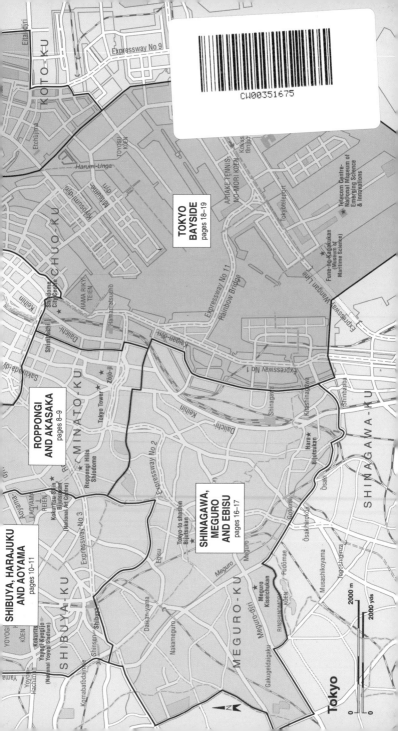

Tokyo

SHIBUYA, HARAJUKU AND AOYAMA
pages 10–11

ROPPONGI AND AKASAKA
pages 8–9

TOKYO BAYSIDE
pages 18–19

SHINAGAWA, MEGURO AND EBISU
pages 16–17

KOTO-KU

CHUO-KU

MINATO-KU

SHIBUYA-KU

MEGURO-KU

SHINAGAWA-KU

Expressway No 9

Eitai-döri

Etchūjima

YŌYŌGI KŌEN

Harumi-Unga

Misaki-döri

Kyöbashi-döri

Shiodome City Center ★
Shimbashi

Daiichi-

Hamamatsuchō

Kaihin

Sakurada-

ARIAKE TENNIS NO-MORI KÕEN

Kokusai-tenjijō

Tokyo Big Sight

Fune-no-Kagakukan (Museum of Maritime Science) ★

Telecom Centre ★
National Museum of Emerging Science & Innovations

Expressway No 11

Rainbow Bridge

Daiba-döri

Expressway Wangan Line

Tokyoteleport

HAMA RIKYŪ TEIEN ★

Zöjö-ji ★

Tokyo Tower ★

Roppongi Hills ★
Shiodome

Kokuritsu Shin Bijutsukan ★
(National Art Centre)

AOYAMA REIEN

Aoyama-döri

Expressway No 3

Expressway No 2

Expressway No 1

Kaihin

Daiichi

Shinagawa

Kaihin

Kita ★
Bijutsukan

Shimbaba

SHINAGAWA-KU

Ōsaki

Tokyo-to shashin Bijutsukan ★

Ebisu

Meguro

Meguro

Gotanda

Ōsaki

Osakihirokoji

Musashikoyama

TogoShinjinza

Meguro Kiseichukan ★

Meguro-döri

RINSHUNOMORI KŌEN

Meguro-döri

Fudōmae

Gakugeidaigaku

Nakameguro

Daikan-yama

Shibuya

Shinsen

Komabatodaimae

Yöyögi Köen

Kokuritsu Yöyögi Kyögijö
(National Yoyogi Stadium)

Hachim...

Yama

2000 m

2000 yds

N

Tokyo

INSIGHT GUIDES

TOKYO
smart guide

APA PUBLICATIONS L
Part of the Langenscheidt Publishing Group

Contents

Areas

Tokyo 4
Imperial Palace, Yurakucho
    and Ginza 6
Roppongi and Akasaka 8
Shibuya, Harajuku
    and Aoyama 10
Shinjuku 12
Ikebukuro and
    Meijirodai 14
Shinagawa, Meguro
    and Ebisu 16
Tokyo Bayside 18
Suidobashi, Ochanomizu,
    Kanda and
    Akihabara 20
Ueno and Yanaka............22
Sumida River, Asakusa,
    Ryogoku and
    East Tokyo 24
Tokyo's Surroundings 26

Below: Meiji Shrine.

A–Z

Architecture 30
Bars 32
Cafés 36
Children 38
Environment 42
Essentials.......................44
Fashion 46
Festivals 50
Film 52
Food and Drink 54
Gay and Lesbian 58
History 60
Hotels 62
Language........................70
Literature 72
Museums
    and Galleries 74

Left: bright lights of the world's largest metropolis.

Atlas

Ikebukuro and
    Meijirodai **134**
Northern Tokyo
    Ueno and Yanaka......**136**
Western Tokyo
    Shinjuku and
    Shibuya **138**
Central Tokyo **140**

*Inside Front Cover:
    City Locator
Inside Back Cover:
    Tokyo Transport*

*Street Index: 142
General Index: 143–4*

Music 82
Nightlife 88
Otaku Culture 90
Pampering 92
Parks and Gardens 96
Restaurants 100
Shopping 108
Sport 112
Temples and Shrines 114
Theatre and Dance........120
Transport 124
Walks and Views 128

Below: making a fashion statement in Akihabara.

Tokyo

A vast concrete, steel and neon sprawl stretching seemingly to infinity, the world's largest megalopolis is a place of superlatives. Until recently steep prices kept it off the beaten track. Now more affordable and welcoming than ever, Tokyo's secrets are beginning to reveal themselves to increasing numbers of visitors. If possible, count yourself among them.

Tokyo Facts and Figures

Population: 12.8 million (35.2 million in the metropolitan area)
Area: 2,168 sq km (837 sq miles)
Number of islands: 27,000
Total GDP: US$1.191 billion
Rail passengers: 22 million per day
Number of international visitors: 4.8 million per year
Average temperature: 16.2°C (61.2°F)
Number of mobile phones: 1,859 per 1,000 households

Ancient and Modern

For all its modernity, Tokyo is a city imbued with the past. Between its postmodernist architecture and elevated expressways lie hundreds of temples, shrines and Buddhist statues. Parts of Tokyo – its formal gardens, remnants of old Edo estates, teahouses, craft shops and schools for the traditional arts – bring the past to life. Meanwhile the skyscrapers, transport system, modern art galleries and hi-tech electronics are bang up to date.

An Eccentric Division

At first glance, the world's largest city, which is built on Japan's largest area of flat land, resembles a haphazard urban sprawl in danger of spinning out of control. Closer examination, reveals a spoke-and-ring system with the Imperial Palace at its centre. The city is made up of 23 wards, which are segmented into districts divided into numbered sections. Individual streets and buildings within their parameters are numbered separately.

The easiest way around Tokyo is to use the subway and the Japan Railways (JR) Yamanote Line. The latter's egg-shaped track takes roughly an hour to complete a full loop around the inner city. Most of Tokyo's main sights, as well as major hotels and nightspots, are located at or near one of its stops.

When to Visit

Spring is ushered in with late March's cherry blossoms. By May, the weather becomes pleasant. June brings *tsuyu* (dew), a rainy season that lasts about a month. Midsummer is hot and humid. Typhoons occur between August and October. The late summer of September is followed by the mellow autumn days of October and November – Tokyoites' favourite time of year. Winter arrives in December with clear blue skies and low humidity. The cold sets in during January and February, although Tokyo only receives occasional snowfalls. March is usually chilly and overcast.

Three times a year almost all of Japan is on holiday. Avoid trips during the New Year (roughly 25 December–4 January), Golden Week (29 April–5 May), and Obon (7 to 10 days centring on 15 August).

Below: neon-lit city streets invite visitors to come out and have fun.

Tokyoites

Visitors to Tokyo are apt to receive the impression of a well-fed, stylishly dressed and orderly society. Tokyo's standard of living remains high, reduced only from the giddy days of the late 1980s. But one segment of the population that has grown in recent years is the homeless. Many of them are elderly or victims of the recession, while more than a few are simply vagrants.

If Tokyoites have one grumble, it is that their city is too crowded. This is particularly true of train stations at peak periods and sightseeing spots during the holiday season. Overcrowding tests Japanese politeness, and may make many Tokyoites appear self-centred.

Tokyo is becoming an increasingly diverse and international metropolis. Farmers from rural areas converge on the city in winter and return for spring planting. Young people are attracted to the city's less restricted lifestyles. Foreign students come to study, expats to fulfil contracts. Travellers make money (by teaching English or working in bars and clubs) and have fun.

Today, the city has 350,000 resident foreigners, with large numbers of Koreans, Chinese, Japanese-Brazilians, Filipinos and some Westerners settling in Tokyo. Although tourists encounter a range of reactions, they are often still treated with honour and accorded a traditionally warm welcome to the city.

Highlights

▲ **The Imperial Palace** Once the world's largest fort, the palace compound is home to the world's oldest monarchy.

▶ **Shibuya** Japanese youth culture begins here amid a din of shopping, dining and nightlife.

▲ **Kamakura** Japan's 13th-century capital is a well-preserved Zen oasis of temples and shrines.

▶ **Foodies' Paradise** Michelin awarding Tokyo the most stars suggests it has the best food: from sushi to fusion to haute cuisine.

▲ **Disney Resort** Tokyo has two of the world's 11 Disney parks.
▶**Tsukiji** The world's largest wholesale fish market handles more than 2,000 tonnes of 450 different types of seafood daily.

Imperial Palace, Yurakucho and Ginza

The atmospheric grounds of the once formidable Imperial Palace compound offer unhurried exploration in the heart of Tokyo. Here, too, are the city's main business districts of Marunouchi and Nihombashi, the elegant shopping nexus of Ginza and the earthier commuter hub of Yurakucho. The area is interspersed with fine museums and glitzy shopping malls, but it also takes in an old theatre devoted to *kabuki* performances, a traditional bathhouse, eateries, cafés and boutiques.

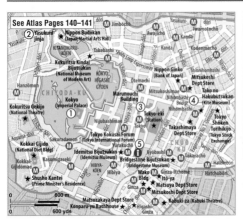

Above: leading up to the Imperial Palace.

Imperial Palace

From the ancient to the ultra-modern, the working class to the super rich, this area spans the extremes that define 21st-century Tokyo. In the middle of this metropolis lies the sprawling **Imperial Palace** ①, home to the world's oldest monarchy. Tokyo's rise began in 1590 when Ieyasu Tokugawa, the future shogun, chose the site as his new headquarters. When the castle was completed in 1640, it was the largest in the world.

To the north and northwest of the palace are several important institutions, including the **National Museum of Modern Art**, the **Japan Martial Arts Hall** ② and the **Yasukuni-jinja Shrine**. The shrine is one of Tokyo's popular cherry-blossom-viewing venues. The **National Theatre**, a centre of traditional Japanese performing arts, stands to the west of the Imperial Palace and the **National Diet Building**, in the area of Nagatacho, is home to government offices and the Prime Minister's Residence.

SEE ALSO ARCHITECTURE, P.30, 31; MUSEUMS AND GALLERIES, P.74; PARKS AND GARDENS, P.96; TEMPLES AND SHRINES, P.114; THEATRE AND DANCE, P.121

> In the 17th century, Edo, as Tokyo was then known, was the world's largest city, with over 1 million people. By 1970, the population of Tokyo had reached 9 million. Today, including the 23 inner wards and the metropolitan area, the figure is said to be 26 million, making Tokyo the world's most densely inhabited capital.

Marunouchi

The Marunouchi business district, from the palace to Tokyo Station, includes the red-brick **Tokyo Station**. Completed in 1914, the station welcomes some 3,000 trains every day.

You may wish to stop in at the soaring **Marunouchi Building** ③, with gourmet

Left: skyscrapers around the Imperial Palace.

glimmer of times past remains in these raucous *yakitori* (barbecued chicken) joints.

Shopping is the overriding diversion in Ginza. **Chuo-dori**, Ginza's main shopping drag, dominates the area known as **Ginza 4-chome**, where people enjoy the pleasures of Gin-bura, or 'strolling in the Ginza'. Two stores dominate: the **Wako Building**, now an elegant shopping edifice, and **Mitsukoshi**, a branch of the famed department store. **Mikimoto Pearls**, the classy **Matsuya** department store, handmade paper specialist **Ito-ya** and a pack of new European designers are further magnets on Chuo-dori.

A few steps beyond the Ginza 4-chome crossing is the **Kabuki Theatre**, a building that, amid Ginza's Fifth Avenue pretensions, looks as if it belongs in Japan.

In the opposite direction along Chuo-dori lies the venerable **Matsuzakaya** department store. Also around Chuo-dori are modern galleries and a pre-Meiji-era bathhouse *(sento)*, the **Konparu-yu Bathhouse**, left from a bygone age.

SEE ALSO SHOPPING, P.109, 111; THEATRE AND DANCE, P.121

food stores, boutiques and restaurants. Near the station, in the Nihombashi disrict, are major department stores, **Takashimaya**, one of Japan's oldest, and **Mitsukoshi**, Tokyo's most luxurious.

On the north bank of the Nihombashi lies the **Nihombashi Bridge** ④ or 'Bridge of Japan', built by Ieyasu as the starting point of the five main roads out of the city. This financial district includes the imposing **Bank of Japan**, the **Tokyo Stock Exchange** and three good museums, the **Bridgestone Museum**, **Idemitsu Museum** and the **Kite Museum**.

SEE ALSO MUSEUMS AND GALLERIES, P.74; SHOPPING, P.109, 110

Yurakucho and Ginza

During the Edo Period, there was little to suggest the elegance and exclusivity that the name Ginza now conjures. Ieyasu established a silver mint *(gin-za)* here in 1612.

In 1872, a European-style quarter was built, with hundreds of fireproof red-brick buildings boasting theatres, cafés, beer halls and shops selling Western goods. By 1894, the district's most famous landmark, the Hattori Clock Tower, later rebuilt as the Wako Building *(see right)*, was already in place. But Ginza was laid to waste in the 1923 Great Kanto Earthquake and during the air raids of 1945.

EXPLORING THE AREA

One of the easiest starting points for exploring Ginza is Yurakucho Station. Close to the station rises the spectacular **Tokyo International Forum** ⑤. Its futuristic 60m-high glass atrium is its visual highlight. An older Yurakucho is south of the station, with cubbyhole restaurants directly under the Yamanote Line. A

Right: shopping in Ginza.

Roppongi and Akasaka

Tokyo's international nightlife centres on Roppongi, an area infamous for its pick-up bars and strip joints. These days, however, the area's carnal pleasures face competition from the upscale Roppongi Hills enclave of offices, luxury housing, upmarket shops, restaurants and museums, and its new rival, the recently completed Tokyo Midtown on the other side of Roppongi Crossing. Down the hill, nearby Akasaka is as busy with office workers by day as it is with restaurant- and bar-goers by night. It also contains an important shrine that draws pregnant women, and the striking Tokyo Broadcasting System Tower and entertainment complex.

Minatoku

In the lower middle of the oval defined by the Yamanote Line is an area favoured by Tokyo's expatriates: **Minato-ku**, a ward made up of Aoyama, Akasaka, Roppongi and Azabu. The area is peppered with embassies and spiced with nightclubs, pubs, music venues and restaurants.

Roppongi Hills

On a hill, **Roppongi**, meaning 'six trees', was once a garrison town for the Meiji gov-ernment. After World War II, the Americans established barracks here, giving it its start as the hub of Tokyo's international nightlife.

Begin exploring at the Rop-pongi Crossing. West along Roppongi-dori is the massive **Roppongi Hills Shiodome** ①, a complex among the brash-est of Tokyo's mini-cities. Its spaceship-like tower, de luxe **Grand Hyatt**, nine-screen cin-ema and over 200 shops form one of the largest develop-ments in Japan.

Every last Thursday and Friday of the month, the **Roppongi Flea Market**, a cornucopia of old bric-a-brac, used kimonos, old aquatint postcards as well as junk, is set up in front of the Roi Building, south of the Roppongi Crossing.

The **Mori Art Museum** in the Mori Tower is a first-rate contemporary gallery. Adja-cent to it, the **Tokyo City View** is an observation deck with a heart-stopping 360-degree view of the city.
SEE ALSO ARCHITECTURE, P.31; FASHION, P.48; HOTELS, P.64; MUSEUMS AND GALLERIES, P.75; SHOPPING, P.110

Tokyo Midtown

Tokyo Midtown ② is about 500m north of Roppongi Hills, with high-end fashion, luxury dining, club **Billboard Live**, the **Ritz Carlton** hotel, extensive gardens and an observation gallery. Within Tokyo Midtown are the **Suntory Museum of Art**, whose exhibits date as far back as the 17th century, and **21_21 Design Sight**, for Japan's foremost designers.
Within walking distance is the **National Art Centre**, arresting for both its architec-ture and its exhibitions. It completes the Art Triangle

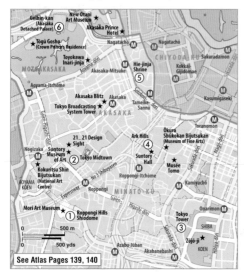

See Atlas Pages 139, 140

8

Left: it's hard to miss the lofty Tokyo Tower.

is the **Tokyo Broadcasting System Tower** and its flying-saucer roof, and one of the city's newest performance venues, **Akasaka Blitz**.

North from the shrine, past Akasaka-Mitsuke subway, you encounter the Benkei-bori moat. Cross the Benkei Bridge to the former estates of aristocrats. The **Grand Prince Hotel Akasaka**, a creation of Kenzo Tange and shaped like a folding fan, is named after one.

The **Hotel New Otani** also lies within the castle's outer moat near Benkei Bridge. Its **New Otani Art Museum** is noted for a small collection of works by European masters.

The museum is near the extensive grounds of the **Akasaka Detached Palace** ⑥, or Geihin-kan. Completed in 1909, the European-style palace hosts visiting heads of state. Between Aoyama-dori and the borders of the palace grounds is the **Toyokawa Inari-jinja Shrine**, while between Akasaka and Akasaka-Mistuke stations is the centre of Akasaka's tamer nightlife.
SEE ALSO FESTIVALS, P.51; HOTELS, P.64; MUSIC, P.85; TEMPLES AND SHRINES, P.115

Roppongi concept, an alternative to the district's nightlife scene.
SEE ALSO ARCHITECTURE, P.31; HOTELS, P.65; MUSEUMS AND GALLERIES, P.75, 76; NIGHTLIFE, P.85;

Shiba

South of the Roppongi Crossing towards **Shiba** is the city's tallest landmark, **Tokyo Tower** ③. Its **Special Observatory** offers exceptional views of Mount Fuji on a clear day. The tower sheds its shabby image at night, when it is illuminated to startling effect. Just behind, in the spacious grounds of Shiba Park, stands the **Zojo-ji Temple**, one of Tokyo's grandest.
SEE ALSO ARCHITECTURE, P.31; TEMPLES AND SHRINES, P.115

Ark Hills

Following Roppongi-dori east from the Roppongi Crossing leads to **Ark Hills** ④, yet another complex of towers, shops, restaurants, offices

and exclusive apartments. The **Japan Foundation Library**, with thousands of books on Japan in English, and the **Suntory Hall** concert venue are within the complex.

Nestled in exclusive residential streets behind Ark Hills is the **Okura Shukokan Museum of Fine Arts**, with fine Asian artefacts, and the **Musée Tomo**, showing a collection of Japanese pottery.
SEE ALSO MUSEUMS AND GALLERIES, P.75; MUSIC, P.83

Akasaka

Following Roppongi-dori north from Ark Hills, a sharp left along Sotobori-dori takes you to **Hie-jinja Shrine** ⑤ on the borders of Akasaka and Nagatacho. Pregnant women come to pray for healthy childbirth, and every two years in June it hosts the great **Sanno Matsuri** festival. Also nearby

Right: cutting-edge art at 21_21 Design Sight.

Shibuya, Harajuku and Aoyama

The epicentre of Japanese youth culture, Shibuya ward is a bustling labyrinth of fashion, entertainment, communications and commerce. It takes in the brassy department stores and discount chains around the station itself, the stately trees and high fashion of Omotesando Boulevard, the funky boutiques and cafés of backstreet Harajuku, and the affluent, sedate district of Aoyama. Shibuya and adjacent Shinjuku are challenging the traditional eastern power centres of Marunouchi and Ginza.

Shibuya

All surrounding avenues slope gently towards **Shibuya Station** ①. It is difficult to imagine that trendy Shibuya was the site of tea plantations on Tokyo's western outskirts only a century ago.

After the 1923 Great Kanto Earthquake, Shibuya, as the site of the terminals for the Inokashira and Toyoko train lines and the Ginza subway line, played a significant role in the growth of the western suburbs. Six railway lines converge on different floors in the station complex.

The plaza in front of the station's north exit and its 'scramble' crossing dominated by huge video screens are the site of an otherworldly concentration of hi-tech advertisements. The streets behind the screens continue the theme, with some of Tokyo's premier fashion and design buildings. Among the shopping venues in Shibuya are **Mark City**, a major complex of lifestyle stores, boutiques and restaurants; **Seibu** department store, with up-to-the-minute fashions; and the Seibu offshoot **Loft**, selling funky household goods. Also nearby is **Parco**, offering designs by world-famous names, and **Tokyu Hands**, specialising in hobby and leisure goods.

Immediately west of the station, the **109 Building** targets the *gyaru* (teenage girl) demographic. Up the **Dogenzaka** slope west of the station is a warren of narrow backstreets offering short-

Above: Tokyu Hands for all kinds of housewares and crafts.

stay rooms in whimsically designed buildings; the area is nicknamed 'Love Hotel Hill'. This tiny but enthralling area has a lively music scene,

---

A popular rendezvous spot at Shibuya Station is a small bronze statue of a dog named Hachiko. Hachiko accompanied his owner to the station each day and waited for his return, until his master died in 1925. Undaunted, Hachiko returned each day to the same spot until he died at age 13.

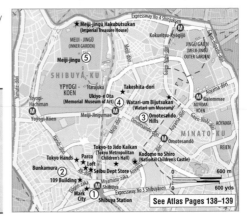

See Atlas Pages 138–139

Left: young shoppers in Harajuku.

Designed in 1924, Harajuku is one of the few Japan Rail stations intact.

The station abuts one of Tokyo's major sights, the **Meiji-jingu Shrine** ⑤, dedicated to the Meiji emperor. It is also one of Tokyo's foremost gathering points for *cosplay* addicts. Across the way is a cluster of striking stadiums erected for the 1964 Tokyo Olympics. SEE ARCHITECTURE, P.30; MUSEUMS AND GALLERIES, P.77; SHOPPING, P.108; TEMPLES AND SHRINES, P.115

Aoyama

A sense of space is apparent along **Aoyama-dori**, which connects Shibuya with Akasaka. The broad avenue leads north from Shibuya Station, and is synonymous with refined shopping, gallery visits and sipping coffee. As you head away from Shibuya, you encounter two child-centric attractions, the **National Children's Castle** and the **Tokyo Metropolitan Chidren's Hall**. The noteworthy avant-garde **Watari-um Museum** and the **Meiji-jingu Shrine Outer Gardens** are further on. SEE ALSO CHILDREN, P.38; MUSEUMS AND GALLERIES, P77; TEMPLES AND SHRINES, P.115

with rock venues like **O-East** and clubs such as **Womb**, with its heavyweight DJs.

Back at the 109 Building, the right fork leads to **Bunkamura** ②, Shibuya's premier cultural centre. The name of this complex means 'Culture Village' in Japanese, and it includes **Bunkamura Orchard Hall** and the **Bunkamura Museum of Art**. SEE ALSO FASHION, P.47; MUSIC, P.83, 86; NIGHTLIFE, P.89; SHOPPING, P.108, 109, 110, 111

Harajuku

One stop north of Shibuya, the youth magnet of **Harajuku** seems to live in the now, but closer scrutiny reveals a coexistence with the traditional. In the 11th century, Harajuku was a well-known post station on the Kamakura Kaido road to the wild northern provinces.

Harajuku is bisected by **Omotesando-dori**, the capital's Champs-Elysées and a

tree-lined boulevard whose chic establishments carry the hallmark of quality. Yet another upscale shopping development is **Omotesando Hills** ③, on the north side.

Among Harajuku's swirl of boutiques and fashion houses are reminders of an older city in the roadside shrines and cultural museums. A short stroll from the intersection of Meiji-dori and Omotesando is the **Ukiyo-e Ota Memorial Museum of Art** ④, with a fine collection of Japanese woodblock prints.

There are more pedestrians towards **Takeshita-dori**. The cheap fashions, cuddly toys, hair salons and fast-food restaurants lure teenagers for a taste of subcultural kitsch. Exiting west out of Takeshita-dori, the mock-Tudor façade of Harajuku Station comes into view.

Right: Omotesando Hills has had a mixed reception.

Shinjuku

Some two million people pass through Shinjuku each day. This unrivalled density makes it a microcosm of all that is Tokyo: soaring high-rises, massive malls, tiny shops, classy boutiques and a maze of entertainment venues. The district is home to infamous Kabuki-cho, Japan's largest red-light district, but just a short stroll away is the imposing Tokyo City Hall and the elegant New National Theatre. While Shinjuku has little historical significance to recommend it, the area is a fertile ground for shopping, dining, people-watching and simply taking in all that is contemporary Japan.

New Lodgings

Shinjuku came into existence because of its position at the junction of two key arteries leading into the city from the west. Shinjuku means 'new lodgings', a reference to a post station built on Koshu Kaido Avenue for horses and travellers on their way to Edo.

Trains first rolled into Shinjuku in 1885. The major factor in its rise, however, was its narrow escape from the 1923 Great Kanto Earthquake. Huge numbers of residents moved in, followed by department stores, theatres and artists' studios. The area's importance made it a target for American bombing, which levelled the entire district on 25 May 1945. Yet by the 1970s it had rebounded.

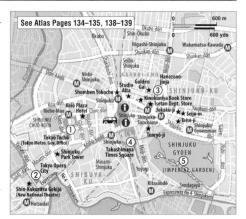

See Atlas Pages 134–135, 138–139

Below: Park Hyatt Tokyo.

Seven railway lines and three subways feed over 2 million passengers through Shinjuku Station every day, making it Tokyo's densest hub.

Western Shinjuku

The first skyscraper here was the **Keio Plaza Hotel**, built in 1971. Many have followed, the most conspicuous being the **Tokyo Metropolitan Government Office** ① (Tocho). Its twin towers are the work of Kenzo Tange, and its 45th-floor observation galleries afford superlative views.

Further west along Koshu Kaido Avenue, the hand of Kenzo Tange surfaces again in the **Shinjuku Park Tower**.

Occupying the top of the Shinjuku Park Tower is the posh **Park Hyatt Tokyo**. On the next block, the **Tokyo Opera City** ② is one of Tokyo's newest culture complexes, housing the **New National Theatre**.

Nestled along the west side of the station, a row of tiny old bars and restaurants cluster along **Shomben**

Japanese trains can be plagued by *chikan*, or gropers. Japanese women often endure the indignity, but recently many train lines have introduced women-only cars during rush hours, usually at the end of the train.

Left: Kabuki-cho hostess bars.

Golden Gai provides a gentle transition into **Kabuki-cho**. In the early post-war years, the plan to rebuild the Kabuki Theatre here was dropped but the name remained. The aspirations of today's Kabuki-cho run to 'pink salons' and 'soap-lands' (read brothels) and extortionate hostess bars.

Take almost any of the narrow roads north from Kabuki-cho and you will soon hit lively **Okubo-dori**. An influx of foreigners – Koreans, Thais and Filipinos among them – have made the area their home. At night, 'ethnic' restaurants release pungent smells into the atmosphere.
SEE ALSO TEMPLES AND SHRINES, P.116

Southern Shinjuku

Facing Shinjuku's south exit is **Takashimaya Times Square** ④. In addition to a department store, the complex includes a branch of **Tokyu Hands**, a Sega virtual reality arcade called **Joypolis**, an even larger Kinokuniya, and an HMV record store.

The **Shinjuku Imperial Garden** ⑤, a short stroll east from Times Square, relieves the concrete oppression of the area, and is a popular spot for cherry-blossom-viewing.
SEE ALSO PARKS AND GARDENS, P.97; SHOPPING, P.109, 111

> Shinjuku-dori becomes a traffic-free zone (*hokoten* or 'pedestrian paradises'), with buskers and all kinds of performers on Sundays.

Yokocho, a narrow passage whose name translates as 'Piss Alley'. You will meet a friendly, if rather offbeat, set of customers here.
SEE ALSO HOTELS, P.66; MUSIC, P.83–4; THEATRE AND DANCE, P.123

Eastern Shinjuku

The east exit of Shinjuki station faces the youth retail edifice, **Studio Alta**, one of Tokyo's best-known rendezvous points, at the head of Shinjuku-dori. The **Kinokuniya Book Store** is on the left as you walk east. Eastern Shinjuku also holds a cluster of department stores, including **Mitsukoshi** and **Isetan**. **Marui** is another of Tokyo's so-called 'fashion buildings'.

This is also the also the centre of Tokyo's vibrant underground gay scene, with its epicentre in **Shinjuku ni-chome**. Over 300 gay bars and clubs are located around its central street, Naka-dori.
SEE ALSO FASHION, P.47; GAY AND LESBIAN, P.58–9; LITERATURE, P.73; SHOPPING, P.108, 109

Northern Shinjuku and Kabuki-cho

The **Hanazono-jinja Shrine** ③, set back from Shinjuku's other main thoroughfare, Yasukuni-dori, is hemmed in by office blocks. Taking the exit behind the shrine leads into the **Golden Gai** area. These few small blocks, crowded with tiny bars and pedestrian alleys, evoke a bygone era. But the spectre of gentrification is evident: several watering holes have been turned into DJ bars.

Right: Tokyo's gay scene is centred on Shinjuku ni-chome.

Ikebukuro and Meijirodai

One of the premier shopping and entertainment centres along the Yamanote Line, Ikebukuro was a relative latecomer to the Tokyo scene. The district only began to expand after the arrival of the railways in the early 20th century, but now, along with Shibuya and Shinjuku, it rounds out the three major hubs that define Tokyo's relentless westward expansion in the wake of the Great Kanto Earthquake and World War II. Leisure choices of a more eclectic nature can be found in this shopping and entertainment area, including a massive Toyota car showroom, a huge mall dubbed 'a city within a city' and a stainless-steel-covered church.

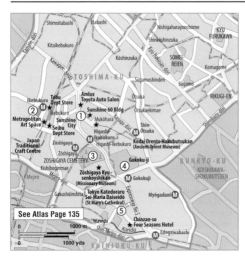

Agricultural Past

The final phase in Ikebukuro's transformation from agricultural hamlet to one of Tokyo's main sub-cities came about through the sibling rivalry of two half-brothers, Yasujiro Tsutsumi and Kaichiro Nezu, respective heads of the Seibu and Tobu commercial groups.

Their first incisions into the area, the Seibu and Tobu train lines, were crowned with two opulent department stores of the same names.

Right: one of the many gyoza food stalls at Gyoza Stadium.

Seibu now dominates the east side, while **Tobu** defends its interests along the western portion of the

tracks. The area also accommodates a **Parco**, a **Mitsukoshi**, and yet another **Tokyu Hands**.
SEE ALSO SHOPPING, P.108, 109, 111

Eastern Ikebukuro

East along **Sunshine 60-dori**, named for the area's tallest skyscraper, takes you to **Amlux Toyota Auto Salon**. This massive five-floor showroom features prototype car designs not seen elsewhere, a 3-D cinema, a virtual driving simulator and a design studio where you can create your own car.

Wandering through **Sunshine City** ①, a self-styled 'city within a city' with four buildings, could take a whole day. One of the world's fastest elevators is in its **Sunshine 60** building to the 60th-

Left: prayer cards at Gokoku-ji Temple.

Higashi-Ikebukuro

At Higashi-Ikebukuro, one stop from Ikebukuro on the Yurakucho Line metro, **Zoshigaya Cemetery** ③, with its graves of famous authors, is a quiet respite from Ikebukuro's crowds. Exit from the east side of the cemetery to the grounds of **Gokoku-ji Temple** ④, an important but surprisingly underrated site that sees few visitors. Another little-visited spot in this older part of the city is **Zoshigaya Missionary Museum**, a lovingly preserved colonial-style house built in 1907 by an American missionary who spent 50 years in Japan.

SEE MUSEUMS AND GALLERIES, P.78; TEMPLES AND SHRINES, P.116

Ikebukuro Station is a veritable labyrinth, with five overhead train tracks and metro lines feeding into it. To add to the confusion, there are over 40 exits. Most arrivals find the first exit at hand and then use the department stores and other cardinal buildings to orient themselves.

---

floor observation gallery. The massive **Sunshine City Prince Hotel** occupies the second building, and the **World Import Mart** the third, where on the 10th floor there is a large planetarium and an aquarium. The **Culture Hall** is another highlight, including the **Sunshine Theatre** and, on the seventh floor, the **Ancient Orient Museum** and its collection of fine pre-Islamic Middle Eastern art.

Half of Sunshine City's **Namco Namja Town** is an indoor food-themed amusement park known as **Gyoza**

Stadium. There are 25 varieties of **gyozas**, Japanese fried dumplings with meat and vegetable fillings, to choose from here.

Further east of Ikebukuro on the Yamanote Line is **Komagome**, with two fine gardens, the **Rikugien Garden** and the **Kyu Furukawa Garden**, a 10-minute walk north of the station.

SEE ALSO HOTELS, P.67; PARKS AND GARDENS, P.97–8

Western Ikebukuro

West of Ikebukuro Station is the **Japan Traditional Craft Centre**, with selections from over 130 different arts and crafts. Two blocks west of Tobu's Metropolitan Plaza is **Metropolitan Art Space** ②, a cultural complex housing concert halls, theatres and exhibition centres. Its 30m-high atrium is a haven of tranquillity among the crowds that swarm Ikebukuro.

SEE ALSO SHOPPING, P.111

Meijirodai

Through the residential backstreets of Mejirodai, you come to **St Mary's Cathedral** ⑤, an early work by Kenzo Tange. The spacious structure is completely covered in stainless steel, an effect intended to symbolise the light of Christ. The design of the cathedral, with a spire as sharp and narrow as a rooster's talon, resembles hands outstretched in prayer.

Across from the cathedral is one of Tokyo's premier hotels, the **Chinzan-so Four Seasons Hotel**, where wedding banquets are held frequently. Interesting, too, is its garden, with pagodas, **rakan** stones, an Inari shrine and sacred trees brought together and arranged in a neat cultural digest. A stone basin, carved for thirsty pilgrims by the wandering monk Mokujiki-shonin, flows with sparkling clear water.

SEE ALSO HOTELS, P.67

15

Shinagawa, Meguro and Ebisu

Comprising the bottom section of the Yamanote Loop Line, this area spans from the older, bayside district of Shinagawa in the south to the uber-trendy reaches of Ebisu and Daikanyama in the north. You can shop in Ebisu's massive all-in-one mall, visit the burial grounds of the 47 samurai, or picnic among trees that were around when Edo was a fishing village. Graceful residential districts abut industrial neighbourhoods, and ambitious new office and retail complexes hide some hidden jewels.

Shinagawa

A key station at the start of the great Tokaido (East Sea Road) that connected Edo with Kyoto, Shinagawa once stood on tidal flats at the edge of the city. The area was founded on fishing, but the main trade soon gave way to services, inns and teahouses catering to travellers. When the feudal system collapsed with the advent of the Meiji era, railways and industry moved in.

Shinagawa and its residential districts of Higashi-Gotanda, Takanawa and Shirokanedai have since come up. Close to Shinagawa Station's west exit is the **Shinagawa Prince Hotel**, while a block north are first-class hotels like **Le Meridien Pacific Tokyo**, all arranged around a lovely garden.

There are several cultural features to what at first appears to be a rather drab district of offices, embassies and hotels. Modern art finds an unusual home in the **Hara Museum of Contemporary Art** ①, a 15-minute walk south of Shinagawa Station.

North of the Hara and a short walk west of Sengakuji

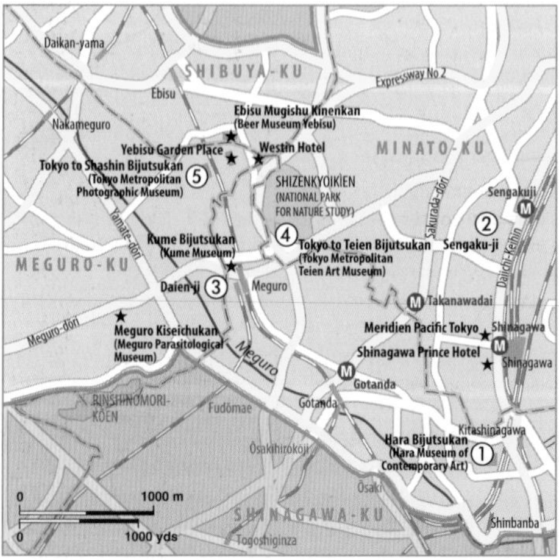

The Happo-en along Meguro-dori, a popular wedding hall, offers a patch of green in crowded Tokyo. Its beautiful Edo Period stroll garden was once part of an estate owned by retainers of Tokugawa shogun.

Station is the **Sengaku-ji Temple** ②. This temple was the setting for one of Edo's best-known true stories. The 18th-century tale tells of the tragic fate of 47 *ronin* ('masterless samurai'), who avenged their lord's ritual suicide but then had to commit suicide themselves.

SEE ALSO HOTELS, P.67; MUSEUMS AND GALLERIES, P.78–9; TEMPLES AND SHRINES, P.116–7

Meguro

The JR Yamanote Line tracks mark the border between Shinagawa and **Meguro** wards. Emerging from Meguro Station, you see the fairy-tale turrets of a medieval European castle, which herald the **Meguro Club Seitei**, one of Tokyo's most flamboyant love hotels. Five minutes southwest of the station, down a steep slope, **Daien-ji Temple** ③ is home to a fabulous creation: 500 lifelike images of a disciple of the Buddha.

Left: Ebisu Garden's large plaza is pretty at dusk.

the superb **Tokyo Metropolitan Photography Museum** ⑤.

SEE HOTELS, P.68; MUSEUMS AND GALLERIES, P.79; SHOPPING, P.110

Daikanyama and Nakameguro

To the north, between Ebisu and Shibuya, are two of the city's most fashionable quarters, **Daikanyama** and **Nakameguro**. Daikanyama is more established, with couture brands such as Tsumori Chisato squeezed between trendy teen stores, chic French restaurants, cafés and wine bars.

The newest starlet among Tokyo's *oshare* (stylish) venues is Nakameguro, one stop down the Tokyu Toyoko Line after Daikan-yama. Here, young entrepreneurs have set up a series of innovative boutiques, alfresco bars and cafes on a tree-lined stretch of the Meguro River.

Just opposite Meguro Station's west exit on the left corner is the **Kume Museum**, housing a collection of paintings by Kume Kuchiro, the first Impressionist Japanese painter, while west and across Shimbashi Bridge is one of the city's strangest institutions, the **Meguro Parasitological Museum**, with a morbid collection of 4,500 parasites. A short distance east of the station is the **National Park for Nature Study**.

At the entrance to the park are signs for **Tokyo Metropolitan Teien Art Museum** ④, the city's finest example of Art Deco architecture.
SEE ALSO MUSEUMS AND GALLERIES, P.79; PARKS AND GARDENS, P.98

Ebisu

One stop up the Yamanote Line from Meguro is **Ebisu**, an old district that has become chic in the last few years.

Ebisu is the name of one of the seven gods of good fortune, but the name of the district derives in fact from the popular Yebisu beer. Ebisu Station, connected by the Yamanote and Hibiya metro lines, was built as a freight depot to transport freshly brewed beer to market.

Redesigned in the late 1990s, the south side of Ebisu now hosts the **Yebisu Garden Place**, a massive shopping, hotel, office and entertainment complex that is filled at weekends with young people and couples enjoying themselves at shops, bars, cafés, a concert hall and the **Westin Hotel Tokyo**.

Befitting its location on the site of the old brewery, the **Beer Museum Yebisu** traces the history of beer around the world. On the eastern side of the plaza is

Right: marking the National Park for Nature Study.

Tokyo Bayside

If the inlets of Tokyo Bay and the bluffs between them were the cradle of old Edo – the site for its great castle and the flatlands that accommodated the bustling merchant classes east of the Sumida River – then the shoreline was the crucible for newer developments. Even today, the area continues to expand. Landfills have been adding new dimensions to Tokyo's urban compression for over 400 years. First, stop at Tsukiji Fish Market at the crack of dawn, before moving on to the artificial beach at Odaiba. There's also Rainbow Bridge, an indoor shopping street with simulated sunsets, and a gigantic Ferris wheel.

Tsukudajima

At the mouth of the Sumida River is a series of islands, which are in fact landfills reclaimed from the bay. The most interesting of these is **Tsukudajima**, meaning 'island of cultivated rice', an allusion to the home of the island's first settlers who came in the early 17th century from Osaka. The island can be reached either by crossing Tsukuda Bridge from Tsukiji, or from Tsukishima Station on the Yurakucho Line. Reminders of the past remain in the narrow alleyways, small fish restaurants and the exquisite Meiji and Taisho Period wooden houses.

Tsukiji

Retracing your steps from Tsukudajima, a short stroll takes you to Tsukiji Station. The Tokyo Bay area has always been a vital point in the fish supply route. At the **Tsukiji Fish Market** ① more than 400 species of seafood

The name Odaiba comes from the cannon emplacements placed in Tokyo Bay in 1853 to defend the city against any attack by Commodore Perry's Black Ships. The remains of two cannons can still be seen.

from all over the world arrive every day. Restaurateurs arrive to buy the day's catch between 7 and 9.30am. It is wonderful to breakfast at one of the sushi restaurants lining the road to the fish market, or at the dozens of makeshift stalls selling bowls of fish soup. Visit this wonderfully atmospheric market while

you can, for it is due to move to a new location.

Exit the main entrance to the market and turn left for the expansive **Hama Rikyu Detached Garden** ②. Another formal garden is a few minutes' walk south of Hama Rikyu, opposite Hamamatsu-cho Station on the Yamanote Line. The **Kyu-Shiba Rikyu**

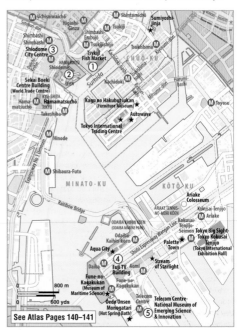

See Atlas Pages 140–141

Left: Stream of Starlight Ferris wheel at Palette Town.

tours of the Telecom Centre's cutting-edge **National Museum of Emerging Science and Innovation**, or Miraikan.

If the past is more appealing, walk over to the extraordinary **Oedo Onsen Monogatari**, a traditional hot-spring bath with outdoor and indoor tubs, a sand bath, mixed healing sauna and a foot-massage bath.

Follow the elevated monorail in the direction of an enormous Ferris wheel called the **Stream of Starlight**. The Ferris wheel is part of **Palette Town**, a shopping complex that includes **Venus Fort**, an indoor street whose 150 shops and cafés are lit by an artificial sky that changes during the day.

Take a short walk along the track to the next chunk of futurism, the **Tokyo Big Sight**. Used as a major trade fair and exhibition space, the vast structure consists of four inverted pyramids standing on a narrow base. Large atriums and an eighth-floor **Observation Bar Lounge** give superb views of the bay.
SEE ALSO CHILDREN, P.39; MUSEUMS AND GALLERIES, P.79; PAMPERING, P.92; SHOPPING, P.110

Garden receives fewer visitors than Hama Rikyu.

Highly visible from the grounds of Hama Rikyu is the futuristic **Shiodome City Centre** ③. Its series of indoor malls and an outdoor piazza at the rear of the complex make for a pleasant place to dine, shop or quaff a cocktail in futuristic surroundings.
SEE PARKS AND GARDENS, P.98; SHOPPING, P.109

Odaiba Island

Hop on the Yurikamome Line at Hinode Station, south of the garden. The ride offers stunning views as it crosses **Rainbow Bridge** to **Odaiba Island**. Odaiba could best be described as a kind of urban laboratory for monumental projects requiring more space than downtown Tokyo can spare.

Alight at Odaiba Kaihinkoen Station, where **Odaiba Marine Park** boasts an artificial beach. There are restaur-

ants and cafés across the road at **Sunset Beach Restaurant Row**, which is part of a themed shopping complex that includes **Joypolis**, a virtual-reality arcade, and **Aqua City**, another centre of mass youth consumption.

Just along is the landmark **Fuji TV Building** ④, yet another Kenzo Tange design. Its two blocks are connected by several sky corridors and girders. Its 32m- diameter, titanium-panelled sphere has a viewing gallery.

You can either walk or take the train on to the Fune-no-Kagakukan station for the **Museum of Maritime Science**, which bears the unmistakable shape of an ocean liner.

The next postmodernist structure on the island is the blue arch of the **Telecom Centre** ⑤. A robot conducts

Right: under a fake sky at Venus Fort.

Suidobashi, Ochanomizu, Kanda and Akihabara

The east–west line of the Kanda River passes across a drained marshland from the districts of Iidabashi and Suidobashi to Kanda, Ochanomizu and Akihabara. This area marks where the traditional High City descends to the Low City. The district harbours isolated gardens and obscure temples as well as the brash Tokyo Dome City sports and entertainment centre and the Akihabara district, world-famous for its hi-tech shops and as a centre of *otaku* culture.

Iidabashi

Easily approached from Iidabashi Station, **Koishikawa Korakuen Garden** is one of the city's finest Edo Period stroll gardens. Another attractive expanse of green, the **Koishikawa Botanical Garden** lies to the north near Hakusan Station.

Exiting the Botanical Garden and turning left, several temples and shrines add to the serenity of the area.

Down the hill from here close to Kasuga Station is an old tree said to be visited by an Inari fox deity. Somehow, locals have kept town planners away from this sacred spot. The tree is a signpost indicating the presence of the **Takuzosu-Inari Shrine**, one of the spookiest spots in the city.
SEE PARKS AND GARDENS, P.98–9; TEMPLES AND SHRINES, P.117

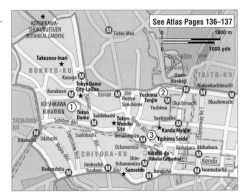

Suidobashi

East of Iidabashi in the **Suidobashi** area is **Tokyo Dome City**, a huge theme park. In addition to rollercoasters, the complex contains the **Tokyo Dome** ①, a venue for rock concerts and baseball games, and **LaQua**, with thrilling water rides and a natural hot spring.

For a more cultural experience, head east from Suidobashi Station along Sotobori-dori, then bear left when you see the signs for **Tokyo Wonder Site**, a facility for up-and-coming artists.
SEE ALSO CHILDREN, P.40; MUSEUMS AND GALLERIES, P.80;

Left: water rides and a natural hot spring at LaQua.

There is a flea market (6am–sunset) on the first Saturday of every month at the Iidabashi Central Plaza Ramla shopping centre next to Iidabashi JR Sobu and Tozai metro stations.

MUSIC, P.87; PAMPERING, P.92; SPORT, P.113

Yushima

The name **Yushima** means 'island of hot water', from the age when water bubbled up from the hills. Even in the early Meiji Period, streams of clear water trickled down to the lowlands. Historically, this was where the trade districts of the Low City people blend into the samurai

Nikolai Cathedral, named after a Russian missionary.

Continuing down Meidai-dori leads to one of Kanda-Jimbocho's main streets, **Yasukuni-dori**. Prominent in its right section is **Sanseido**, a bookshop with a large stock of foreign-language titles, accompanied by many tiny English-language bookshops. A well-loved pastime here is to hang out in the numerous coffee shops busy with students from the nearby universities.
SEE ALSO TEMPLES AND SHRINES, P.117

Akihabara

The eastern edge of this area is **Akihabara**, meaning 'field of autumn leaves', but its English name, 'Electric Town', better captures Akihabara's status as a showcase for Japanese technology.

Located at the intersection between the Yamanote and Sobu lines, Akihabara's postwar black market developed into stalls under the railway tracks selling spare radio parts. Despite its tech pretensions, the district remains close to its roots, with strident shop assistants hawking goods to passers-by. Hundreds of discount stores, ranging from multi-storey affairs to hole-in-the-wall businesses, are shoehorned into a few blocks. At night, the multinational throngs, smoky food stalls and neon billboards evoke street scenes from the 1982 movie *Blade Runner* – a perfect setting for *otaku* pursuits.
SEE OTAKU CULTURE, P.90–1

zones, marking the transition from the High City to the Shitamachi (Low City).

Modern buildings now obscure the historical backdrop, but the slopes from the **Yushima Tenjin Shrine** ②, the city's great shrine of learning, to the flatlands impart a sensation of descending.
SEE ALSO TEMPLES AND SHRINES, P.117

Ochanomizu

One stop east of Suidobashi Station on the Sobu or Chuo lines is the district **Ochanomizu**, which means 'honourable tea water'. Water for the shogun's tea is said to have been drawn from the area's deep wells. Ochanomizu is also long associated with academia and faith, as far back as the Meiji Period when some of today's leading universities, such as Meiji University, were set up here.

In Soto-Kanda is one of Tokyo's most important places of worship, the **Kanda Myojin Shrine**, dedicated to a rebel general who fought against the imperial forces for the oppressed Kantoites. Just across the street from Kanda Myojin is the **Yushima Seido Shrine** ③, a fascinating building and one of the few Confucian centres left in Tokyo. Two blocks south of Hijiri Bridge is the unlikely

Ueno and Yanaka

Heading north from Tokyo Station, one passes through the glare of Akihabara and then comes to Ueno. Occupying a bluff, Ueno Park contains the largest concentration of museums in Japan, easily taking a full day. Further north is the charming old district of Yanaka, a dignified preserve of reclusive artists and literati. These western districts of Taito Ward together with the Tokyo University in neighbouring Bunkyo Ward form Tokyo's traditional bastion of art and learning. Yet the area also includes the earthy street market of Ameyoko and boisterous celebrations that pack Ueno Park with drunken revellers during the cherry-blossom season.

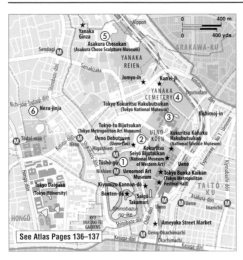

Above: watching the animals at Ueno Zoo.

Around Ueno Park

Eight minutes on the Yamanote Line from Tokyo Station is Ueno Station. The area around the station seems down to earth – this was once the commoners' part of town, the Shitamachi (Low City).

Tucked under the JR railway tracks is **Ameyoko**, one of Tokyo's liveliest street markets. It did a roaring trade in confectionery in the post-war years and also thrived as a black market for American goods. Over 500 shops, many selling foodstuffs, cram into the 400m strip.

The centrepiece of Ueno is **Ueno Park**, a fine place for people-watching. In spring, the park is cherished among Japanese for its many cherry-blossom trees. The park contains **Kiyomizu Kannon Hall**, an imitation of the far grander Kiyomizu-dera Temple in Kyoto. The temple offers a fine view of the freshwater

Shinobazu pond and its island, which is home to the **Benten Hall**, dedicated to Benten, patron of the arts and goddess of beauty.

North of the pond is the **Tosho-gu Shrine** ①, a magnificent structure interesting for its Chinese-style Karamon, a gate decorated with dragons.

North of the shrine, **Ueno Zoo** has over 900 species of wildlife, with some 1,200 animals on view. Children will enjoy the enclosure where they can pet small animals.

On the east side of Ueno Park is a row of institutional-style buildings – the **Tokyo Metropolitan Festival Hall**, whose main attraction is a classical music concert hall, the **National Museum of**

Ueno Zoo is famous for its giant pandas. If you want to see them eat, 3pm is their feeding time. On Fridays, they take a day off from the public.

Left: view of the serene lake in Ueno Park.

Cemetery ④. The graveyard, with its moss-covered tombs, leafy paths and eroded statues, is steeped in the past.

The **Asakura Choso Sculpture Museum** ⑤, exhibiting the work of Fumio Asakura, is close by.

Return to the road that runs from the station, turn left and continue until you see a flight of steps leading to a narrow but lively shopping street. This is **Yanaka Ginza**, full of small restaurants, teashops and traditional crafts stores.

Down the slope is Shinobazu-dori. Just to the right of the traffic lights is **Nezu-jinja Shrine** ⑥, known for its azalea festival in late April, when more than 3,000 bushes bloom. The shrine was rebuilt by Japan's fifth shogun, Tsunayoshi, in 1706. SEE ALSO MUSEUMS AND GALLERIES, P.80

Hongo

Return to Nezu Station for the short, uphill walk to **Hongo**. With cheap eateries, student lodging houses and second-hand bookshops, Hongo is a residential area and an intellectual centre. **Tokyo University** campus is a pleasant place to stroll under the shade of its gingko trees.

Western Art and the **National Science Museum**. On the other side of the park, the **Tokyo Metropolitan Art Museum** ② completes the set of Kunio Maekawa designs in Ueno Park.

For the colossal **Tokyo National Museum** ③, in the park, you need to allow at least half a day. The museum is said to house the world's largest collection of Japanese art and archeology. SEE ALSO CHILDREN, P.40; MUSEUMS AND GALLERIES, P.80, 81; PARKS AND GARDENS, P.99; TEMPLES AND SHRINES, P.118

Yanaka

The backstreets around **Kan'ei-ji Temple**, northwest of the National Museum, provide a back door into Yanaka, one of the best-preserved quarters of Tokyo. This time capsule is populated with wooden houses and shops, private galleries, temples, bathhouses and back alleys.

The town was one of the few old quarters to have come through both the Kanto Earthquake and the fire-bombing of 1945 relatively unscathed. As temple lands were reduced, Yanaka became a fashionable but pleasantly reclusive district for artists, writers, professors and intellectuals.

One of the area's highlights is the **Yanaka**

Right: ancient sculptures in Yanaka Cemetery.

Sumida River, Asakusa, Ryogoku and East Tokyo

The Sumida River forms a north–south strip with a number of sights, most falling within the area of the old Low City to the east of the channel. Once famous for its temples and pleasure quarters, the district now bears few vestiges of its Shitamachi past after the destruction of the Great Kanto Earthquake and World War II. Still, along the river you can find Tokyo's most visited temple complex, a superb garden and a myriad of tiny temples tucked between the modern residential blocks.

See Atlas Page 137

See Atlas Pages 137, 141

Asakusa

In the north is **Asakusa**, which from the mid-1800s until World War II was the centre of all fine things in Tokyo, a nucleus of theatre, literature, cuisine and other sensual delights. By the 1930s, Asakusa was the largest entertainment district in Japan; now it's Shinjuku *(see p.12–13)*.

The heart of old Tokyo is here in this working-class district. Asakusa is a part of the Shitamachi or 'downtown'; a word that also means 'home of the common people'.

The **Asakusa Kannon Temple** ①, also known as Senso-ji, lies to the west of Asakusa station and the Sumida River. Pass beneath the **Kaminarimon** (Thunder Gate), a weathered wooden entrance flanked by statues of meteorological gods, and stroll along **Naka-mise**, an avenue of tiny souvenir shops, to the temple compound.

Step into the main temple grounds through the last grand gate, the **Hozomon** (Treasury Gate). Founded in 628, the Asakusa Kannon Temple was a place where people came to worship but also for the local entertainment.

Also in the compound are the 17th-century **Asakusa-jinja Shrine** ②, one of the few buildings in the complex to have remained intact, the **Five-Storey Pagoda** and one of the temple's best-kept secrets, the **Denbo-in Monastery** ③.

Every year in May, Asakusa holds the dynamic **Sanja Matsuri** festival. The Asakusa Kannon Temple and the roads

Left: Five-Storey Pagoda in Asakusa Temple compound.

housed in an ultra-contemporary building that looks like the bridge of a space ship.
SEE ALSO MUSEUMS AND GALLERIES, P.81; SPORT, P.112

East Tokyo

Further south on the main north–south road of Kiyosumi-dori is the **Kiyosumi Garden**. The garden, which is fed by water from the Sumida River, was first built in 1688 and is a typical **kaiyushiki teien**, or 'pond walk around garden'.

Roughly a kilometre east of the garden, hugging a stretch of Mitsume-dori, in the district of Kiba, the **Tokyo Museum of Contemporary Art** ⑥ is located on land that was once a marsh. This futuristic museum features ambitious shows of Japanese and international artists.

Situated close to Monzen-Nakacho Station on the Tozai Line, the **Tomioka Hachiman-gu-jinja Shrine** used to be the official venue for sumo wrestling. It is the focus of the **Fukagawa Matsuri**, a great traditional festival held every third year in August, drawing huge crowds.
SEE ALSO MUSEUMS AND GALLERIES, P.81; PARKS AND GARDENS, P.99; TEMPLES AND SHRINES, P.119

around it are the heart of this enormous four-day spectacle.
SEE ALSO ARCHITECTURE, P.30; TEMPLES AND SHRINES, P.118

East Bank

Follow the Sumida River south towards Azuma Bridge and, on the east bank, you will see one of the city's most striking structures. Philippe Starck's **Asahi Super Dry Hall** ④, named for the beer, towers above the Shuto Expressway. Aggressively surrealistic, with a giant inverted pyramid base, it is topped with a sculpture resembling a gold flame.

Continue tracking the expressway and you will see trees on your left, against the outer wall of **Kyu Yasuda Garden**. This tiny, peaceful, Edo Period stroll garden was acquired in the 1850s by

Left: shopping along Naka-mise. **Right:** Edo-Tokyo Museum tells the history of the city.

During the Fukagawa Matsuri and Sanja Matsuri festivals, men with full-body tattoos carry the shrines along the streets around the temples.

banker Yasuda Zenjiro, Yoko Ono's grandfather.

Ryogoku

Further south, the district of **Ryogoku** is primarily known for its history of sumo wrestling. Just north of the station is the green roof of the vast **National Sumo Stadium** ⑤, home to Japan's national sport. If you cannot catch a tournament, there is always the small but intriguing **Sumo Museum** here. There are also several sumo stables in the area, where wrestlers work out and live.

Opposite the Sumo Stadium is Ryogoku's enormous **Edo-Tokyo Museum**, a must for anyone interested to learn how the city evolved. It is

Tokyo's Surroundings

Tokyo's concrete can seem unending, but thanks to an efficient rail system, nearby getaways offer easily accessible escapes. Depending on one's fancy, choose from rambunctious Tokyo Disneyland, old-world Kawagoe, the laid-back port town Yokohama, Zen-like Kamakura, majestic Mount Fuji and temple-crammed Nikko. All of these – not to mention broad Pacific beaches and soaring peaks – are within two hours' reach of downtown. It should be remembered, however, that getting out of the city can be challenging – especially at weekends, when it seems as if all of Tokyo has the same idea.

Chiba

Over 100 million people have visited **Tokyo Disneyland** ① since it opened in 1983. It is located in suburban Chiba prefecture to the east of the capital. Next door, the new and very popular **DisneySea** offers attractions designed along aquatic themes.

The nearby **Narita-san Temple** is one of the most important temples in the region, drawing throngs of worshippers during the New Year period.

South of Narita, the hilly **Boso Peninsula** boasts **Mount Nokogiriyama**, with Japan's largest figure of the Buddha, and on the eastern, Pacific coast of Boso, some of the most underrated beaches in the Tokyo area. SEE ALSO CHILDREN, P.41; TEMPLES AND SHRINES, P.119

Kawagoe

A favourite of TV directors looking for nostalgic backdrops, the former castle town of **Kawagoe** ② northwest of Tokyo prospered as a supplier of goods during the Edo Period. It is known as 'Little Edo' due to its main street of well-preserved buildings and ageing temples.

> The ascent to Mount Fuji's summit takes about five to seven hours, so don't attempt the climb unless you are reasonably fit. According to a Japanese saying, there are two kinds of fools: the ones who never climb Mount Fuji and the ones who climb it twice in a lifetime.

Yokohama

West of Tokyo along the Pacific is **Yokohama** ③, one of the greatest international seaports of Asia. Yokohama is Japan's second most populous city, and offers a laid-back port atmosphere.

The Yokohama bay area has been totally revamped by the massive Minato Mirai 21 development. Highlights include majestic sailing ship the **Nippon Maru**, **Yokohama Museum of Art**, and charming old red-brick custom houses that now serve as shops, restaurants and boutiques. No visit to Yoko-

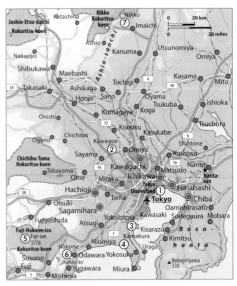

Left: the iconic Mount Fuji.

nearly perfect cone at 3,776m, Fuji-san is said to watch over Japan. Those who wish to see the rising sun from Fuji's peak start in the afternoon and complete the climb once it is dark.

Hakone ⑥ and **Lake Ashino**, a beautiful caldera lake set against the backdrop of Mount Fuji, have long been popular for rest and recreation, with their numerous hot springs. Also in Hakone are the landmark **Fujiya Hotel**, a place where time has stood still, and the **Hakone Open-Air Museum**, a glorious outdoor sculpture garden.

Nikko

No visit to Japan would be complete without a trip to the delightful temple town of **Nikko** ⑦, a treasure house of art and architecture produced during the Tokugawa era. Nikko's fortunes improved when it was chosen in 1617 as the burial place of the first shogun, Ieyasu Tokugawa. The clan built an astonishingly elaborate memorial, the **Toshogu-jinja Shrine**, which was completed in 1636, and nestles atmospherically in a grove of towering cedar trees at the base of a mountain range.

hama would be complete without a meal in **Chinatown** (Chukagai), the largest and best Chinatown in Japan.

Kamakura

Further down the coast from Yokohama, **Kamakura** is flanked by wooded mountains and the blue Pacific. In the 13th century, Kamakura was the de facto political and cultural capital of Japan. The administration built impressive temples, filled with Zen-influenced art.

Kamakura's 65 Buddhist temples and 19 Shinto shrines, interspersed through quiet hills, are swamped with visitors at weekends. Most begin from Kita-Kamakura Station, nearest to the great Zen temples of **Engaku-ji**, **Tokei-ji** and **Kencho-ji**.

Alternatively, take the Enoden Line and drop off at

Hase Station, which is closest to the Daibutsu (Great Buddha), cast in 1252. On the east side of Kamakura Station is the broad boulevard of Wakamiya-dori leading to the **Tsurugaoka Hachiman-gu Shrine**, the physical and spiritual centre of Kamakura.

Mount Fuji and Hakone

It would be hard to find a mountain more praised than **Mount Fuji** ⑤. Sweeping up from the Pacific to form a

Right: Hakone Open-Air Museum, filled with sculptures.

27

A–Z

In the following section Tokyo's attractions and services are organized by theme, under alphabetical headings. Items that link to another theme are cross-referenced. All sights that are plotted on the atlas section at the end of the book are given a page number and grid reference.

Architecture	30
Bars	32
Cafés	36
Children	38
Environment	42
Essentials	44
Fashion	46
Festivals	50
Film	52
Food and Drink	54
Gay and Lesbian	58
History	60
Hotels	62
Language	70
Literature	72
Museums and Galleries	74
Music	82
Nightlife	88
Otaku Culture	90
Pampering	92
Parks and Gardens	96
Restaurants	100
Shopping	108
Sport	112
Temples and Shrines	114
Theatre and Dance	120
Transport	124
Walks and Views	128

Architecture

Contemporary Tokyo is a quilt of streets and neighbourhoods devoid of urban planning. A vast, ugly sprawl punctuated by the occasional cluster of skyscrapers when viewed from afar, Tokyo reveals itself at street level. The quintessentially Japanese attention to detail has resulted in a profusion of new concrete, glass and steel edifices, many of which are in glitzy Omotesando. But residential areas also conceal a blend of modern and historical houses interspersed with tiny gardens, particularly in parts like Yanaka or the backstreets of Harajuku, which have survived wartime bombing and the ravages of post-war development.

Asakusa Kannon Temple
2-3-1 Asakusa, Taito-ku; tel: 3842 0181; station: Asakusa; map p.137 E3
Formally titled Senso-ji, Asakusa Temple is said to be Tokyo's oldest, founded in 628. The current building is a ferro-concrete replica of the 1692 temple, which was destroyed in World War II. Brightly painted Senso-ji, Asakusa-jinja Shrine and Five-Storey Pagoda are the centrepiece of historic Asakusa and continually thronged with visitors who come to pray to Kannon, the Buddhist goddess of mercy, or shop at the many souvenir stands that line the entrance.
SEE ALSO TEMPLES AND SHRINES, P.118

Imperial Palace
Station: Tokyo; map p.140 B3
The seat of the world's longest continuous monarchy, the Imperial Palace, or *Kokyo*, is the eye around which the heart of Tokyo revolves. Hidden behind walls on a spacious plot of land, the palace is a fortified castle built by the shoguns who ruled Japan during the

Edo era. Completed in 1640, it was the largest fort in the world, with 110 entry gates, 30 bridges, 21 watchtowers and 28 armouries. It became the imperial palace when the Shogunate was overthrown in the Meiji Revolution of 1868, and houses the Imperial Residence of the emperor and empress, and various other official buildings. Access is restricted, but one can get close by crossing Nijubashi, one of the massive stone bridges that span the moat around the palace. Grounds are open to the public on 2 January and 23 December.
SEE ALSO PARKS AND GARDENS, P.96

Left: Asakusa Temple.

Meiji-jingu Shrine
1-1 Yoyogi-Kamizono-cho, Shibuya-ku; www.meijijingu.or.jp; 5.40am–5.20pm (spring and autumn), 4am–5pm (summer), 6am–5pm (winter); station: Harajuku; map p.138 B2
Approached through the massive Ichi-no-torii gate made from 1,700-year-old Taiwanese cypress trees, the shrine is an oasis of tranquility set in gardens and forests that are one of central Tokyo's largest green spaces. It is dedicated to the Meiji emperor and empress, and although it dates from only 1920, it is a superb example of Shinto architecture. Its plain cypress pillars, sweeping copper roof and gravel courtyard often host Japanese weddings. During the days following New Year, 3 million people come to pray for good luck.
SEE ALSO TEMPLES AND SHRINES, P.115

National Art Centre
7-22-2 Roppongi, Minato-ku; tel: 5777 8600; www.nact.jp; Wed–Mon 10am–6pm; station: Nogizaka; map p.139 D1

Left: the Imperial Palace.

tower housing the **Mori Art Museum** and the **Grand Hyatt Hotel**. Guided tours start from the Roppongi Hills Tour Counter (2F Mori Tower; tel: 6406 6677).

SEE ALSO FASHION, P.48; HOTELS, P.64; MUSEUMS AND GALLERIES, P.75, SHOPPING, P.110

Tokyo Midtown
www.tokyo-midtown.com; station: Roppongi; map p.140 A2
The equally sumptuous and slightly taller Tokyo Midtown was built in 2007. Containing Tokyo's first **Ritz-Carlton** hotel, **the Suntory Museum of Art**, the **Design Hub** exhibition space and the **Billboard Live** Tokyo supper club, the rectilinear structure was built on the site of the old Self-Defence Forces headquarters with designs by star architects like Tadao Ando.

SEE ALSO HOTELS, P.65; MUSEUMS AND GALLERIES, P.75–6; MUSIC, P.85

Tokyo Tower
4-2-8 Shiba-Kouen, Minato-ku; tel: 3433 5111; observatories open daily 9am–10pm; station: Akabanebashi; map p.140 B1
The Tokyo Tower was built in 1958 as a broadcasting tower. At 333m it is the city's most prominent landmark. A red-and-white steel lattice by day, it transforms into a multicoloured spire by night.

Japanese 'starchitects' like Kenzo Tange, Tadao Ando and Shigeru Ban have increasingly put their imprint on cities the world over. In Tokyo, where buildings like Kenzo Tange's inspired Tokyo City Hall and Shinjuku Park Tower (the location for the film *Lost in Translation*) punctuate the cityscape.

Designed by renowned architect Kisho Kurokawa and completed in 2007, the National Art Centre was hailed as Tokyo's most inspired building of the new millennium. Fronted by a sweeping, multi-storey wave of glass meant to evoke a sea cliff, the NACT is the largest art space in Japan. With no collection of its own, it is given over entirely to large-scale exhibitions.

SEE ALSO MUSEUMS AND GALLERIES, P.75

National Diet Building
1-7-1 Nagatacho, Chiyoda-ku; tel: 3581 3111; www.sangiin. go.jp; Mon–Fri 8am–5pm, except national holidays; station: Nagatacho; map p.140 B2
The centre of Japanese power, *Kokkai-gijido* is a 65m-

tall edifice combining aspects of Western and Japanese architecture in the Kasumigaseki government office district. Completed in 1936 after 18 years of work, the Diet is made of domestic materials. The north wing houses the more powerful House of Representatives and the south wing the House of Councillors. There are free, one-hour guided tours of the House of Councillors.

Roppongi Hills Shiodome
tel: 6406 6677; www.roppongi hills.com; station: Roppongi; map p.140 A1
Roppongi Hills and Tokyo Midtown *(see right)* are two new museum and shopping complexes in the Roppongi entertainment district, symbolising the ambitions of the city's barons to sweep away urban clutter. Built by leading Japanese developer Minoru Mori in 2003, Roppongi Hills is a lavish, 11-hectare glass-and-steel complex with a Virgin Cinema, luxury shopping and residential units topped by a 54-storey spaceship-like

Right: Roppongi Hills.

Bars

Japan is a place where dignified executives and college students alike get staggeringly drunk without any shame. Liberal attitudes towards alcohol contribute to one of the world's highest bar-per-capita ratios. From the local pub *(izakaya)* to 'water-trade' *(mizu shobai)* places, where women and men have their egos tickled by winsome young hosts and hostesses, to trendy DJ bars and expat watering holes, Tokyo caters to the young and old, the rich and poor. All-you-can-drink establishments abound, but Tokyo is also a place for connoisseurs of rarified sake to microbrews and tropical cocktails.

Imperial Palace, Yurakucho and Ginza

The Irish House
2-8-9 Shimbashi, Minato-ku; tel: 3503 4494; Mon–Thur 6pm–2am, Fri 5pm–3am, Sat 5–11.30pm; station: Shimbashi; map p.140 B2
A cheerful place to experience nostalgic Ireland. This pub tries to reconstruct that green, misty mood with its distinctive brews and food.

Mizuho
5-5-8 Ginza, Chuo-ku; tel: 3571 2660; Mon–Sat noon–2.30pm and 5.30–10.30pm, Sun and holidays noon–2.30pm; station: Ginza; map p.141 C2
Tucked into a narrow building along Ginza's West 5th Street, close by the Chanel and Hermès stores, Mizuho specialises in only the Fukumitsuya brand of sake. Try the slightly cloudy variety called *ukiyo* for starters. Also serves food specially created to accompany sake.

Old Imperial Bar
1-1-1 Uchisaiwai-cho, Hibiya, Chiyoda-ku; tel: 3504 1111; www.imperialhotel.co.jp; daily 11.30am–midnight; station: Hibiya; map p.140 C2

A legendary bar in the Imperial Hotel. Part of the design has been preserved from the original Lloyd Wright design that was lost in the 1960s. Famous personalities, from Igor Stravinsky to Tom Wolfe, have patronised this bar.

Roppongi and Akasaka

Agave
B1F Clover Building, 7-15-10 Roppongi, Minato-ku; tel: 3497 0229; daily 6.30pm–2am, (Fri–Sat until 4am); station: Roppongi; map p.139 E1
A Mexican and Latin inclination is evident here in the decor and music, and in the astonishing selection of tequilas. But cocktails like mojitos and daiquiris, and other rum-based concoctions, suggest strong Caribbean leanings.

Fiesta International Karaoke Bar
3F Crest Roppongi-1, 7-9-3 Roppongi, Minato-ku; tel: 5410 3008; www.fiestaroppongi.com; Mon–Sat 7pm–5am; station: Roppongi; map p.139 E1
This legendary English-language karaoke bar with over 10,000 international hits and 70,000 Japanese songs

An evening of bar-hopping in Roppongi or Shinjuku's Kabuki-cho district also means running the unlikely gauntlet of the many African touts who will try to lure you into one of numerous strip joints with enticements of 'titties and beer'. The standard charge is ¥5,000 for one all-you-can-drink hour, with extra fees for 'private dances'.

caters to an international crowd. There's a good sound system and two 50-inch TVs.

Geronimo
2F Yamamuro Building, 7-14-10 Roppongi, Minato-ku; tel: 3478 7449; www.geronimoshotbar.com; Mon–Fri 6pm–6am, Sat–Sun 7pm–6am; station: Roppongi; map p.139 E1
A short stroll from Exit 4 of Roppongi Station, this is a very popular bar for both expats and local business people. Happy hours (6–8pm) are especially crowded when the drinks drop to half-price.

Grace
7-13-7 Roppongi, Minato-ku; tel: 5775 2949; www.grace-roppongi.com; restaurant daily

Mon–Sat 6pm–2am, Sun and holidays 5pm–2am; station: Shibuya; map p.138 B1
East End London-style pub in the heart of the youth Mecca, Shibuya. There are familiar ales and stouts, plus a menu of pub grub, including the usual fish 'n' chips and Aldgate's vegetarian dishes. Huge collection of British rock CDs and English Premier League football matches on TV add to its appeal.

Bar Den Inmu
B2F Aoyama KT Building, 5-50-8 Jingumae, Shibuya-ku; tel: 5766 1616; daily 7pm–5am (Sun and holidays until 2am); station: Omotesando; map p.138 C1
Over-the-top retro '60s bar that recalls the Austin Powers flicks. Low-slung sofas and disco lighting complete the effects at this hang-out for Aoyama fashionistas.

Cozmos Café
1-6-3 Shibuya, Shibuya-ku; tel: 3407 5166; www.cozmos cafe.com; Mon–Sat 6pm–12am (Thur–Sat until 2am); station: Shibuya; map p.138 C1
A sleek, arty expat bar with funky furnishings, run by expat American Ronna Beth Fujisawa. Extremely friendly staff serve glasses of gin

from 5pm, bars and clubs from 8pm; station: Roppongi; map p.139 E1
This five-floor entertainment complex is the hip-hop palace of Roppongi. Drawing a mixed local and international crowd of Snoop Dogg and Beyoncé wannabes, club Midas is the centrepiece. Also on the premises are Ristorante Ruby and Crystal Lounge.

Hotel New Otani Bar
40F Tower 5, 4-1 Kioi-cho, Chiyoda-ku; tel: 3265 1111; www.newotani.co.jp; Mon–Fri 5pm–midnight, Sat–Sun and holidays noon–midnight; station: Akasaka-mitsuke; map p.140 A3
A full range of drinks, including some excellently shaken cocktails, are available here, but the main draw is the night view from the bar stools and tables of Akasaka and the illuminated Rainbow Bridge. There is also a Trader Vic's (tel: 3265 4707) in the hotel.

Paddy Foley's
B1F Roi Building, 5-5-1 Roppongi, Minato-ku; tel: 3423 2250; www.paddyfoleystokyo. com; Mon–Fri 5pm–2am (Fri until 4.30am), Sat 1pm–4.30am,

Sun 1pm–2am; station: Roppongi; map p.139 E1
Because of its Roppongi location, Paddy's can get quite congested even on weekdays. But this is a testament to its fine Guinness and other Irish brews, and its dependable, no-frills British food. This is one of the oldest British pubs in town, and one of the friendliest places to meet locals.

Wall Street
B1F Com Building, 3-11-5 Roppongi, Minato-ku; tel: 3478 7659; www.wstokyo.com; daily 6pm–8am; station: Roppongi; map p.139 E1
As suggested by its name, Wall Street is a big, brash place, where traders go to unwind and ladies look for sugar daddies. Over 200 varieties of drinks are mixed by expert bartenders, while DJs spin a crowd-pleasing house mix.

Shibuya, Harajuku and Aoyama

The Aldgate
B1F World Building, 12-9 Udagawa-cho, Shibuya-ku; tel: 3462 2983; www.the-aldgate.com;

Drinking etiquette in Japan requires that one takes turns pouring beer and other alcoholic beverages for one's partners. Usually the member lowest in the social hierarchy is expected first to pour for his or her superiors. The favour may then be returned.

and vermouth, Bass Pale Ale, and a curious line of coffee cocktails like Tiramisu Martini, which is a mix of espresso, kahlua, vodka and foamed milk. Bands, DJs and even belly dancers might enliven your evening here.

Insomnia Lounge
B1F Inkushin Bldg, 26-5 Udagawa-cho, Shibuya-ku; tel: 3476 2735; station: Shibuya; map p.138 B1

A basement lounge bar completely decorated from its walls to its thick shag carpet in screaming crimson, right on the main drag of Shibuya. If this is not your colour, stay away.

Office
5F, Yamazaki Bldg, 2-7-18 Kita-Aoyama, Minato-ku; tel: 5786 1052; www.transit-web.com; Mon–Sat 7pm–3am; station: Gaienmae; map p.139 D2

Below: media haunt, The Pink Cow in Shibuya.

A big green light in the window is the giveaway to this eccentric bar that, as its name suggests, makes you feel as if you've never left the office. Desks, bookshelves and a copy machine complete the effect.

The Pink Cow
B1F Villa Moderna, 1-3-18 Shibuya, Shibuya-ku; tel: 3406 5597; www.thepinkcow.com; Tue–Sun 5pm until late; station: Shibuya; map p.138 C1

Loved by the art, fashion and media crowd, the Pink Cow is the brainchild of Californian artist-sculptor Traci Consoli. This café-bar offers a good range of wine, beers and cocktails as well as food. Events include poetry readings, jazz concerts, book launches and art exhibitions.

Sasagin
1-32-15 Uehara, Shibuya-ku; tel: 5454 3715; station: Yoyogi-Uehara

Arguably the best sake bar in Tokyo, although only a small number of cognoscenti know it. The warm, sand-coloured, Zen-style interior is the setting for a very choice selection of sweet, dry, sparkling and cloudy sake. The master, Narita-san, speaks English.

Velours
B1F Almost Blue, 6-4-6 Minami-Aoyama, Minato-ku; tel: 5778 4777; Sun–Thur 6pm–2am, Fri–Sat until 4am; station: Omotesando

This glitzy bar/restaurant/nightclub recalls the go-go days of Japan's economic bubble, with marble floors, mirrors and chandeliers. Week nights are for chilling, while weekends draw a more committed, trendy and international clubbing crowd.

Shinjuku

The Dubliners'
2F Shinjuku Lion Kaikan, 3-28-9 Shinjuku, Shinjuku-ku; tel: 3352

6606; www.dubliners.jp/ shinjuku; Mon–Sat noon–1am, Sun and holidays 5pm–midnight; station: Shinjuku

Guinness and other draught beers, a lively after-work international crowd and frequent performances of Celtic music are the draw at this flagship of the highly successful Dubliners' chain.

La Jetée
1-1-8 Kabuki-cho, Shinjuku-ku; tel: 3208 9645; www.lajetee.net; Mon–Sat 7pm–2am; station: Shinjuku; map p.134 C1

Cosy Golden Gai bar patronised by film buffs, including visiting luminaries like Jim Jarmusch and Francis Ford Coppola. Incidentally, the second language here, spoken by the master of the establishment, is French.

New York Bar
52F park Hyatt Hotel, 3-7-1-2 Nishi Shinjuku, Shinjuku-ku; tel: 5323 3458; tokyo.park.hyatt.com; Sun–Wed 5pm–midnight, Thur–Sat 5pm–1am; station: Hatsudai

Located on the upper floors of the luxurious Park Hyatt Hotel in West Shinjuku, this spot is popular because of its night views over Tokyo. The drinks list is impressive and the service impeccable.

Ikebukuro and Meijirodai

Bobby's Bar
3F Milano Building, 1-18-10 Ikebukuro, Toshima-ku; tel: 3980 8875; www.geocities.com/ bobbys2002jp/BAR.html; station: Ikebukuro

A well-known friendly bar patronised by a mix of expats, travellers and Japanese. Drinks are moderately priced.

Shinagawa, Meguro and Ebisu

Bonsai-ya
4F Takara Building, 2-8-9 Nishi-Ebisu, Shibuya-ku; tel: 3464 7377; www.alles.or.jp/~bonsai/

Above: stylish Velours is a glamorous spot, relaxing during the week but busy with clubbers at the weekends.

If the expat haunts of Roppongi or the trendy bars of Shibuya aren't your bag, try your luck at one of Japan's countless *izakaya* (literally 'drinking shops'). Recognisable by the clouds of tobacco smoke pouring out of the doors and the crowd of elbow-to-elbow *sarariman* (salarymen), these plebeian joints serve inexpensive Japanese food to be washed down with beer or cocktails made with cheap *shochu* spirits.

page004.html; Tue–Sun 7pm–2am; station: Hiroo
Located in hip Hiroo, Bonsai-ya offers a serene, Zen-like experience to accompany the lovingly prepared cocktails. Drinkers are surrounded by examples of

Tourists wishing to try their luck with the locals or meet fellow foreigners should head to the meat markets of Roppongi. So-called *roppongi gyaru* (Roppongi girls) are well versed in the ways of Western men, while Japanese men who hope to meet foreign women also frequent these establishments. Caution is advised: Roppongi is an exception to Tokyo's safe image; its dangers made headlines worldwide in 2000 when the body of Englishwoman Lucy Blackman was found, decapitated, on a beach near Tokyo. She had probably been murdered by a Japanese patron of one of Roppongi's many hostess bars where she worked.

Japan's famous miniature tree art.

Chano-ma
6F, 1-22-4 Kami-Meguro, Meguro-ku; tel: 3792 9898; Sun–Thur noon–2am (Fri–Sat until 4am); station: Naka-Meguro
Just around the corner and high above the station in uber-hip Nakameguro (Nakame to the initiated) is Chano-ma, a lounge bar and café for the students and creative types who populate the area. Wash your light food down with expertly mixed cocktails and chai lattes as you lounge on cushions that afford great views out of both sides of the narrow, retrofitted building.

The Footnik
1F Asahi Building, 1-11-2 Ebisu, Shibuya-ku; tel: 5795 0144; www.footnik.net; Mon–Fri 11.30–1am, Sat, Sun and holidays 3pm–1am; station: Ebisu
Low-key British football pub draws expats and Japanese

football fans alike with big-screen TVs. With another location in Osaki (1F ThinkPark, 2-1-1 Osaki, Shinagawa-ku; tel: 5759 1044).

What The Dickens
4F Roob 6 Building, 1-13-3 Ebisu Nishi, Shibuya-ku; tel: 3464 1012; www.whatthedickens.jp; Tue–Sat 5pm–late, Sun 5pm–midnight; station: Ebisu
A Tokyo expat institution, this British pub has a loyal following, who come for its draught beer and traditional English pies, as well as the live music featured on most nights of the week. Its location is rumoured to have formerly been used by Aum Shinrikyo, the terrorist group responsible for the Tokyo subway gas attack.

Xex Daikanyama
La Fuente Daikanyama 3D, 11-1 Sarugakucho, Shibuya-ku; tel: 3476 0065; www.ystable.co.jp/restaurant/xexdaikanyama/bar.html; Mon–Fri 2.30pm–4am, Sat–Sun 11.30am–4am; station: Daikanyama
The spot of choice for the young and moneyed set of trendy Daikanyama, Xex is a stylish restaurant/bar complex with an indoor bar and outdoor, Southeast Asian-themed terrace featuring a reflecting pool.

35

Cafés

Since arriving from the West in the late 19th century, the coffee bean has overtaken the tea leaf as the country's perk of choice. The heart of Japan's coffee culture lies in its old-fashioned *kissaten* and its trendy European-style cafés. *Kissaten*, dark, atmospheric establishments devoted to pricey, gourmet coffee and often jazz, proliferated in the post-war period as Japan rescinded its ban on the 'enemy's beverage'. By the late 1980s there were over 150,000 *kissaten*, but in recent years they have come under attack by generic chains and, over the past few years, chic cafés where the fashionable go to be seen.

Imperial Palace, Yurakucho and Ginza

Café De L'Ambre

8-10-15 Ginza, Chuo-ku;
tel: 3571 1551; Mon–Sat
noon–10pm, Sun and hols
noon–7pm; station: Ginza; map
p.140 C2

When the now 96-year-old Ichiro Sekiguchi launched his 'coffee only' Café De L'Ambre in 1948, Ginza was the centre of the action in Tokyo. A half-century later the café remains the archetypal *kissaten*, with baristas swirling slow streams of water from custom-built kettles over coffee beans aged as old as 30 years into cups of fine china. For this premium product one must of course be prepared to pay premium prices.

Café Paulista

Nagasaki Centre, 8-9-16 Ginza,
Chuo-ku; tel: 3572 6160;
Mon–Sat 8.30am–10pm, Sun
noon–8pm; station: Ginza; map
p.140 C2

This venerable Ginza coffee shop dates back to 1914 and has survived earthquakes and wars. Only the finest coffee beans imported directly from Brazil are used, making

Above: delicious cakes to accompany your coffee.

for one of the most aromatic, atmospheric and affordable brews around.

Roppongi and Akasaka

Arumondo Roppongi

6-1-26 Roppongi, Minato-ku;
tel: 3402 1870; station: Roppongi; map p.139 E1

A Roppongi institution, *Aru-mondo* at Roppongi Crossing is the area's most widely recognised landmark and meeting point. That's perhaps the best that can be said about it; most prefer not to step inside for the chain's mediocre take on coffee and pastries.

Shibuya, Harajuku and Aoyama

Anniversaire Café

3-5-30 Kita-Aoyama, Minato-ku;
tel: 5411 5988; daily 10am–
11.30pm; station: Omotesando;
map p.139 C1

The best European-style pavement café on Omote-sando, which is Tokyo's most successfully European-style boulevard, Anniversaire is a place for lingering and people-watching over well-prepared but costly cups of coffee.

Dragonfly Café

2F, 3-13-14 Minami-Aoyama,
Minato-ku; tel: 5412 7527; Mon–
Thur 11.30am–9pm, Fri–Sat and
holidays until 10pm; station:
Omotesando; map p.139 C1

This is tucked down an alley just off the Omotesando-Aoyama street intersection and up a flight of stairs. An oasis of trendy Tokyo refine-ment, this part-art book-shop, part-café with a lovely, tree-shaded balcony, has hip young servers offering fan-tastic if pricey cappuccinos and chai lattes along with contemporary Japanese light dining. Another branch can be found in the

Left: outdoor tables beside the canal at Canal Café.

fees and cakes, an assortment of English reading material and a lively calendar of exhibitions, poetry readings and the like make Ben's a perennial favourite.

New Dug
B1F, 3-15-12 Shinjuku, Shinjuku-ku; tel: 3341 9339; Mon–Sat noon–2am, Sun noon–midnight; station: Shinjuku; map p.134 B1

Founded in 1967, Dug recalls a time when *kissaten* meant *jazu kissa*. The cool strains of jazz waft out of a cosy, brick basement on the main drag of Yasukuni-dori; live performances are featured at the nearby basement annexe.

Manga *kissa* and their more recent incarnation, the *netto café*, places where people come to read manga and surf the Internet for cheap hourly fees, have recently come under scrutiny due to the phenomenon of 'net café refugees'. This controversial term refers to the thousands of homeless people who now rely on these comfortable establishments, which often have private rooms and showers, as cheap lodgings.

Marunouchi business district (1F, 2-3-2 Marunouchi, Chiyoda-ku; tel: 5220 2503).

Violette
5-63-10 Yoyogi, Shibuya-ku; tel: 5738 3295; Tue–Sat 11.30am–11pm, Sun–Mon 11.30am–10pm; station: Yoyogikouen; map p.138 B1

Lovely, languorous Violette, located next to the greenery of Yoyogi Park, is the kind of establishment you find only in Tokyo: a combined 'café-restaurant and hairmake'. But don't be fooled, the staff pay keen attention to their cappuccinos and cakes – the baked gorgonzola cheese-

cake is to die for – and Violette's lunch sets are nothing short of superb.

Shinjuku
Ben's Café
1-29-21 Takadonobaba, Shinjuku-ku; tel: 3202 2445; www.benscafe.com; Mon–Thur, Sun 11.30am–11.30pm, Fri–Sat 11.30am–12.30am; station: Takadanobaba; map p.134 C3

Although Ben has long since returned to the US, Ben's Café remains one of the most popular expat haunts in the Takadanobaba student district. Lovingly prepared coffee

Below: relax at Violette near Yoyogi Park.

Suidobashi, Ochanomizu, Kanda and Akihabara
Canal Café
1-9 Kagurazaka, Shinjuku-ku; tel: 3260 8068; Mon–Sat 11.30am–11pm, Sun and holidays 11.30am–9.30pm; station: Lidabashi; map p.136 B2

Delightfully situated alongside one of the remaining canals in an older section of the city, Canal Café offers the outdoor café experience minus exhaust fumes. Competently done beverages, reasonably priced Italian cuisine and friendly staff make this a place to remember.

Deco's Dog Café (2-20-14 Ebisu-Nishi, Shibuya-ku; tel: 3461 4551) in Daikanyama was one of the first, but with the rapid growth in dog ownership, 'dog cafés' have now spread across the fashionable parts of Tokyo. At some cafés, it is more common to see owners with their designer pooches decked out in brand names than it is to see parents with children.

Children

Tokyo wouldn't rank high on a list of kid-friendly municipalities. A lack of public parks and playgrounds means families have to turn to private facilities for entertainment. These are many, and for older children, Tokyo itself is like a giant hi-tech theme park in which kids are roller-coastered about on futuristic trains and monorails, greeted by flashing screens at every turn. If the city isn't interesting enough, there's always Disneyland, zoos and aquariums, as well as shopping. Tokyo's safety, its abundant and clean public toilets, and its many pharmacies for infant necessities also recommend it to families.

Imperial Palace, Yurakucho and Ginza

Hakuhinkan Toy Park

8-8-11 Ginza, Chuo-ku; tel: 3571 8008; www.hakuhin kan.co.jp; daily 11am–8pm; station: Shinbashi; map p.140 C2
Located in staid Ginza, Tokyo's top toy store offers kids nine floors of toys and games, with an emphasis on local products such as the trendy Licca-chan and Jenny doll series. Restaurants and a theatre on the top floor for Japanese kids' shows means a trip to Hakuhinkan could occupy the best part of a day.

Pokémon Centre

3-2-5 Nihonbashi, Chuo-ku; tel: 6430 7733; www.pokemon. co.jp/pokecen/tokyo.html; Mon–Fri 11am–8pm, Sat–Sun and holidays 10am–8pm; station: Hamamatsucho; map p.141 D3
Products and merchandise from the ever-popular TV programme: films, games and branded items like Pokémon-themed cell phones, many of which you will find exclusively here. Note that only Japanese-language versions are available.

Shibuya, Harajuku and Aoyoma

Kiddy Land

6-1-9 Jingumae, Shibuya-ku; tel: 3409 3431; www.kiddyland. co.jp; daily 10am–9pm, closed 3rd Thur; station: Omotesando; map p.138 C2
A veritable palace of toys, games, novelties and the latest electronic gadgets aimed at older children (and many adults, too) in the heart of Omotesando.

National Children's Castle

5-53-1 Jingumae, Shibuya-ku; tel: 3797 5666; www.kodo mono-shiro.or.jp; Tue–Fri 12.30–5.30pm, Sat–Sun

Left: teddies at Kiddy Land.

10am–5.30pm; entrance charge; station: Omotesando
A privately run indoor play facility, Kodomo no Shiro with its five floors of jungle gyms, music and arts workshops, rooftop pools and go-karts is a lifesaver for tired Tokyo parents and tourists alike.

Tokyo Metropolitan Children's Hall

1-18-24, Shibuya, Shibuya-ku; tel: 3409 6361; www.fukushi hoken.metro.tokyo.jp/jidou; July–Aug 9am–6.30pm, Sept–June 9am–5pm, closed 2nd and 4th Mon; station: Shibuya; map p.138 C1
Conveniently located in Shibuya, this *jidokan* (indoor play space) is slightly worn but boasts six amusement-filled floors, with art studios, fun mazes, jungle gyms and mini kitchens outfitted with rubberware items suitable for small children.

Ikebukuro and Meijirodai

Toshimaen

3-25-1 Koyama, Nerima-ku; tel: 3990 8800; www.toshi

Left: Tokyo Dome City entertainment complex.

their hands along the backs of starfish and other sea creatures.

Tokyo Bayside

Joypolis
1-6-1 Daiba, Minato-ku; tel: 5500 1801; sega.jp/joypolis/tokyo; daily 10am–10.15pm; entrance charge; station: Odaiba Kaihin Koen

Artificial island Odaiba in Tokyo Bay includes among its postmodern monuments game-maker Sega's Joypolis, one of four around the country. With attractions and rides like Halfpipe Canyon and Aquarena themed around its game software, Joypolis is a three-storey indoor amusement park that makes for a great rainy day alternative for parents at a loss as to how to entertain restless children.

Kidzania
Lalaport Toyosu 3F, Urban Dock, 2-4-9 Toyosu, Koto-ku; tel: 3536 2100 (9am–7pm); www.kidzania.jp; 10am–3pm (1st shift), 4–9pm (2nd shift); entrance charge; station: Toyosu

maen.co.jp; Thur–Sun (hours vary); entrance charge; station: Toshimaen

There is nothing particularly notable about this suburban amusement park except during the summer months, when its outstanding Hydropolis water park provides relief from the heat and humidity. Thirty-one slides are complemented by a wave pool and hot-spring facility.

Shinagawa, Meguro and Ebisu

Akachan Honpo
5F T.O.C. Building, 7-22-17 Nishi-Gotanda, Shinagawa-ku; tel: 3778 0365; www.akachan.jp; daily 10am–6pm, Sat–Sun and hols until 7pm; station: Gotanda

Japan's largest retailer of baby goods, maternity wear and pre-school items has a number of shops in Tokyo known for their reasonable prices and helpful staff. The easiest to reach is in Gotanda on the Yamanote Ring Line.

Fukugawa Edo Museum
1-3-8 Shirakawa, Koto-ku; tel: 3630 8635; www.kcf.or.jp/fukugawa/english.html; daily

9.30am–5pm, closed 2nd and 4th Mon; entrance charge; station: Kiyosumi Shirakawa

Explore a 19th-century Edo neighbourhood of white-walled warehouses and canals in a wonderfully realistic reproduction, including lighting and sound effects. A traditional theatre presents performances of *rakugo* comedy, period music and plays.

Shinagawa Aquarium
3-2-1 Katsushima, Shinagawa-ku; tel: 3762 3433; www.aquarium.gr.jp; Wed–Mon 10am–4.30pm; entrance charge; station: Omori-kaigan

Adjacent to Tokyo Bay is one of the city's best aquariums. A giant Tunnel Water Tank with a walk-through tunnel affords overhead views of stingrays and giant groupers, while other displays feature tropical fish and the marine inhabitants of the bay itself. Also sure to please kids are the Dolphin & Sea Lion Stadium, with shows of charming marine-mammal antics, and a Touching Pool where children can gently slide

Japan's ingenious designers have created not only some of the world's more innovative adult fashions, but some of its most colourful and well-made children's clothes and accessories, too. Two of the best names are the more mainstream Miki House, with its cheerful reds, blues and yellows and its iconic bears, and the offbeat Boofoowoo, with bohemian and rock-influenced lines ranging from Back Alley to Natural Boo. Miki House can be found in department stores, while Boofoowoo has a delightful outlet in the backstreets of Harajuku.

Above: thrills and spills at Tokyo Dome City.

The brainchild of a Mexican entrepreneur, Kidzania is a role-playing theme park where children get to try their hands at more than 80 jobs, including pilot and TV anchor, and get paid in 'Kidzos'. Wildly popular since opening in Tokyo in 2006, Kidzania is most recommended for kids with some understanding of the Japanese language.

Suidobashi, Ochanomizu, Kanda and Akihabara

Tokyo Dome City
1-3-61 Koraku, Bunkyo-ku; tel: 5800 9999; www.tokyo-dome.co.jp; daily 10am–10pm; stations: Suidobashi, Korakuen; map p.136 B2

Still known to locals by its former name Korakuen, Tokyo Dome City is part of the entertainment complex that includes the **Tokyo Dome** stadium and **LaQua** hot spa theme park. Although limited in scope, TDC has a lofty, spokeless Ferris wheel that affords endless views of the city, and a compact but terrifying roller-coaster that slices right through the centre of the wheel and the wall of a building.

SEE MUSIC, P.87; PAMPERING, P.92; SPORT, P.113

Ueno and Yanaka

Ueno Zoo
9-83 Ueno Koen, Taito-ku; tel: 3828 5171; www.tokyo-zoo.net; Tue–Sun 9.30am–5pm; entrance charge; station: Ueno; map p.137 D3

Children who've suffered through a family visit to Ueno's museums can be rewarded with a tour of the granddaddy of Japanese zoos. Its cramped premises pale in comparison to Tama Zoo, but Ueno Zoo (founded in 1882) nonetheless boasts a fine collection of creatures, from pandas to okapis. Kids can also enjoy interacting with sheep and goats at the petting zoo.

Sumida River, Asakusa, Ryogoku and East Tokyo

Asakusa Hanayashiki
2-28-1 Asakusa, Taito-ku; tel: 3842 8780; www.hanaya shiki.net; daily 10am–6pm; entrance charge; station: Asakusa; map p.137 E3

Tokyo's oldest amusement park dates back to 1853, when it opened as a flower park (*hana* means flower), with entertainment and animal exhibits. Now seeing a nostalgia-based return to popularity, Hanayashiki is a good way to conciliate kids who have been dragged along to the historical sites of Asakusa. It's a cosy park, with rides like merry-go-rounds and Ferris wheels most recommended for tots.

Tokyo's Surroundings

Fuji-Q HighLand
5-6-1 Shin-Nishihara, Fujiyoshida-shi, Yamanashi prefecture; tel: 05-5523 2111; www.fuji-q.com; daily 9am–5pm, Sat–Sun and holidays until 8pm; entrance charge; station: Shinjuku, then the Fuji Goko line

About and hour and a half from Tokyo, near scenic Lake Kawaguchi at the foot of Mount Fuji, Fuji-Q contains some of the world's biggest and baddest roller-coasters. Among them are the 79m- Fujiyama and the Dodonpa, which reaches speeds of 172km per hour. Also on location is the world's first **Thomas Land**, themed around the famous children's illustrated train books.

Sanrio Puroland
1-31 Ochiai, Tama-shi; tel: 042-339 1111; www.puroland.co.jp; daily 10am–5pm, Sat–Sun and holidays until 8pm; entrance charge; station: Tama Centre

Left: see giant pandas for real at Ueno Zoo.

For further English resources see www.tokyowithkids.com, an 'interactive online community for English-speaking parents in Tokyo'. The site is packed with practical suggestions such as babysitting services, entertainment options and links to seasonal festivals that would appeal to kids. Some of the information, however, can be out of date.

The young and young-at-heart can meet world-famous Miss Kitty and her friends Keroppi and others at Japan's home-grown version of Disneyland. Among the attractions at this indoor theme park on the outskirts of Tokyo are Kitty's House, the Sanrio Character Boat Ride and The Time Machine of Dreams.

Tama Zoo
7-1-1 Hodokubo, Hino-shi; tel: 042-591 1611; www.tokyo-zoo.net; Thur–Tue 9.30am–5pm; entrance charge; station: Tama Dobutsu Koen

A spacious 'natural habitat' zoo located amid the rolling Tama hills on the outskirts of Tokyo, complete with safari-park rides. The collection here features reticulated giraffes, cheetahs and chimpanzees in the African Garden and Amur tigers, Asiatic elephants and orang-utans in the Asiatic Garden.

Tobu World Square
209-1 Kinugawa Onsen Ohara, Nikko City; tel: 02-8877 1055; www.tobuws.co.jp; daily 9am–5pm (11 Nov–19 Mar until 4pm); entrance charge; station: Kosagoe

Not so far from Nikko's temples, adjacent to the Kinugawa hot-spring resort about a two-hour trip from central Tokyo, Tobu World Square has 42 finely crafted 1:25 scale models of UNESCO World Heritage Sites like Egypt's Pyramids, along with dioramas of famous cities. They are peopled by 140,000 miniature figurines, each a distinct individual, including a few enacting a robbery on the streets of a diminutive New York! Perhaps not worthy of a trip on its own, but an exciting diversion for kids bored by Nikko.

Tokyo Disneyland
1-1 Maihama, Urayasu-shi, Chiba prefecture; www.tokyo disneyresort.co.jp; daily 9am–10pm (schedule changes according to season; check website for details); entrance charge; station: Maihama

Sprawling over a massive, windblown stretch of flats by Tokyo Bay about 30 minutes from downtown are the iconic Disneyland and its sister theme park, DisneySea, which can be experienced only in Tokyo. With its Thunder Mountain ride and the like, Disneyland is a perfect replica of its overseas brethren, while **DisneySea** has offered a slightly more adult-oriented, marine-themed experience since opening in 2001. DisneySea's two dozen or so attractions are grouped around seven 'ports of call', including a Mediterranean Harbour and an Arabian Coast themed around Disney's smash animated film *Aladdin*. As both parks become heinously crowded at weekends and holidays, weekday mornings are the best time to go, especially in the winter. Hardcore Disney-holics may also want to consider staying at one of the excellent nearby Disney-themed resort hotels. Tickets for both parks may be purchased on arrival, or one can buy advance tickets from **Tokyo Disneyland Ticket Centre** (Hibiya Mitsui Building, 1-1-2 Yurakucho, Chiyoda-ku; tel: 3595 1777). One-day tickets restrict entry to either Disneyland or DisneySea, while multi-day tickets allow entry to both parks.

Tokyo Sea Life Park
6-2-3 Rinkai-cho, Edogawa-ku; tel: 3869 5152; www.tokyo-zoo.net; Thur–Tue 9.30am–5pm; entrance charge; station: Kasai Rinkai Koen

A visit to this striking modernist aquarium built on a slab of landfill next to Tokyo Bay can be combined with a day at nearby Disneyland. Pleasantly uncrowded, its main attraction is a giant, round tank inhabited by some 200 tuna.

Right: Tokyo Disneyland.

Environment

The year 2007 was Tokyo's second-hottest year and the first time the city went snowless. For a metropolis whose CO_2 emissions equal those of Sweden, global warming is more than an inconvenient truth. It is a reality felt daily by city dwellers sweltering through 'heat island' summers and ever-warmer winters. A report by the Tokyo Metropolitan government put the average temperature rise in the capital over the course of the 20th century at 3°C. Thanks to the city's rapid development, the number of days over 35°C has gone up to more than 35 a year, compared to the 14 days recorded in 1975.

Air

Tokyo has come a long way in cleaning up its act since the 1970s, when the Kawasaki industrial belt was one of the world's most polluted areas. Strict limits have been placed on industrial emissions, resulting in an air quality that compares favourably for a city of its size.

More recently under maverick right-wing governor Shintaro Ishihara, the Tokyo Metropolitan government has imposed further limits on diesel exhaust, resulting in a noticeable improvement in the capital's air quality. The widespread use of public transport and bicycles also helps Tokyo's air quality.

Nonetheless, Tokyo is still plagued by photochemical smog, particularly in the hot and humid summer typhoon season that follows the cool June rainy season, making spring with its legendary cherry blossoms and autumn with its foliage the most pleasant seasons to visit.

The world's fifth-largest emitter of greenhouse gases, Japan is unlikely to meet its

Above: spring is cherry-blossom time in Japan.

Kyoto Protocol emissions targets, despite being the country where the landmark agreement was signed. With the government's global environmental initiatives getting mixed reviews, some Tokyo citizens and companies are taking matters into their own hands. gConscious, Inc. (11-7 Shinsencho, Shibuya-ku; tel: 5459 4078; gconscious.jp) in Shibuya Ward and Carbon Offset Japan (www.co-j.jp) in Minato Ward offer novel ways for both Tokyoites and visitors who wish to balance the pollution created by their long flights to Japan, to offset their CO_2 emissions.

Under the scheme, participants help Japan reach its reduction target by purchasing offsets to compensate for their own CO_2 emissions. Carbon offsets take the form of the funding of tree-planting projects or hydroelectric power plants. To offset 1 tonne of CO_2 emissions, gConscious charges ¥5,000, and Carbon Offset Japan ¥4,200.

Under the Kyoto Protocol, Japan must cut its emissions by 6 percent from 1990 levels between 2008 and 2012, yet levels have already exceeded those of 1990 by an equal figure. In order to meet this target, the government plans to purchase emissions offsets of 100 million tonnes within five years, leaving plenty of room for travellers to Japan to have a carbon-neutral holiday.

Water

The water quality in Tokyo's 120 rivers, 700 natural springs and Tokyo Bay has improved markedly since the 1970s, thanks to the control of factory discharge and

Left: traffic is heavy and congested in the city.

(kitchen waste, cloth, paper), non-burnables (plastics, metals, ceramics) and recyclables (PET bottles, newspaper, cardboard, batteries).

Earthquakes

A July 2007 earthquake that shook Japan's largest nuclear power plant only a few hundred kilometres from Tokyo was only the latest reminder of the city's vulnerability to a major tremor.

Japan lies above the confluence of four tectonic plates: the Eurasian, North American, Philippine and Pacific. Home to 20% of the world's most powerful earthquakes, the country's most recent massive jolt was the 1995 Great Hanshin Earthquake that took over 5,000 lives.

The Great Kanto Earthquake of 1923 flattened large parts of Tokyo and claimed over 58,000 lives. Even with improved building regulations and techniques it is estimated by the Japanese government that a quake measuring 7.3 on the Richter scale hitting the city at evening rush hour would kill 13,000 inhabitants and cause $US 1 trillion worth of damage. One need only look to the horizon to see Mount Fuji, an active volcano, to be reminded of the precarious state in which Tokyoites have always gone about their lives.

If you are caught in an earthquake first get under a desk to protect your head, then open doors and windows and turn off gas and electricity to prevent fire. Even the largest quakes last for only a minute or so. Try not to panic and then evacuate using the stairs.

gConscious, Inc. and Carbon Offset Japan follow the model established by groups such as Responsibletravel.com in their carbon-offset schemes. Responsibletravel.com estimates that a 19,161-km round trip from London to Tokyo generates 2.8 tonnes of CO_2. The per-passenger cost to offset this amount of CO_2 is calculated to be £20.94.

sewage treatments. Progress stalled in the 1980s, and Tokyo Bay still has high concentrations of nitrogen and phosphorus, and suffers from chronic eutrophication leading to plankton outbreaks. The traveller won't notice any overt signs of water pollution, except in the hot summer months when Tokyo's rivers and Bayside become a bit dank, and the drinking water, sourced from a reservoir in the mountains, is clean and safe.

Waste Management

Tokyo Bay is also home to the euphemistically named Dream Island (Yume no Shima), composed entirely of rubbish. Launched in the 1960s as a solution to Tokyo's mounting waste problem, Yume no Shima has since been covered by topsoil and now hosts a sports park, tropical greenhouse and waste facility. The building of more 'Dream Islands' in Tokyo Bay continues.

In the past few decades, garbage-disposal rules have become increasingly stringent, and tourists should do their part by separating their rubbish into burnables

Below: cycling is a common way of getting around.

43

Essentials

Tokyo's profile as an international city of business and culture puts it on par with New York and London, but don't expect most people to speak English. The single greatest hurdle most visitors will encounter is the language barrier. Happily, the few English-speakers around will often go out of their way to help bewildered visitors. Learning how to say 'please' *(onegaishimasu)*, 'thank you' *(arigato)* and 'excuse me' *(sumimasen)* will also go a long way in easing your visit. Besides the language problem, tourists can expect smooth, timely transport, fastidious service and remarkably safe and clean streets.

Addresses

Japanese addresses start with the area and work down to the street. The typical order is: prefecture *(to)*, ward *(ku)* and city (depending on name); then district, city block and building, by number. For example, Tokyo Central Post Office is: Tokyo-to, Chiyoda-ku, Marunouchi 2-7-2. This guide gives addresses Western-style, beginning with the building number.

Embassies and Consulates

Australia: 2-1-14 Mita, Minato-ku; tel: 5232 4111
Canada: 7-3-38 Akasaka, Minato-ku; tel: 5412 6200
UK: 1 Ichiban-cho, Chiyoda-ku; tel: 3265 5511
US: 1-10-5 Akasaka, Minato-ku; tel: 3224 5000

Emergency Numbers

Police: 110; **Fire/ambulance:** 119; **Hospital info:** 5285 8181; **The Japan Helpline:** 0120-461-997

Entry and Customs

All visitors need a passport, but nationals of most Western countries do not need a visa for a short visit. On arrival, visitors are usually granted temporary visitor status, good for 90 days. Anyone wishing to extend their stay should apply at the **Tokyo Immigration Bureau** (Immigration Information Centre, tel: 5796 7112). Non-residents entering the country are given a duty-free allowance of 200 cigarettes; three 760ml bottles of alcohol; 2oz of perfume; and gifts whose total value is less than ¥200,000. (For more information: Tokyo Customs Headquarters, tel: 3529 0700.)

Health

No vaccinations are required to enter Japan. Tap water is safe, and medical care is good. Hospitals with English-speaking staff: Japanese Red Cross Medical Centre (Nihon Sekijujisha Iryo Centre); tel: 3400 1311; St Luke's International Hospital (Seiroka Byoin), tel: 3541 5151; Tokyo British Clinic, tel: 5458 6099; and Tokyo Medical and Surgical Clinic, tel: 3436 3028.

Money

The Japanese yen is available in 1-, 5-, 10-, 50-, 100- and 500-yen coins and 1,000, 2,000, 5,000 and 10,000 bank-notes. Money can be exchanged at banks and authorised exchangers. Many shops do not accept credit cards, so carry a reasonable amount of cash. Major credit cards and cash cards linked to Cirrus, PLUS, Maestro and Visa Electron networks can be used at post office and Seven Bank (located at 7-Eleven stores) ATMs. Traveller's cheques are accepted by leading banks, hotels and stores. Tipping is not practised in Japan.

Postal Services

Postal services are efficient but expensive. Local post offices open Mon–Fri 9am–5pm; some Sat mornings. Larger central post offices open Mon–Fri 9am–7pm and

Tokyo (like the rest of Japan) is +9 hours GMT, +14 hours EST (New York) and +17 PST (Los Angeles). Japan does not have summer daylight-saving time.

in Japan. If calling Tokyo from overseas, dial +81-3 before the local number. To make overseas calls from Tokyo, first dial the access code of one of the international call-service providers below, then the country code and the number: KDDI 010, NTT 0033, IDC 0061.

MOBILE PHONES

NTT DoCoMo and SoftBank Mobile allow visitors to use their own numbers and SIM cards with their 3G services, though you will need to rent or buy a phone in Japan. Alternatively, rent a phone with a Japan-based number at Narita Airport to use during your stay. Most mobile phone numbers begin with 090.

Tourist Offices

The **Tourist Information Centers** (TIC) run by the **Japan National Tourist Organisation** (JNTO), provide information and can organise hotel reservations. **Japan National Tourist Organisation (JNTO)** 2-10-1 Yurakucho, Chiyoda-ku, tel: 3216 1903; www.jnto.go.jp **Tourist Information Centre (TIC)** 2-10-1 Kotsukaikan Building, 10F, Yurakucho, Chiyoda-ku, tel: 3201 3331.

Sat 9am–noon. (Tel: 3241 4891 for Tokyo postal information.)

The Tokyo Central Post Office (2-7-2 Marunouchi, Chiyoda-ku, tel: 3284 9539, accepts mail round the clock.

For 24-hour, 365-day international mail services, Tokyo International Post Office (Kokusai Yubin-kyoku) is just north of Tokyo Station at 2-3-3 Otemachi, Chiyoda-ku.

EXPRESS MAIL/COURIER

Larger post offices offer express mail services. International parcel post may not exceed 20kg per package. For heavier packages use a commercial courier service. **Federal Express:** tel: 053-298 1919; www.fedex.com. **UPS Yamato Express:** tel: 0120-271 040; www.ups.com.

Telephones

The main domestic carrier is **Nippon Telegraph and Telephone** (NTT). Local calls start from ¥10 per minute.

Public phones take telephone cards, though some may accept ¥10 and ¥100 coins. Each carrier issues its own prepaid cards: NTT and

DDI (domestic) and KDD (international). The cards can only be used at the appropriate telephone booth. For Directory Assistance:
• NTT Information Service: tel: 0120-505506. In English.
• Local directory assistance: tel: 104. Ask for an English-speaking operator.
• International directory assistance (English-speaking) tel: 0051.
Note: Local numbers beginning with 0120, 0088 or 0053 are toll-free calls that can be dialled only within Japan. Long-distance calls (over 60km) are cheaper after peak hours. If calling from one province to another, dial the area code first (with the zero). When calling within Tokyo, don't dial the city's area code (03). Area codes: Tokyo 03, Yokohama 045, Narita 0476.

INTERNATIONAL CALLS
• International dialling code for Japan is 81.
• For the international operator dial 0051 from anywhere

Fashion

Compared to fashion capitals like London, Paris and New York, Tokyo's signature styles may not be readily apparent. This is partly due to the frenetic pace of its trend cycles. In the past few years, the Western media have become enthralled with Tokyo youngsters in bizarre attire strolling around bustling streets and funky boutiques. This stereotypical scene can be found in Harajuku, but it's just a part of the whole picture. The Japanese take fashion seriously, and the city offers shopping opportunities to satisfy a wide range of demand, from eccentric street labels to design-forward and couture brands.

Japanese Designers

Comme des Garçons

5-2-1 Minami-Aoyama, Minato-ku; tel: 3406 3951; daily 11am–8pm; station: Omotesando; map p.139 C1

Rei Kawakubo, creator of the brand, is one of the pioneers who contributed to the rise of internationally renowned Japanese designers since her controversial Paris collection debut in 1981. Kawakubo's avant-garde yet classic suits and formal wear have inspired many young local and international designers, and claim hardcore fans from across the globe.

Dress Camp

5-5-1 Minami-Aoyama, Minato-ku; tel: 5778 3717; www.dress camp.org; daily 11am–8pm; station: Omotesando; map p.139 C1

Dress Camp's Toshikazu Iwaya is a graduate of the prestigious Bunka Fashion Institute, where many of Japan's groundbreaking designers are trained. Iwaya's extravagant style was a huge success at the autumn 2007 Japan Fashion Week; like his predecessors, he is aiming for international success.

Issey Miyake

3-18-11 Minami-Aoyama, Minato-ku; tel: 3423 1407; www.isseymiyake.co.jp; daily 11am–8pm; station: Omotesando; map p.139 C1

Without any doubt one of the most famous Japanese designers in history, Hiroshima-born Miyake's bold and experimental approaches to clothing fuse beauty with technology and functionality. The Tokyo flagship store offers many limited items that cannot be found anywhere else in the world.

Tsumori Chisato

4-21-25 Minami-Aoyama, Minato-ku; tel: 3423 5170;

Left: inspirational Comme des Garcons collection.

www.a-net.com; daily 11am–8pm; station: Omotesando; map p.139 C1

Tsumori started her career as fashion tycoon Issey Miyake's protégé, and eventually established her fame with distinctively feminine, bohemian styles, building a strong fan base in Europe and North America. Tsumori also has lines of loungewear, bags and accessories, and is extremely popular among Japanese girls in their late teens and twenties.

Yohji Yamamoto

5-3-6 Minami-Aoyama, Minato-ku; tel: 3409 6006; www.yohji yamamoto.co.jp; daily 11am–8pm; station: Omotesando; map p.139 C1

Yamamoto's conceptual style, often characterised by oversized silhouettes and dark solid colours, earned him the status of top-notch Japanese designer along with his comrades Issey Miyake and Rei Kawakubo in the 1980s. In recent years, Yamamoto's expanded his

HANEL

Left: couture as well as high fashion is available in Tokyo.

Shinjuku; map p.134 C1
This complex has been one of the most trusted department stores in Tokyo for decades. In terms of its size, service and trend-savvy selections it is always reliable. The men's tower is a metrosexual heaven, boasting Shinjuku's largest and finest collections of both Japanese and foreign brands. There is a foreign customer service desk for language assistance and tax-refund procedures, located on the sixth floor of the main building.

SEE ALSO SHOPPING, P.109

Laforet Harajuku
1-11-6 Jingumae, Shibuya-ku; tel: 3475 0411; www.laforet. ne.jp; daily 11am–8pm; station: Harajuku; map p.138 C2
Fashion-obsessed teenagers all dressed in their best outfits travel from all over the country to visit Laforet, on the corner of Omotesando and Meiji-dori. This is where any sort of eccentric and excessive style is considered normal. The multilevel complex is home to many of the Harajuku brands that fashion people in the West are talking about.

Marui
2-7-1 Yurakucho, Chiyoda-ku; tel: 3212 0101; www.0101.co.jp;

Looking for fashion news in English? Bilingual webzine Arica (www.arica.jp) is a new kid on the block, but has already become a trusted resource for keeping up on the latest buzz in the land of the rising sun. In addition to its stylish layout and insightful content, Arica offers a superb online shopping experience, with orders from local designers shipped worldwide.

---

visions outside the couture world, launching the casual Y-3 collection in 2003. He's also designed costumes for some of director Takeshi Kitano's acclaimed film productions.

Malls and Department Stores

109 Building
2-29-1 Dogenzaka, Shibuya-ku; tel: 3477 5111; www.shibuya 109.jp; daily 10am–9pm; station: Shibuya; map p.138 B1

Right: classic fashions as well as cutting-edge styles.
Far right: Laforet draws fashion-crazed teenagers.

This landmark in the heart of Shibuya embodies the trends and culture of the teenage girls who play a leading role in Japanese consumer culture. If you are looking for the newest styles in relatively low price ranges, this Forever 21-like store-cum-mall is the place to hit. Even if you don't fit into the targeted demographic, just walking through the countless boutiques filled with young fashionistas and echoing with loud dance music is quite an adventure.

Isetan
3-14-1 Shinjuku, Shinjuku-ku; tel: 3352-1111; www.isetan. co.jp; daily 10am–8pm; station:

F

Above: the Hysteric Glamour rock chick look in Roppongi Hills.

Tokyo may be expensive, but low-budget travellers can still earn the title of fashionista. Indeed, many fashion students and the like gather at Yoyogi Park every Sunday to score vintage outfits at its famous flea market, which can easily be purchased for 1,000 yen or less. Remember: it's not what you wear, it's how you wear it.

Mon–Fri 11.30am–9pm, Sat 11am–8.30pm, Sun and holidays 11am–8pm; station: Yurakucho; map p.138 B4
This national-chain department store caters to trend-savvy people in their 20s and early 30s who prefer more clean-cut and mass-marketed styles than Laforet and 109 Building (see p.47). The newly opened Yurakucho branch at Itocea complex especially draws the area's young professionals seeking a head-to-toe smart look for business and social occasions. (Also at: 1-21-3 Jinnan, Shibuya-ku; tel: 3464 0101; Mon–Sat 11.30am–9pm, Sun and hols 11.30am–8.30pm; station: Shibuya)

Roppongi Hills
6-10-1 Roppongi, Minato-ku; tel: 6406 6000; www.roppongihills.com; daily 11am–9pm; station: Roppongi; map p.140 A1
Although it was slightly overshadowed by the launch of the Tokyo Midtown complex in 2007, this Roppongi city within a city contains all the upscale shops and leading Japanese brands that you would expect, including a large outlet of the rock 'n' roll-flavoured Hysteric Glamour brand.

Casual and Street Fashion

A Bathing Ape
Manivia 1F, 5-5-8 Minami-Aoyama, Minato-ku; tel: 5464 0335; www.bape.com; daily 11am–7pm; station: Omotesando
Multi-talented Tomoaki 'Nigo' Nagao's urban hip-hop clothing line has evolved into a brand that represents 'cool Japan', with colourful and retro-patterned hoodies and baseball caps. Patronised by Japanese B-boys and American hip-hop stars (Kanye West is a friend) alike. (Also at: Rice Building, 13-7 Udagawacho, Shibuya-ku; tel: 6415 6041; daily 11am–7pm; station: Shibuya)

Beams
1-15-1 Jinnan, Shibuya; tel: 3780 5500; www.beams.co.jp; daily 11am–8pm; station: Shibuya; map p.138 B1
This mega-chain boutique introduces the newest and hippest styles, mostly focused on home-grown designers, to a Japanese college age through young professional crowd. Beams often collaborates with designers and artists to create limited-collection items; anything from the boutique featured in a fashion magazine becomes an instant hit among the targeted demographic. (Also at: 3-25-12 Jingumae, Shibuya-ku; tel: 3646 5851; daily 11am–8pm; station: Harajuku)

Loveless
3-17-11 Minami-Aoyama, Minato-ku; tel: 3401 2301;

Right: a city within a city at the Tokyo Midtown complex.

Mon–Sat noon–9pm, Sun and holidays noon–8pm; station: Omotesando; map p.139 C1
This multilevel underground boutique is known for its eccentric and inspirational window displays facing glamorous Omotesando in the Harajuku/Aoyama district. The basement floor is filled with tons of great up-and-coming Japanese brands that are not yet widely known to the public. It's also a popular shopping spot among stylists and other folks in the fashion industry.

Restir
Tokyo Midtown Galleria D-0102, 9-7-4 Akasaka, Minato-ku; tel: 5413 3708; www.restir.com; Mon–Sun 11am–9pm; station: Roppongi; map p.139 E1
One of Tokyo's finest boutiques, produced by French interior designer Laur Meyrieux, is fully equipped with VIP dressing rooms,

48

making it a perfect destination for those looking for an extravagant shopping experience or just for inspiration. This 'ultra closet' for both top-notch local and import attire is like walking through a posh nightclub or a strobe-lit, electronica-thumping catwalk show. (Also at: Yayoi Building, 4-2-2 Ginza, Chuo-ku; tel: 5159 0595; Mon–Sat 11.30am–8.30pm, Sun and holidays 11am–8pm; station: Ginza; map p.137 D3)

Uniqlo UT Store

6-10-8 Jingumae, Shibuya-ku; tel: 5468-7313; http://ut.uniqlo.com; daily 11am–9pm; station: Harajuku; map p.138 B1

Japan's answer to the Gap and H&M became a phenomenon with low-priced fleece jackets in the late 90s. Recently it has remodelled its flagship Harajuku store in 2007 and launched its innovative new UT line. In collaboration with up-and-coming artists, this paradise for Tokyo's budget shoppers is taking T-shirts to the next level, with plans to introduce 1,000 designs for graphic Ts each year, packed in futuristic plastic bottles and sold for ¥1,500 each.

Accessories

ABC Mart

27-6 Udagawa-cho, Shibuya-ku; tel: 5784 4361; www.abc-mart.com; daily 11am–9pm; station: Shibuya; map p.138 B1

Mega-chain shoe store in the middle of Shibuya's bustling Center-gai street is a heaven for shoe-lovers on a low budget. They've got everything from brand-name running shoes to leather loafers in all sizes and styles. If you are serious about getting the best deal, try the special sale

section, which usually occupies the entrance area. (Also at: 4-7-1 Ueno, Taito-ku; tel: 3832 0686; daily 10am–8pm; station: Ueno; map p.137 D3)

CA4LA

6-29-4 Jingumae, Shibuya-ku; tel: 3406 8271; www.ca4la.com; daily 11am–8pm; station: Harajuku; map p.138 C2

If you are looking for trendy headgear, this is the place to get the most wicked and newest hats in the city. The store is always crowded with funky Japanese youth looking for unique but still affordable headwear ranging from simple beanies to decorative trilby hats. (Also at: 2F Isetan, 3-14-1 Shinjuku, Shinjuku-ku; tel: 3351 8138; daily 11am–8pm; station: Shinjuku; map p.134 C1)

Daichu

16-13 Udagawa-cho, Shibuya-ku; tel: 3463 8756; www.daichu-co.co.jp; daily 11am–9pm; Shibuya; map p.138 B1

Bargain-hunters looking for something trendy but dirt-cheap should head to Daichu. Located in the heart of Shibuya's Spain-zaka, this store is filled with teenagers trying to score a cute dress, ballet flats and chandelier earrings, all for under 1,000 yen. Don't expect great quality here, though. (Also at: 3-16-26 Roppongi, Minato-ku; tel: 3584

0725; daily noon–10.30pm; station: Roppongi; map p.139 E1)

Queen's Himiko

3-5-6 Ginza, Chuo-ku; tel: 5524 3334; www.himiko.co.jp; Mon–Sun 11am–8pm; station: Ginza; map p.141 C2

Tokyo's status as one of the world's most fashion-forward cities makes it a paradise for footwear fanatics. But as any foreign woman in Tokyo knows, it can be extremely hard to find the right size. The Ginza branch of Himiko though offers ladies shoes up to 27cm. The shop has a range of designs suitable for both casual and formal wear at relatively affordable prices.

Titicaca

2-26-2 Kitazawa, Setagaya-ku; tel: 3465 7432; www.titicaca.jp; daily 11am–8pm; station: Shimokitazawa

Japan's favourite chain boutique specialising in clothes and accessories from Africa, South America and Asia. The vast array of cheap jewellery and costumes sold at the shop play a huge role in completing the earthy 'Shimokita' style, which often consists of vintage Ts and jeans with obscure jewels and scarves rolled up on the head. (Also at: 6-20 Udagawacho, Shibuya-ku; tel: 3476-3449; daily 11am–8pm; station: Shibuya; map p.138 B1).

Right: watching Tokyo's fashion tribes gives plenty of inspiration.

Festivals

Matsuri (festivals) have always been integral to the life of Tokyo, and hardly a week goes by without a celebration. Linked to the seasons and to Shinto religious beliefs, their function is not only to give thanks, petition the gods for favours and promote community solidarity; they also celebrate the sheer joy of life. There are also local festivals, especially in the summer, celebrating local gods that often seem more like community street parties, with plenty of food and drink. Something extraordinary happens to the decorous Japanese when they attend festivals and their usual inhibitions vanish.

Public Holidays

1 Jan: New Year's Day; **2nd Monday of Jan:** Coming-of-Age Day; **11 Feb:** National Foundation Day; **20 or 21 Mar:** Vernal Equinox Day; **29 Apr:** Showa Day; **3 May:** Constitution Memorial Day; **4 May:** Greenery Day; **5 May:** Children's Day; **3rd Monday of July:** Marine Day; **3rd Monday of Sept:** Respect for the Aged Day; **23 or 24 Sept:** Autumnal Equinox Day; **2nd Monday of Oct:** Health-Sports Day; **3 Nov:** Culture Day; **23 Nov:** Labour Thanksgiving Day; **23 Dec:** Emperor's Birthday.

Festivals and Events

JANUARY/FEBRUARY

New Year's Day (Ganjitsu): A national holiday. People don traditional attire to visit temples and shrines to make wishes for the New Year.

Coming-of-Age Day: Girls aged 20 put on their best kimono for an 'adulthood' ceremony at a shrine.

Setsubun: On 3 Feb, this is a ceremony to purify the home. Beans are thrown out of the windows and doors to shouts

Above: kimonos at a procession for Cherry-Blossom-Viewing.

of 'Oni wa soto' (Devils, go out), followed by, 'Fuku wa uchi' (Good luck, come in).

Valentine's Day: On 14 Feb, it is the custom for women to give men gifts of chocolate.

Plum Viewing: In mid-Feb view floral displays and tea ceremonies at Yushima Tenjin Shrine.

MARCH

Girls' Day: 3 Mar is Hina Matsuri, when hina dolls representing imperial court figures are displayed.

White Day: On the 14th, men give women chocolates in

The traditional matsuri spirit has translated itself into a growing number of contemporary events. Among them are the Fuji Rock Festival (see Music, p.85), a three-day party on the last weekend of July, the Asakusa Samba Carnival at the end of August, and the endless round of ethnic festivals that celebrate Tokyo's growing diversity each summer weekend at Yoyogi Park.

return for what they received on Valentine's Day.

Golden Dragon Dance: Held on the 18th in the precincts of Asakusa Kannon Temple.

APRIL/MAY

Cherry-Blossom-Viewing: From early to mid-Apr is Ohanami, an important spring rite. Japanese picnic, drink sake and sing under the pink cherry blossoms. Some famous spots are Aoyama Cemetery, Chidorigafuchi Park, Ueno Park and Yasukuni-jinja Shrine.

Birthday of Buddha: 8 Apr is Hana Matsuri, with commemorative services at tem-

Left: procession of *mikoshi* during the Sanja Matsuri.

7th people write wishes on coloured paper and hang them on bamboo branches before floating them down a river the next day.

Sumida River Fireworks: The last Saturday is Sumidagawa Hanabi Taikai – biggest fireworks display in Tokyo. Best views are from the Komagata Bridge and between Kototoi and Shirahige bridges.

Obon: Between 13–16 Aug people return to their hometown to clean ancestral graves and offer prayers. *Bon odori* dance festivals are organised locally.

ples such as Senso-ji and Hommon-ji.

Horseback Archery Event: On the 19th, *yabusame*, mounted archers in samurai costumes, in Sumida Park.

Golden Week: 29 Apr marks the first day of the Golden Week holiday period.

Meiji Shrine Spring Festival: From 2 Apr to 3 May, this colourful celebration features *yabusame* and other displays.

Children's Day: 5 May is *Kodomo no hi*. Carp banners are flown so that boys will grow up strong like the fish.

Summer sumo tournament: In mid-May, catch the 15-day Natsubasho at Kokugikan.

Sanja Matsuri: On the third Saturday and Sunday, shrine processions, traditional dancing and music at Senso-ji Temple. The festival is one of Tokyo's 'Big Three' events.

Kanda Matsuri: Another of Tokyo's Big Three events. In mid-May during an odd-numbered year. Parades start at the Kanda Myojin Shrine.

JUNE

Torigoe-jinja Taisai: This night-time festival based at the Torigoe-jinja Shrine falls on the second Sunday, when the biggest *mikoshi* (portable shrine) is carried through the streets of Tokyo.

Tsukiji Festival: Held in the fish market, this 7–8 June event is boisterous. Drum performances, portable shrines and sushi-cutting.

Sanno Matsuri: During 10–16 June, this festival (last of the Big Three) has people parading in traditional garb at the Hie-jinja Shrine on Saturday.

JULY/AUGUST

Tanabata Matsuri: On the

OCTOBER/NOVEMBER

Chrysanthemum-Viewing: In mid- to late Oct head for Shinjuku Imperial Garden, Meiji-jingu and Asakusa-jinja for the best views.

Shichi-Go-San: On the 15th, this ceremony ('Seven-Five-Three') is when five-year-old boys and three- and seven-year-old girls are taken to visit local shrines.

DECEMBER

Joya no Kane: At midnight on the 31st, temple bells toll 108 times to represent the 108 evil human passions.

Below: picnics under the cherry-blossom trees.

Film

Tokyo has been the backdrop for a number of English-language films (and many music videos). Mostly it is a mythologised Japan recreated in a studio lot. Then the 2003 Bill Murray and Scarlett Johansson vehicle *Lost In Translation* brought renewed attention to Tokyo as an atmospheric location. By contrast, Tokyo's allure has not been lost on Japanese directors. As the centre of Japan's film industry, including *anime* or animated works, the metropolis has been the location for numerous Japanese masterpieces, many of whose directors are regarded as among film history's most creative and influential.

Made in Tokyo

After World War II, a rush of Hollywood flicks explored Japan's traditions and its rush to modernise. Most notable among those filmed in Tokyo is *The Barbarian and the Geisha*. This 1958 John Huston film stars John Wayne as Townsend Harris, the first US consul in Japan, and Eiko Ando as Okichi, the tragic geisha chosen as his mistress.

You Only Live Twice, the 1967 Bond movie with Sean Connery, features Japanese actors and Tokyo locations, including Hotel New Otani in Akasaka and Yoyogi Stadium.

In the 2003 film *Lost In Translation*, Sofia Coppola explores the closeness that develops between two Americans who find themselves adrift in Tokyo.

Arthur Golden's book *Memoirs of a Geisha* became a sweeping romantic epic in 2005 starring Ziyi Zhang.

The 2006 Brad Pitt vehicle *Babel* created a new star in Rinko Kikuchi, who plays a deaf Japanese high-school student trying to overcome her mother's suicide.

Above: Rinko Kikuchi, who appeared in *Babel*.

Japanese Films

Japanese film began in the 19th century but had a 'golden age' in the 1930s when directors, including Kenji Mizoguchi and Yasujiro Ozu, produced naturalistic works of great sensitivity.

Propaganda films of World War II were followed by the rise of the major studios – some of them still active today – including Daiei, Nikkatsu, Shochiku and Toho. This era also saw the emergence of the director who is most associated overseas with Japanese cinema, Akira Kurosawa.

One of the most famous of the films of the 'golden age' is Ozu's *Tokyo Story (Tokyo Monogatari)* made in 1953, which starts as a story about the generation gap but transposes into a meditation on mortality. Another classic is Kurosawa's *Seven Samurai (Shichinin no Samurai)* from 1954, which made a star of Toshiro Mifune as one of seven unemployed samurai recruited to defend a poor village from bandits.

The 1970s and 80s saw the domestic film industry lose ground to a wave of Hollywood imports, but recent decades have seen a rebirth in Japanese film. Directors including Juzo Itami, Hirokazu Kore-eda and Takeshi Kitano have all made highly original work that is attracting a growing international audience.

The success of Japanese *anime* speaks for itself. Hayao Miyazaki's 2001 masterpiece *Spirited Away* was the highest-grossing Japanese film of all time, and won a 2003 Academy Award for Best Animated Feature.

Left: romantic 2005 film *Memoirs of a Geisha*.

Uplink
1F, 2F Totsune Building, 37-18 Udagawacho, Shibuya-ku; tel: 6821-6821; www.uplink.co. jp; station: Shibuya; map p.138 B1
This fascinating 'micro café theatre' contains two tiny cinemas. It screens and distributes Japan's most innovative indie films, documentaries and experimental works. With regular workshops, lectures and performances.

SHINJUKU
Cinema Square Tokyu
3F, Tokyu Milano Building, 1-29-1 Kabukicho, Shinjuku-ku; tel: 3203 1189; tokyucinemas. net/shinjuku/index.html; station: Shinjuku; map p.138 B4
Tokyo's first independent cinema presents everything from Hollywood mainstream to offbeat features.

IKEBUKURO AND MEIJIRODAI
Shin-Bungeiza
3F, Maruhan-Ikebukuro Building, 1-43-5 Higashi-Ikebukuro, Toshima-ku; tel: 3971 9422; www.shin-bungeiza.com; station: Ikebukuro
Art-house cinema screens Japanese and Western films.

Below: from *Spirited Away*, directed by Hayao Miyazaki.

The **Tokyo International Film Festival** (www.tiff-jp.net) attracts international talent to Roppongi Hills and Bunkamura in Shibuya in early November. TIFF and its lesser but in some ways more innovative rival **Tokyo Filmex** (www.filmex.net) both screen Japanese and international films with English subtitles.

Cinemas

IMPERIAL PALACE, YURAKUCHO AND GINZA
Ginza Théâtre Cinema
5F Ginza Theatre Building, 1-11-2 Ginza, Chuo-ku; tel: 3535 6000; www.cinemabox.com; station: Kyobashi; map p.141 C2
An alternative and independent selection of films. There are also late-night showings here.
Hibiya Chanter Ciné
2F Chanter Ciné Building, 1-2-2 Yurakucho, Chiyoda-ku; tel: 3591 1511; www.chanter cine.com; station: Hibiya; map p.140 C2
A tasteful assortment of international films are screened at this triplex.

National Film Centre
3-7-6 Kyobashi, Chuo-ku; tel: 5777 8600; www.momat.go.jp; station: Kyobashi; map p.140 B4
Located at the National Museum of Modern Art, this has an excellent programme of Japanese classics shown with English subtitles.

SHIBUYA, HARAJUKU AND AOYAMA
Ciné Amuse
2-23-12 Dogenzaka, Shibuya-ku; tel: 3496 2888; www.cine amuse.co.jp; station: Shibuya; map p.138 B1
Fresh international fare and Japanese standards.
Cinema Rise
13-17 Udagawacho, Shibuya-ku; tel: 3464 0051; www.cinema rise.com; station: Shibuya; map p.138 B1
Independent Japanese and foreign films by young directors for a young crowd.
Le Cinema
6F, Bunkamura, 2-24-1 Dogenzaka, Shibuya-ku; tel: 3477 9264; www.bunkamura.co.jp; station: Shibuya; map p.138 B1
Venue for European movies and the Tokyo International Film Festival.

Food and Drink

When it comes to the variety and quality of food, Tokyo is unrivalled. Even in simple eateries, the quality is remarkable; in the best places, it is exceptional. Japanese cuisine is a sensation for the eyes and the taste buds. Seasoning is minimal, and every chef takes freshness very seriously. Tokyo claims many Japanese dishes as its own, but its cuisine also reflects that of the entire country. Tokyo's gastronomic offerings encompass other Asian cuisines as well as those of Europe, Africa and the Americas. You can also explore the traditional and sample the contemporary in this city.

Where to Eat

Eating out in Tokyo is not as expensive as one would expect, especially the budget-priced lunch sets for under ¥1,500. Dinner is more expensive; expect to pay about ¥3,000 per head. Some of the top places can go up to ¥10,000 per person; if there is no menu posted at the entrance, look elsewhere.

Neighbourhood Japanese diners have little ambience, but prices are low. Noodle shops are found everywhere, ranging from venerable establishments to cheap stand-and-slurp counters.

Conveyor-belt sushi is good value, and *okonomiyaki* pancakes make for fun dining.

In the evening, *izakaya* (restaurant-pubs) serve reasonably priced local food and alcohol. They identify themselves with a string of red lanterns hanging over the door. *Izakaya* do not serve full-course meals, and there is no pressure to eat quickly. Order beer or sake, and sample a few dishes such as sashimi, grilled fish, *yakitori* or tofu. End your meal with rice or noodles.

SEE ALSO RESTAURANTS, P.100–107

Japanese Cuisine

The building blocks of any Japanese meal are rice, a bowl of miso soup, a small plate of pickles and a cup of green tea. Even on their own, these are enough for a square meal.

Japanese cooking focuses on accentuating the inherent flavours rather than enhancing them with sauces. Meals are based on fish, vegetables, seaweed and tofu. Eggs, meat and poultry are used in limited quantities, while dairy foods play no part in the traditional diet. Portions are small and served in bite-sized morsels.

Ingredients reflect the seasons. Seafood and produce are generally at their best in spring and autumn, while local gourmets look forward to hearty hotpots in winter and the aroma of grilled eel in midsummer.

Presentation is equally important. Plates, bowls and utensils are made of ceramic, glass, stone, wood or lacquer.

Left: a line of red lanterns indicates a neighbourhood *izakaya*.

Left: sushi and sashimi is best enjoyed as fresh as possible.

Yanagawa-nabe, made with *dojo* (an eel-like loach).

A favourite among locals – and an acquired taste for visitors – is *oden*. Made with *daikon*, potatoes, whole hard-boiled eggs, tofu and other ingredients, this hotpot is one of the standard dishes served at *yatai* street stalls and convenience stores.

GRILLED FOOD

The classic dish of summer is *unagi*, grilled eel served on a bed of rice. Since Edo times, this has enjoyed a reputation for giving energy during summer months.

Another summer food is *yakitori*, skewers of chicken, often grilled over charcoal. Almost every part of the bird is eaten, from the breast to the heart. Gourmet versions can be had in upscale restaurants, but most people prefer the smoky street stalls.

NOODLES

Noodles are the original Japanese fast food. Wholesome, quick to prepare and even quicker to eat, they make a good, light meal. Thin, greyish-brown *soba* noodles are made with buckwheat flour. The best *soba* is *te-uchi*, freshly prepared and chopped by hand. Top-quality *soba* needs little seasoning. It is cooked, chilled and served on

If you like a frisson of fear with your food, enjoy the dangerous delicacy known as *fugu*. Although the flesh of the puffer fish is safe, its internal organs are so poisonous that it can only be prepared at licensed restaurants. If ingested, the toxin paralyses the nervous system, leading to heart failure. Once a skilled chef has removed the dangerous parts, *fugu* is served as sashimi. *Fugu-sashi* is a great delicacy with a subtle flavour. The rest of the fish goes into a casserole that is served with a spicy dip.

Like the ingredients, they are changed to fit the season.

SUSHI AND SASHIMI

The Japanese love seafood and wish to eat it as close as possible to its natural state – either as sashimi served with a dip of soy sauce and *wasabi* (horseradish), or on vinegared rice, as sushi.

The best-known sushi is the Tokyo style known as *nigiri-sushi*. The concept of eating small patties of rice topped with cuts of raw seafood originated in the days of Edo and is still called Edomae sushi, because the seafood was caught in the bay in front of the city. Some of the best *sushiya* (sushi shops) are found near the central fish market in Tsukiji.

There are two approaches at a *sushiya*: either sit at the counter and choose each serving from the seafood in front of you; or sit at a table and order a set course. Good sushi demands that ingredients are absolutely fresh. That may mean a dauntingly expensive experience. The alternative is a *kaiten-sushi* shop, where small dishes of sushi pass by on a conveyor belt, often for as little as ¥10 per plate.

HOTPOT

One of the pleasures of visiting Japan in the cold season is the variety of hearty hotpots served throughout the winter. Known as *nabe-ryori* (casserole cuisine), every area has its own distinctive variations. Styles range from Hokkaido's salmon-based *ishikari-nabe* to Tokyo's

If Tokyo lacks anything, it is choices for vegetarians. An increasing number of restaurants are catering to visitors who cannot afford the vegetarian delights of *shojin ryori* (traditional temple cuisine), but menus may not always match expectations. A 'vegetarian salad' may be topped with ham.

a bamboo tray, accompanied by a dip made with soy sauce, *mirin* (sweet sake) and *katsuobushi* (shaved flakes of dried bonito), together with *wasabi* (horseradish) and thinly sliced spring onions. Prepared like this, it is known as *zaru-soba*. The same noodles may also be served with lightly battered and fried tempura-style shrimp and grated *daikon*.

In colder weather, *soba* is eaten with a hot broth, topped with tempura, *sansai* herbs, *wakame* seaweed, deep-fried tofu (*kitsune*) or with a raw egg cracked into it (*tsukimi*). The classic dish, however, is *kamo-nanban*, in which the hot broth contains slices of duck meat and sliced leeks.

Chunky *udon*, made from white wheat flour, are a cold-weather favourite, served in a hot soy-based broth with spring onions and a variety of toppings.

The classic hot-weather noodle is the fine vermicelli known as *somen*, also made from wheat flour, served in iced water, with strips of omelette, shrimp and green vegetables and a sesame-flavoured dip. It is light and refreshing on a summer's day.

One other type of noodle is more popular than all the others. Despite its Chinese roots, *ramen* has become part of the Japanese diet, especially at late-night diners. It is served in a very hot, soy-flavoured broth, typically with pickled bamboo, chopped spring onion and slices of *cha-shu* (roast pork).

No meal is complete without a serving of *tsukemono* (pickles) to add nutrition and texture, cleanse the palate and assist digestion. A wide variety of produce goes into it, including cucumber, turnip, cabbage and aubergine.

KAISEKI RYORI

This celebration of the seasons finds ultimate expression in the formal cuisine known as *kaiseki ryori*, derived from banquets served as part of the tea ceremony. The taste and visual appeal of the dishes are created to ensure perfect harmony.

Kaiseki ryori is composed of numerous small courses, some little larger than a mouthful, and each prepared differently. They follow a prescribed order. First, a selection of appetisers; next, some sashimi and a clear soup; then follow dishes that have been grilled; seasoned with a thick dressing; simmered; steamed; deep-fried; and dressed with vinegar.

Sake is served alongside the dishes but never with the final course, which consists of rice, a bowl of miso soup and a few pickles. Hot green tea is served alongside, and dessert is usually a small portion of fresh fruit.

Grocery Markets

Kinokuniya
3-11-13 Minami-Aoyama;
Minato-ku; tel: 3409 1231;

Below: tempura and noodles.

Left: presentation is very important in Japanese cuisine.

www.e-kinokuniya.com; 9.30am–8pm; station: Omotesando; map p.139 C1
Food from the world over, with special gift boxes for Japan's traditional gift-giving season.

National Azabu
4-5-2 Minami-Azabu, Minato-ku; tel: 3442 3186; www. national-azabu.com; daily 9am–8pm; station: Hiroo
The ultimate in international supermarkets and mainstay of the wealthy and expatriate clientele in the area.

Seijo Ishii
3F Atre Ebisu Building, 1-5-5 Ebisu-Minami, Meguro-ku; tel: 3448 1070; www.seijiishii. co.jp; daily 8am–11pm; station: Ebisu
Imported food and wines.

Sake Shops

Hasegawa
3F Omotesando Hills, 4-12-4 Jingumae, Shibuya-ku; tel: 5785 0833; www.sekkobai. ecnet.jp/E-home.html; daily 11am–10pm; station: Omotesando; map p.138 C2
Well-stocked sake retailer in the chic Omotesando Hills shopping centre. Offers sake-tasting at a stand-up bar.

Shochu Authority
1F Kitchen Street, 1-9-1 Marunouchi, Chiyoda-ku; tel: 5208 5157; www.shochu.tv; daily 10am–9pm; station: Tokyo
Over 2,000 varieties of potent *shochu* spirits and dozens of locally produced microbrews. Inside Tokyo Station, with another branch in the Shio-dome complex in Shimbashi.

Suzuden
1-10 Yotsuya, Shinjuku-ku; tel: 3351 1777; Mon–Sat 10am–8pm; station: Yotsuya

Right: bottles of sake from a specialist retailer.

> esake.com is run by noted sake expert John Gauntner. It has hundreds of reviews of Japanese sake brewers and sake bars, a 'Sake Knowledge' section and links to online sake shops in the US and elsewhere.

A stand-up tasting bar at the back and chilled wine cellars below are the highlights of this well-stocked specialist.

Bakery

Viron
33-8 Udagawacho, Shibuya-ku; tel: 5458 1770; daily 9am–10pm; station: Shibuya; map p.138 B1
This two-floor *boulangerie* (bakery), *patisserie* (pastry shop) and brasserie is a temple to all things French in the heart of Shibuya. Viron imports flour directly from its own mill in France – no wonder its baguettes are to die for.

Japanese Sweets

Japanese sweets or *wagashi* ('wa' stands for things Japanese, 'gashi' means sweets) are based mostly on the *azuki* bean. Mixed into *anko*, a sweet paste made with sugar that is pressed into *anman* wheat buns and *mochi* rice flour shells, or processed into *yokan* (gelatin) and *higashi* (hard

sweets), *azuki* forms the basis of a universe of sweets. Confections are created according to the seasons: around cherry-blossom-viewing, *wagashiya* (sweet shops) will be selling cherry-flavoured treats, maybe wrapped in cherry leaves. *Wagashi* also have an ancient history. They often accompany the tea ceremony, and were given by samurai as gifts.

Toraya
Akasaka 4-9-22, Minato-ku; tel: 3408 4121; www.toraya-group.co.jp; Mon–Fri 8.30am–8pm, Sat, Sun and holidays 8.30am–6pm; station: Akasaka-mitsuke; map p.139 E2
Japan's oldest traditional confectionery provides sweets to no less than the emperor himself; the company has followed the imperial family from Nara to Kyoto and then to Tokyo. No less than 20 specific seasons have their respective recipes at Toraya, which dates back to the 16th century.

Cooking Courses

A Taste of Culture
www.tasteofculture.com
Culinary classes in *washoku* home-style cooking, tasting programmes and market tours by Elizabeth Andoh in English (tel: 5716 5751).

Gay and Lesbian

The gay and lesbian scene has a low profile in Japan, and gays in Tokyo do not promote themselves as much as they do in other international cities. Homosexuality is not actively acknowledged and supported here. However, Tokyo is fairly tolerant of gay and alternative lifestyles and has a thriving scene with a selection of clubs, events and support networks. It is mainly centred around Shinjuku in an area called ni-chome, near to Shinjuku-Sanchome Station. Most of the bars, clubs and saunas here cater to the local gay community, but there are also a number of places for non-Japanese-speakers.

Bars and Clubs

Most of Shinjuku ni-chome's 300 or more hole-in-the-wall gay clubs, host bars and restaurants are difficult to seek out, and generally do not welcome casual visitors or foreigners who do not speak Japanese. The gay visitor should visit *gaisen* ('into foreigners') venues or the more anonymous saunas and sex clubs. The following venues are both welcoming and relatively easy to find.

Advocates Café

1F 7th Tenka Building, 2-18-1 Shinjuku, Shinjuku-ku; tel: 3358 3988; advocates-cafe.com; Wed–Sun 6pm–4am; station: Shinjuku San-Chrome; map p.134 C1

A well-known and friendly spot among the expat and local gay crowd, and a good place to begin your Shinjuku ni-chome wanderings.

Arty Farty

2-11-7 Shinjuku, Shinjuku-ku; tel: 5362 9720; www.arty-farty. net; Mon 7pm–midnight, Tue–Fri 7pm–5am and Sat–Sun 5pm–5am; entrance charge; station: Shinjuku San-Chrome; map p.134 C1

A foreigner-friendly gay bar with a mostly male clientele, though an exception is made on Sundays when women accompanied by gay male friends are allowed in.

GB

B1F, Business Shinjuku Plaza Building, 2-12-3 Shinjuku, Shinjuku-ku; tel: 3352 8972; www.techtrans-japan.com/GB/index.htm; Mon–Thur and Sun 8pm–2am, Fri–Sat 8pm–3am; station: Shinjuku San-Chome

As its motto 'Where international friends meet' suggests, this is one of the favourite spots in Tokyo for meetings between foreigners and locals. Attached to a business hotel that offers short-term stays. Men only.

Below: a good place for foreign gay male visitors to go.

The Lounge Arty Farty

The Japanese language offers a depictive vocabulary of gay slang. An *okama* or 'kettle' is an effeminate gay man – often a drag queen – while an *onabe* ('pot') refers to lesbians. An *okage* ('burnt rice that sticks to the bottom of a pot') is a fag hag, while *nyuhaafu* ('new half') refers to people of transgender status.

Kinswomyn

3F Daiichi Tenka Building, 2-15-10 Shinjuku, Shinjuku-ku; tel: 3354 8720; Wed–Sun 8pm–3am; station: Shinjuku San-Chome

Tokyo's most popular lesbian bar. A relaxed, easy-going place that sticks to its women-only rule. Its counterpart for men is the nearby **Kinsmen** (2F, 2-18-5 Shinjuku, tel: 3354 4949).

New Sazae

2F Ishikawa Bldg, 2-18-5 Shinjuku, Shinjuku-ku; tel: 3354 1745; new_sazae.at.infoseek.co.jp; Mon–Sat 9pm–6am, Sun 10pm–6am; entrance charge; station: Shinjuku San-Chome

The gay writer Yukio Mishima, who killed himself after a failed

Left and below: out and proud at the Tokyo Pride Parade.

range of new films, and provides an excuse for some of the summer's best parties after winding up at the Spiral building in Aoyama.

Tokyo Pride Parade
http://parade.tokyo-pride.org
Although it pales in comparison to its New York or Sydney cousins, Tokyo's annual midsummer celebration of all things camp and outré is still a great party. The event draws thousands for a day of symposiums, live music, DJs and dancing. Afterwards, participants head to ni-chome for a night of revelry.

Information

AIDS Hotline
Tel: 0570-000 911; daily 24 hrs
Advice and information.

Otoko Machi Map (OMM)
Guide to gay venues across the nation. Useful even if you cannot speak Japanese.

Utopia
www.utopia-asia.com/japn toky.htm
Online gay community's Tokyo page has a range of listings and travel tips.

coup attempt in 1970, is said to have frequented the former incarnation of this legendary, eccentric bar. Also popular with cross-dressers and drag queens, this is a foreigner-friendly bar with good music.

Saunas
24 Kaikan
2-13-1 Shinjuku, Shinjuku-ku; tel: 3354 2424; www.juno.dti.ne. jp/~kazuo24/index.htm; daily 24 hrs; station: Shinjuku San-Chome; map p.134 C1
Occupying three different buildings in Shinjuku, Asakusa (2-29-16 Asakusa, Taito-ku; tel: 5827 2424) and Ueno (1-8-7 Kita-Ueno, Taito-ku; tel: 3847 2424), Niju-yon Kaikan are gay saunas, community baths (sento), hotels, tanning salons and karaoke bars all in one. After paying the ¥2,000–3,000 entry fee, guests are greeted at the entrance to the seven-storey Shinjuku edifice with a condom. A vast bath area has shower cubicles built to accommodate two men. Another highlight is a 'starlight room' where ultraviolet light sets off bodies as black forms against white bed sheets. The

crowd is varied in terms of age and nationality.

Events
Goldfinger
www.goldfingerparty.com
Venerable Goldfinger, with its infamous, pole-dancing 'Bond Girls', is Tokyo's longest-running women-only party, and has even toured South Korea. It is held on the last Saturday of the month at a changing series of venues.

Red
www.joinac.com/red
Launched in 1998, Red continues to be one of Tokyo's most popular gay-mix parties. The event takes place at Unit (www.unit-tokyo.com) in Daikanyama on the second Saturday of the month, and sees an affable (and buff) gang of go-go boys and drag queens getting down to house, techno and electro.

Tokyo International Lesbian & Gay Film Festival
Tel: 5380 5760; www.tokyo-lgff.org/e/
Since 1992 the annual LGFF in mid-July has been a high-point of the GLBT community calendar. It screens a wide

History

300–538
Kofun period. Japan is united for the first time under the Yamato court in Nara.

628
Senso-ji (Asakusa Kannon) Temple is founded in the Asakusa district.

710–784
Nara period. Nara is declared the imperial capital.

794–1185
Heian period. The capital relocates to Kyoto (Heian).

1180
The first recorded use of the name Edo (Tokyo).

1192–1333
Kamakura period. The capital moves to Kamakura near Edo.

1338–1573
Muromachi period. The capital reverts to Kyoto.

1590
Warlord Toyotomi Hideyoshi makes Edo his base.

1592–98
Toyotomi Hideyoshi occupies Korea.

1603–1867
Edo period. Tokugawa Ieyasu becomes the shogun and establishes government in Edo.

1720s
Edo is proclaimed the largest city in the world.

1804-29
Bunka-Bunsei period marks the zenith of Edo merchant culture.

1854
Treaty of Kanagawa. US Commodore Perry and his 'Black Ships' open Japan to trade and diplomacy. The shogunate is weakened.

1855
An earthquake kills over 4,000 in Edo. Floods and epidemics follow.

1868–1912
Meiji Period. The shogunate is overthrown and the emperor brought to power in the Meiji Restoration. The capital is renamed Tokyo.

1869
The now-controversial Yasukuni shrine is established to honour Japan's war dead.

1872
The samurai class is abolished. The first train service connects Shinbashi to Yokohama.

1883
The Rokumeikan, Tokyo's first Western-style building, is completed in Hibiya.

1889
The Meiji Constitution is enacted.

1894
Marunouchi becomes the site of a European-style business quarter known as 'London Town'.

1894–95
Japan wins the Sino-Japanese War.

1904–05
Japan wins the Russo-Japanese War.

1910
Korea is annexed.

1912–26
Taisho period. Taisho emperor ascends the throne.

1914–18
Japan joins the Allied forces in World War I.

1923
The Great Kanto Earthquake levels Tokyo, leaving 140,000 dead and the city destroyed.

1926–89
Showa period. Showa emperor ascends the throne.

1927
Asia's first subway line opens in Tokyo, between Asakusa and Ueno.

1931
Manchurian Incident. Japan occupies Manchuria and leaves the League of Nations.

1937
Second Sino-Japanese War begins. The Rape of Nanking occurs.

1941
Japan attacks Pearl Harbour; the US joins in World War II as a result. Within a year, Japan occupies most of East Asia and the western Pacific.

1945

Japan surrenders after the firebombing of Tokyo and the dropping of atomic bombs on Hiroshima and Nagasaki. General MacArthur sets up headquarters in Tokyo. The US occupation begins.

1946
A new constitution under the Allied occupation forces is enacted.

1952
The US occupation ends. The San Francisco Peace Treaty settles war-related issues; Japan returns to sovereignty, except for some Pacific islands, including Okinawa. Japan regains pre-war industrial output.

1956
Japan joins the United Nations.

1964
The Olympic Games are held in Tokyo. The Shinkansen bullet train service is launched.

1972
US returns Okinawa to Japan but establishes a base.

1980s
Japan's economy becomes the world's second-most powerful. Banks extend loans to corporations and smalll companies based on inflated land values.

1989
Heisei period. Heisei emperor ascends the throne.

1990
Bubble economy comes to an end, leading to an economic slowdown.

1995
The Aum Shinrikyo cult releases sarin gas in the Tokyo subway system, killing 12.

1999
A nuclear accident at a uranium processing plant near Tokyo claims two lives.

2001

Junichiro Koizumi, a self-proclaimed reformist, is elected as prime minister.

2002
Japan and Korea co-host the World Cup.

2006
Shinzo Abe takes over as prime minister. He upsets Asian countries with revisionist comments about Japan's wartime activities.

2007
Elections are held for Tokyo governor; controversial right-winger Shintaro Ishihara is re-elected for a third consecutive term. Abe suddenly resigns and is replaced by centrist Yasuo Fukuda.

Hotels

There is no lack of places to stay in Tokyo, with some of the world's top brands in the market. Accommodation ranges from de luxe palaces to no-frills business lodgings and budget 'capsule hotels'. Older establishments exude a distinctive Japanese ambience, while business hotels come with clean and functional bedrooms. Traditional Japanese inns, or *ryokan*, provide a different experience. At their best, they epitomise the essence of Japanese hospitality. You sleep on futon mattresses on tatami mats, bathe in a traditional bath, and are served exquisite *kaiseki ryori* meals in your room by attendants in kimonos.

Imperial Palace, Yurakucho and Ginza

Conrad Hotel
1-9-1 Higashi-Shimbashi, Minato-ku; tel: 6388 8000; www.conradtokyo.co.jp; ¥¥¥; station: Shimbashi; map p.140 C1
Shiodome's high-end accommodation doesn't come more luxurious than this 37-floor marvel. Immaculate service from a multilingual staff, designer rooms with hardwood finishing, private cedar baths and views across the Hama-Rikyu Garden, Odaiba and the bay are just part of the pampering environment this new hotel provides.

Diamond Hotel
25 Ichibancho, Chiyoda-ku; tel: 3263 2211; ¥¥; station: Hanzomon; map p.140 A4
Just minutes from the Imperial Palace and the British Embassy. Nice quiet area.

Imperial Hotel
1-1-1 Uchisaiwai-cho, Chiyoda-ku; tel: 3504 1111; www.imperialhotel.co.jp; ¥¥¥¥; Station: Hibiya; map p.140 B2
Japan's first Western-style hotel (1890) is now in its third incarnation, with top

service and restful rooms in the new tower. Its central location near Hibiya Park and subway station, the palace and the chic Ginza shopping area makes it a favourite of both travellers and businesspeople. Until recently showing signs of wear and tear, this landmark underwent a major facelift to compete with the Western luxury incursion.

Mitsui Garden Hotel Ginza
13-1 Ginza, Chuo-ku; tel: 3543 1131; www.gardenhotels.co. jp/ginza; ¥¥¥; station: Shimbashi; map p.140 C2
Located between Shimbashi with its new Shiodome development and traditional Ginza

Left: the Conrad Hotel.

is one of the area's best-value accommodation options. Managed by worldwide hotel group Novotel, Mitsui Garden Hotel's rooms may be shoebox-size, but with sleek, modern interiors created by Italian designer Piero Lissoni and dazzling views, you're sure to nestle in.

Mitsui Urban Hotel Ginza
8-6-15 Ginza, Chuo-ku; tel: 3572 4131; www.granvista.co.jp; ¥¥; station: Shimbashi; map p.140 C3
One of the best of this business hotel chain, right in the backstreets of Ginza. Quite comfortable if you don't mind forgoing some of the frills.

Palace Hotel
1-1-1 Marunouchi, Chiyoda-ku; tel: 3211 5211; www.palace hotelstokyo.com; ¥¥¥; station: Tokyo; map p.140 C3

Price categories are for a double room without breakfast:	
¥¥¥¥	over ¥30,000
¥¥¥	¥20–30,000
¥¥	¥10–20,000
¥	under ¥10,000

Left: expect five-star service at The Peninsula in Yurakucho.

commercial district is intimate and elegant as well as discreet. Expect impeccable service, though the well-equipped rooms are not particularly spacious considering the astronomical rates.

Yaesu Fujiya Hotel
2-9-1 Yaesu, Chuo-ku; tel: 3273 2111; www.yaesufujiya.com; ¥¥; station: Tokyo; map p.141 C2
This two-decade-old hotel has some elegant touches like its majestic, red-carpeted staircase descending into the lobby. Rooms are relatively small, but each has cable TV with CNN access.

Yaesu Terminal Hotel
1-5-14 Yaesu, Chuo-ku; tel: 3281 3771; www.yth.jp; ¥¥; station: Tokyo; map p.141 C3
The rooms in this business hotel may be on the small side, but they are tasteful, cheerful and great value. Excellent amenities, including flat-screen TV.

Roppongi and Akasaka

Akasaka Excel Hotel Tokyu
2-14-3 Nagatacho, Chiyoda-ku; tel: 3580 2311; www.tokyuhotels japan.com; ¥¥¥; station: Akasaka-Mitsuke; map p.140 A3
Reliable quality, efficient service and reasonable rates compared to the de luxe hotels nearby. Rooms away from the road are quieter. Good shops and restaurants in the downstairs mall, and bars on the upper levels. The station is conveniently located in the basement.

Akasaka Yoko Hotel
6-14-12 Akasaka, Minato-ku; tel: 3586 4050; www.yokohotel. co.jp; ¥¥; station: Akasaka; map p.140 A2
The friendly Yoko is well positioned for visits not only to Roppongi's restaurants, gal-

Western-style hotels in Japan charge on a per-room basis, but at traditional *ryokan* inns and pensions, customers are charged per person, with the rate usually including dinner and breakfast.

Well-established hotel with spacious guest rooms and calmer ambience than at other top hotels. Upper levels allow prime views of the Imperial Palace grounds. So does the Crown Bar on the top floor, a popular place to spend an evening. The interior, despite the sweeping views, can seem a little gloomy at times.

The Peninsula Tokyo
1-8-1 Yurakucho, Chiyoda-ku; tel: 6270 2888; tokyo. peninsula.com; ¥¥¥¥; station: Yurakucho; map p.140 C3
A branch of the Hong Kong flagship, the Peninsula began receiving bookings a full year before it opened its doors to business at the end of 2007, a measure of the esteem this

hotel is held in. Its Yurakucho location, equidistant from the palace and the shopping and restaurant streets of Ginza and served by JR and subway lines, is hard to match. Try to get one of the middle- or upper-level rooms, from where the views are outstanding.
SEE ALSO PAMPERING, P.94

Seiyo Ginza
1 Ginza, Chuo-ku; tel: 3535 1111; www.seiyo-ginza.com; ¥¥¥¥; station: Ginza-Itchome; map p.141 C2
More like a private club than a hotel, this 77-room oasis in the heart of Ginza and within walking distance of the entertainment and shopping options of the Marunouchi

Right: exclusive and expensive Seiyo Ginza.

Left: the imposing Grand Hyatt in Roppongi.

leries and night-time entertainment, but also to two famous Shinto shrines: Nogi and Hie. Though not large, the rooms are affordable, clean and comfortable, with Internet connections.

Arca Torre

6-1-23 Roppongi, Minato-ku; tel: 3404 5111; www.arktower. co.jp/arcatorre; ¥¥; station: Roppongi; map p.140 A1

Ideal for nightlife addicts, this is located close to the busy Roppongi Crossing, making it a little noisy at times. But the large semi-double beds in the standard single rooms perhaps make up for it. Helpful, multilingual staff.

Asia Center of Japan Hotel

8-10-32 Akasaka, Minato-ku; tel: 3402 6111; www.asiacenter. or.jp; ¥; station: Nogizaka; map p.140 A2

Popular lodging for low-budget travellers amid the lively buzz of a student dorm atmosphere. Reservations can be hard to secure. Rooms in the newer wing are

Price categories are for a double room without breakfast:	
¥¥¥¥	over ¥30,000
¥¥¥	¥20–30,000
¥¥	¥10–20,000
¥	under ¥10,000

a notch up from the older, cramped ones. A few minutes' walk from the subway, the location is good for both Roppongi and Aoyama areas.

Grand Hyatt

6-10-3 Roppongi, Minato-ku; tel: 4333 1234; tokyo.grand. hyatt.com; ¥¥¥¥; station: Roppongi; map p.140 A1

The grandest of the three Hyatt hotels in Tokyo, this cavernous property is truly spectacular in an understated manner. Wood, glass and marble in the public areas form clutter-free and contemporary lines. Bedrooms feature flat-screen TVs (including one in the bathroom), CD players and high-speed internet, plus capacious bathrooms. An array of excellent in-house restaurants and facilities means you never have to leave the hotel premises.

Grand Prince Hotel Akasaka

1-2 Kioi-cho, Chiyoda-ku; tel: 3234 1111; www.prince japan.com; ¥¥¥¥; station: Akasaka; map p.140 A2

The showpiece of the Prince Hotel chain has an ultra-modernist design, courtesy of Kenzo Tange, and great cityscape views from every room. Elegant furnishings and decor with a decidedly contemporary touch. Complex also includes a convention centre and restaurants.

Ibis Hotel

7-14-4 Roppongi, Minato-ku; tel: 3403 4411; www.ibis-hotel. com; ¥¥; station: Roppongi; map p.140 A1

A good, mid-range option in the heart of the Roppongi area and right above all the action. Well-designed, if smallish rooms. Good business facilities, including

Responding to increasing health and safety concerns, many hotels now offer non-smoking rooms and women-only floors.

modem ports and multi-lingual staff. Good value for this part of Tokyo.

InterContinental ANA Tokyo

1-12-33 Akasaka, Minato-ku; tel: 3505 1111; www.ana intercontinental-tokyo.jp; ¥¥¥¥; station: Tameike-Sanno; map p.140 B2

This five-star hotel owned by All Nippon Airways is set in Ark Hills, an office and shopping complex close to the business and entertainment districts (and the interminable drone of the Shuto Expressway), just two minutes' walk from the subway station. The huge, brightly lit lobby is a foretaste of the large rooms; those on the upper storeys have great views.

New Otani

4-1 Kioi-cho, Chiyoda-ku; tel: 3265 1111; www.newotani. co.jp/en; ¥¥¥¥; station: Akasaka; map p.140 A3

A massive complex with many restaurants and extensive Japanese gardens – one need never leave the hotel. On the borderline with Akasaka, but within a 10-minute walk of the Imperial Palace, the location is ideal for both sightseeing and nightlife. Though beginning to show signs of wear and tear, especially on its exterior, its luxury remains subtle and understated. Former guests include diplomats, business leaders and rock stars.

Okura

2-10-4 Toranomon, Minato-ku; tel: 3582 0111; www.hotel okura.co.jp; ¥¥¥¥; station: Roppongi-Itchome; map p.140 B1

Long held to be one of the world's great hotels, it sits in the middle of an area favoured by embassies. Also close to the Roppongi restaurant and nightlife district. An atmospheric blend of traditional Japanese decor and 21st-century facilities, the Okura is also famous for its cuisine.

Ritz Carlton
Tokyo Midtown, 9-7-1 Akasaka, Minato-ku; tel: 3423 8000; www.ritzcarlton.com/en/Properties/Tokyo; station: Roppongi; map p.140 A1
Occupying the top nine floors of the Midtown Tower, Tokyo's tallest building, is yet another ultra-luxury import to the ever-busier top echelon of the market. Perfect rooms are accented by the Ritz's famous afternoon teatime service, with views of Tokyo at the The Lobby Lounge & Bar on the 45th floor.

Shiba Park Hotel
1-5-10 Shiba-Koen, Minato-ku; tel: 3433 4141; www.shibaparkhotel.com; ¥¥; station: Onarimon; map p.140 B1
A little-known hotel, despite its attractive location just four minutes from the Onarimon subway and the impressive Sangedatsu Gate leading into Zojo-ji Temple. Quiet and cosy, and the staff here are helpful and attentive.

Shibuya, Harajuku and Aoyama

Arimax
11-15, Kamiyama-cho, Shibuya-ku; tel: 5454 1122; ¥¥¥; station: Shibuya; map p.138 B1
A small hotel with elite European pretensions, the atmosphere is that of a mellow cigar club: pleasantly intimate but sedative. Neoclassical and English Regency-style room interiors with full facilities. Notable in-house French

restaurant called Polyantha. A quick 10-minute walk west of JR Shibuya's Hachiko exit.

Capsule Land Shibuya
1-19-14 Dogenzaka, Shibuya-ku; tel: 3464 1777; ¥; station: Shibuya; map p.138 B1
A 15-minute walk from the station, this capsule hotel might be a last resort, or a once-in-a-lifetime experience. Adequate facilities: communal showers, capsule TVs, coin lockers, a restaurant and vending machines dispensing beer and noodles. Men only.

Cerulean Tower Tokyu Hotel
26-1 Sakuragaoka-cho, Shibuya-ku; tel: 3476 3000; www.ceruleantower-hotel.com; ¥¥¥¥; station: Shibuya
Shibuya's most upmarket hotel has the finest views in this part of town. The hotel section of the tower runs from the 19th to 37th floors. Spacious, fully-equipped and tastefully decorated rooms. On the premises are bars and several Japanese and Western eating options, including a modern *kaiseki* restaurant. There is even a noh theatre on the premises. Expect excellent service. A three-minute walk from Shibuya Station's south exit.

Hotels can be booked online via international websites like Expedia (www.expedia.com), Japanese websites such as the Japan Hotel Association (www.j-hotel.or.jp) or directly at the hotel's websites.

Hotel Mets Shibuya
3-29-17 Shibuya, Shibuya-ku; tel: 3409 0011; www.hotelmets.jp/shibuya; ¥¥; station: Shibuya
Besides the moderate cost, there are several advantages to staying in this roomy, mid-range business hotel: its location beside JR Shibuya station, Internet access in each unit and a price that includes breakfast.

Shibuya City Hotel
1-1 Maruyamacho, Shibuya, Shibuya-ku; tel: 5489 1010; ¥; station: Shibuya; map p.138 B1
A small, friendly boutique hotel seven minutes from Shibuya Station. Opposite the Bunkamura complex, the location is ideal for taking in the arts, shopping and nightlife of Shibuya.

Shibuya Excel Tokyu
1-12-2 Dogenzaka, Shibuya-ku; tel: 5457 0109; www.tokyuhotelsjapan.com; ¥¥; station: Shibuya; map p.138 B1
Well-priced accommodation for business travellers and those who want to be in the

Below: New Otani is a well-located hotel complex.

65

Left: stunning views from the Park Hyatt Tokyo.

thick of Shibuya. A part of the Mark City complex attached to the Shibuya Station. Offers two floors solely for women. Bar, restaurants and all the amenities you would expect from this chain.

Shinjuku

Green Plaza Capsule Hotel

1-29-2 Kabuki-cho, Shinjuku-ku; tel: 5457 0109; www.hgpshinjuku.jp; ¥; station: Shinjuku; map p.134 B1

Although it's just minutes from Shinjuku Station, this hotel is designed to accommodate those who miss their last train home, a common occurrence. Located in the heart of Kabuki-cho. Surprisingly comfortable once you get used to the idea of being supine in a plastic case. For men only.

Hilton Tokyo

6-6-2 Nishi-Shinjuku, Shinjuku-ku; tel: 3344 5111; www.hilton.com; ¥¥¥; station: Shinjuku; map p.134 B1

Set among the skyscrapers of west Shinjuku, this is said to be the largest Hilton in Asia. The rooms are Western

Traditional *ryokan* inns and *minshuku* bed-and-breakfasts may not accept credit cards. If staying at one, it is best to check in advance.

in style, but with Japanese accents, all with modem lines and cable TV. Great Sunday brunch in the newly refurbished lobby. Just five minutes' walk from JR Shinjuku, Marunouchi Line's Nishi-Shinjuku Station and the Oedo line's Tochomae Station.

Hyatt Regency Tokyo

2-7-2 Nishi-Shinjuku, Shinjuku-ku; tel: 3348 1234; www.tokyo.regency.hyatt.com; ¥¥¥; station: Shinjuku; map p.134 B1

In the heart of west Shinjuku, a short walk from the main Shinjuku Station or the Oedo line's Tochomae Station, this is one of Tokyo's most praised hotels, though you wouldn't realise it from the outside. The interior, with its soaring atrium lobby, is a different story. The posh executive floors are exclusive, with separate facilities and king-sized beds. Famed for its superlative service, it's a good place to spoil yourself.

Keio Plaza Hotel

2-2-1 Nishi-Shinjuku, Shinjuku-ku; tel: 3344 0111; www.keioplaza.co.jp; ¥¥¥; station: Oedo; map p.134 B1

Right next to Tochomae station on the Oedo line, this large, 45-storey skyscraper on the west side of Shinjuku has a good location. This older, established property

is well maintained. Health club and business facilities, outdoor swimming pool and an array of fine restaurants and bars.

Park Hyatt Tokyo

3-7-1-2 Nishi-Shinjuku, Shinjuku-ku; tel: 5322 1234; www.tokyo.park.hyatt.com; ¥¥¥¥; station: Shinjuku

Fantastic setting on the top 14 floors of the 52-storey Park Tower, with sky walks through glass atriums. Expect top-class facilities and very efficient service. The spacious, well-appointed rooms all have DVDs and videos, but you'll probably spend most of the time staring out of the windows. This is where the award-winning film *Lost in Translation* was shot. Home to the excellent **New York Grill** restaurant. A short stroll from the Oedo line's Tochomae or JR Shinjuku stations.

SEE ALSO RESTAURANTS, P.104

Shinjuku Prince Hotel

1-30-1 Kabuki-cho, Shinjuku-ku; tel: 3205 1111; www.princejapan.com; ¥¥; station: Shinjuku; map p.134 B1

Look down from your room at the goings-on in Kabuki-cho, the heart of Shinjuku nightlife. Right next to Shinjuku Station, the location may not be picturesque, but there is never a dull moment in this exciting part of town. Adequate rooms, good facilities. The restaurant on the 25th floor has the best views this side of Shinjuku.

Tokyo International Youth Hostel

Central Plaza, 18F, 21-1 Kagurakashi, Shinjuku-ku; tel: 3235 1107; www.tokyo-ih.jp; ¥; station: Iidabashi; map p.136 B2

If the idea of a youth hostel in a skyscraper appeals, and you don't mind sharing a room, the clean, dormitory-style bunk beds here may suit. Right next to JR Iidabashi Station. No access to the building between 10am and 3pm, and there is also an 11pm curfew to bear in mind.

Ikebukuro and Meijirodai

Chinzan-so Four Seasons Hotel

Chinzan-so, 2-10-8 Sekiguchi, Bunkyo-ku; tel: 3943 2222; www.fourseasons.com/tokyo; ¥¥¥¥; station: Edogawabashi; map p.135 D3

A superlative low-rise hotel in an unparalleled setting, overlooking the woodlands of the Chinzan-so garden with its pagoda, waterfall and Buddhist statuary. Western luxury is combined with Japanese attention to detail. A drawback is the rather remote location, a 10-minute walk from Edo-gawabashi Station.

Kimi Ryokan

2-36-8 Ikebukuro, Toshima-ku; tel: 3971 3766; www.kimi-ryokan.jp; ¥; station: Ikebukuro

One of Tokyo's best-loved budget places, the helpful English-speaking staff are a

godsend. Clean communal toilets and bathrooms. This inexpensive, homely *ryokan* is very popular, so book in advance. Located in a quiet backstreet off Tokiwa-dori, and a 10-minute walk to the JR station.

Sunshine City Prince Hotel

3-1-5 Higashi-Ikebukuro, Toshima-ku; tel: 3988 1111; www.princejapan.com; ¥¥; station: Ikebukuro; map p.135 D4

Efficient, well run and well equipped with business facilities. Conveniently located in the Sunshine City complex, with its array of shops and restaurants. JR station is an eight-minute walk away.

Shinagawa, Meguro and Ebisu

Excellent Hotel

1-9-5 Ebisu-Nishi, Minato-ku; tel: 5458 0087; ¥¥; station: Ebisu

Nothing fancy about this hotel with its plain, rather small rooms and only basic facilities. Besides its helpful staff and attractive rates, its location near the Yamanote Line, just one stop from Shibuya, with access to trendy Ebisu, makes it popular. It is good for exploring the western reaches of Tokyo. Close to Ebisu Station's west exit.

Grand Prince Hotel

New Takanawa, 3-13-1 Takanawa, Minato-ku; tel: 3442 1111; www.princejapan.com; ¥¥¥; station: Shinagawa

One in a complex of three Prince hotels all in the same beautifully landscaped gardens. The facilities are excellent, the rooms luxurious and spacious. The service is highly reputed. Guests at one of the Prince buildings can use facilities in the other two. Located in an affluent residential district, there is not much nightlife in this area. It is, however, only five minutes from the JR station.

Le Meridien Pacific Tokyo

3-13-3 Takanawa, Minato-ku; tel: 3445 6711; www.starwood hotels.com; ¥¥¥; station: Shinagawa

A gleaming high-rise dominating the Shinagawa district, with 41 suites and six restaurants. Its 30th-floor Sky Lounge affords night views over Tokyo Bay. A large, manicured garden lends tranquillity to a lively area five minutes from the Shiodome shopping and leisure complex.

Meguro Gajoen

1-8-1 Shimo Meguro, Meguro-ku; tel: 3491 4111; www.megurogajoen.co.jp; ¥¥¥¥; station: Meguro

A very old and beautiful *ryokan*, the traditional lodgings here are very expensive. Lovely gardens, artwork and a refined atmosphere add to the sublime experience. European and Japanese-style rooms

Left: pricey but elegant, the Meguro Gajoen *ryokan*.

67

> Many hotels provide *yukata* robes in rooms. These are not part of the amenity kit and should be left in the room after use.

available; ask for the latter. Only a three-minute walk from the JR station.

Sansuiso Ryokan
2-9-5 Higashi-Gotanda, Shinagawa-ku; tel: 3441 7475; www.sansuiso.net; ¥; station: Gotanda

Cosy *ryokan* conveniently located five minutes from Gotanda Station. Traditional Japanese-style rooms that offer a choice of private or shared facilities.

Sheraton Miyako Hotel Tokyo
1-1-50 Shiroganedai, Minato-ku; tel: 3447 3111; www.miyakohotels.ne.jp; ¥¥¥; station: Shirokaneda

Affiliated with Kyoto's famous Miyako Hotel, this Tokyo equivalent successfully attempts to replicate the prototype. Located in a pleasant, quiet neighbourhood near the Happo-en Garden and the National Park for Nature Study, this location makes for a lovely retreat. Only 10 minutes from Shirokanedai subway station.

Westin Hotel Tokyo
1-4-1 Mita, Meguro-ku; tel: 5423 7000; www.starwood hotels.com; ¥¥¥; station: Ebisu

Spacious guest rooms, sophisticated interiors, personalised service and a peaceful setting opposite a fake chateau (housing a restaurant) and the soaring office blocks of Yebisu Garden Place. The Westin models itself on grand European-style hotels, offering gracefully designed rooms, an elegant lobby and tastefully decorated public spaces.

Above: water-side views from Nikko Tokyo.

Tokyo Bayside

InterContinental Tokyo Bay
1-16-2 Kaigan, Minato-ku; tel: 5404 2222; www.inter continental.com; ¥¥¥¥; station: Takeshiba

Overlooking the mouth of the Sumida River and Tokyo waterfront, all its rooms have panoramic views of Odaiba Island and Rainbow Bridge. Rooms are spacious and stylishly appointed. The hotel is part of a complex that faces the east exit of Takeshiba station; a short walk to the Hama-Rikyu Garden.

Le Meridien Grand Pacific Tokyo
2-6-1 Daiba, Minato-ku; tel: 5500 6711; www.starwood hotels.com; ¥¥¥¥; station: Odaiba

Right opposite Odaiba station's south exit, the five-star Meridien is another towering hotel on Odaiba with breathtaking views of the bay and waterfront skyscrapers from its middle- to upper-level rooms and the 30th-floor Sky Lounge. Luxurious rooms and superb service. Situated between Decks Tokyo and the Museum of Maritime Science.

Nikko Tokyo
1-9-1 Daiba, Minato-ku; tel: 5500 5511; www.jalhotels. com; ¥¥¥¥; station: Odaiba

Smack-bang in front of Odaiba Station on the Yurikamome Line, and a stroll up from the leisure complexes of Palette Town and Aquacity, the Nikko has one of the best views of the waterfront. The terrace restaurant and Captain's Bar are romantic settings popular with couples. First-rate service and food. Convenient access to all Odaiba sights.

Tokyo Bay Ariake Washington Hotel
3-1 Ariake, Koto-ku; tel: 5564 0111; www.wh-rsv.com; ¥¥; station: Ariake

A comfortable business hotel on Odaiba, this has the same facilities as you would find in its other branches, but this one, at 20 storeys, is one of the larger buildings. There are several Western and Japanese restaurants on site. It's popular with those attending exhibitions at the Tokyo Big Sight venue next door. Located just a short walk away from Ariake Station.

Capsule hotels have become a famous symbol of crowded Japan. Located near big stations, they provide fully equipped sleeping cells at rock bottom prices, mostly for drunken men who miss the last train home to the suburbs.

Suidobashi, Ochanomizu, Kanda and Akihabara

Hotel Metropolitan Edmont

3-10-8 Iidabashi, Chiyoda-ku; tel: 3237 1111; www.edmont. co.jp; ¥¥¥; station: Suidobashi; map p.136 B2

A five-minute walk southwest of Suidobashi Station, this large hotel is efficiently run with comfortable, well-equipped rooms, but it is a little impersonal. Outside the mainstream area – thus few foreign tourists – but still easy accessible to the JR and subway lines. It's location is within walking distance of the Yasukuni Shrine and the Kanda-Jimbocho bookshop district.

Hotel My Stage Ochanomizu

2-10 Kanda, Awajicho, Chiyoda-ku; tel: 3258 3911; ¥¥; station: Ochanomizu; map p.137 D1

In a quiet location and yet only a five-minute walk to the noise and hustle and bustle of Akihabara's electronics stores. Japanese and Western restaurant on site. A three-minute walk to Ochanomizu Station.

Sakura Hotel

2-21-4, kanda-Jimbocho, Chiyoda-ku; tel: 3264 2777; www.sakura-hotel.co.jp; ¥; station: Jimbocho; map p.136 C1

Given its location, this is a surprisingly good deal, although the rooms – all non-smoking – are tiny. It is

popular with salarymen and tourists. Located close to exit A6 of Jimbocho Station. English-speaking staff.

Tokyo Green Hotel Ochanomizu

2-6 Kanda-Awajicho, Chiyoda-ku; tel: 3255 4161; www.greenhotel.co.jp; ¥¥; station: Ochanomizu; map p.136 C1

This place is remarkably good value given its location, a stone's throw away from the teeming Ochanomizu streets, Nikolai Cathedral and the Kanda-Jimbocho used-book district. The wood and paper-screen interiors create a tranquil setting, and the friendly and bilingual staff are a bonus.

Yama-no-ue (Hilltop) Hotel

1-1 Surugadai, Kanda, Chiyoda-ku; tel: 3293 2311; www.yamanoue-hotel.co.jp; ¥¥; station: Ochanomizu; map p.137 D1

Just five minutes southwest of Ochanomizu Station, this secluded hotel has genuine period charm. A favourite of writers and artists, including the late novelist Yukio Mishima. The service is impeccable and the cuisine is of a high standard. On clear days, the upper-storey rooms give good views of Mount Fuji.

Ueno and Yanaka

Ryokan Katsutaro Annex

3-8-4 Yanaka, Taito-ku; tel: 3828 2500; www.katsutaro.com; ¥; station: ; map p.137 D4

This modern *ryokan* combines the best of Japanese decor with tatami flooring and paper-screen windows. There are also private bathrooms and broadband Internet access in each room, along with free Internet usage and coffee in the entrance area. The hotel is located just

around the corner from Yanaka Ginza, a lively street with craft and tea shops.

Sawanoya Ryokan

2-3-11 Yanaka, Taito-ku; tel: 3822 2251; www.tctv.ne.jp/ members/sawanoya; ¥; station: Nezu; map p.137 C4

Small but comfortable rooms with tatami mats in this friendly *ryokan* situated in a residential neighbourhood close to the old quarter of Yanaka. The ¥300 self-service breakfast is good value. It's about a seven-minute walk from Nezu Station.

Ueno First City Hotel

1-14-8 Ueno, Taito-ku; tel: 3831 8215; www.uenocity-hotel.com; ¥¥; station: Yushima; map p.137 D2

Close to Yushima Station's exit 6, this is a smart business hotel that prides itself on its comfort and efficiency. Within walking distance of both the Ueno district and the area around the Yushima Tenjin Shrine. Look out for its red-brick façade. The restaurant, bar and coffee shop are as intimate as the hotel itself.

Asakusa

Asakusa View Hotel

3-17-1 Nishi-Asakusa, Taito-ku; tel: 3842 2117; www.view hotels.co.jp/asakusa; ¥¥; station: Asakusa; map p.137 E3

Well situated for sightseeing and shopping in downtown Asakusa. Traditional Japanese rooms are also available on the sixth floor, where there are aerial gardens. The bar on the 28th floor offers an excellent river view.

Price categories are for a double room without breakfast:		
¥¥¥¥	over ¥30,000	
¥¥¥	¥20–30,000	
¥¥	¥10–20,000	
¥	under ¥10,000	

Language

With its three alphabets, Japanese is a notoriously difficult language. However, don't let this put you off trying to master a few simple words and phrases. As a spoken language, Japanese is simple, and when used strategically even in a basic form will often be greeted by the locals with joy. Japan has poured billions of dollars into learning English in recent decades, but it is still not widely spoken. Some people will understand written English, and it can be useful to write down what you're trying to communicate. After hundreds of years of isolation, Japan's language barrier is high, but it's beginning to come down.

Japanese

Japanese is spoken almost exclusively, though in the conduct of international business, English is used. Signs on streets, stations and public buildings are generally written in Roman letters, often with English translations. The level of spoken English is generally poor, but has shown marked improvement in recent years.

Japanese uses three different forms of writing (four, including Roman letters): two simple home-grown syllabaries (phonetic scripts) known as *hiragana* and *katakana*, each of which consists of 46 basic characters; plus Chinese characters *(kanji)*. Knowledge of just under 2,000 of these (plus their numerous compounds) is required to read a newspaper.

While it is unnecessary to memorise more than a very few simple *kanji* characters (those for 'man' and 'woman' are useful at hot-spring resorts and public toilets), it is not so daunting to learn the two *kana* scripts. This will help you read station names and some menu listings.

Hiragana is used for transliterating most *kanji* and for connectors that cannot be written with *kanji*. *Katakana* is used primarily for representing foreign names and loan words (e.g. *takushi*/taxi).

Pronunciation Tips

Apart from a few consonants, Japanese is easy to pronounce. The vowels in standard Japanese are always regular. The most important aspect is to give each syllable equal stress and to avoid the intonation patterns of English and other Western languages.

Consonants do not exist on their own, with the exception of n which only follows a vowel, but are always accompanied by one of the five basic vowel sounds. These are pronounced much as they would be in English, with the following notes:

chi – as in cheese
g – always hard (as in get)
ji/ju/jo – as in jeans/June/joke
n – pronounced like m before b or p (*tenpura* is read 'tempura'; *shinbun* (newspaper) is pronounced 'shimbun')
tsu – like 'it's' (without the i)

The basic vowel sounds are pronounced much as in Spanish.

Below: even a few words of Japanese will be well received.

Left: English is not widely spoken in Tokyo.

Where is the toilet?
Toire wa doko desu ka?
Where is the ...? *... wa doko desu ka?*
Airport *Kuukou*
Station *Eki*
Bank *Ginko*
Food *Tabemono*
Drink *Nomimono*
Water *Omizu*
How much does this cost?
Ikura desu ka?
Is there an English menu?
Eigo no menyu wa arimasu ka?
Oishi *Delicious*
The bill, please
Okanjo kudasai
Thank you for the meal
Gochiso sama deshita
Rice *gohan* (cooked), *kome* (raw)
Noodles *Men*
Bread *Pan*
Fish *Sakana*
Beef *Gyuniku*
Pork *Butaniku*
Chicken *Toriniku*
Vegetables *Yasai*
Water *Omizu*
Black Tea *Kocha*
Green Tea *Ocha*
Coffee *Kohi*
Sukiyaki Simmered meat (usually beef) hotpot, served with raw egg
Shabushabu Thinly sliced meat (usually beef) and vegetable hotpot, served with sauce
Gyudon Beef on rice
Kare curry, but much sweeter
Kushiage Deep-fried kebab
Tempura Batter-fried seafood and vegetables
Teppanyaki Grilled food
Tonkatsu Breaded, deep-fried pork
Yakosoba Fried noodles

Japanese do not usually use first names, but the family name, followed by '-san', which can stand for Mr, Mrs, Miss or Ms. The suffix '-chan' may be used by close friends.

a – like the a in about
e – like the e in egg
i – like the i in ink
o – like the o in orange
u – like the u in butcher
In combination the vowels are pronounced as follows:
ai – like 'eye'
ae – almost the same as ai, but with a slight e sound at the end
ao – like the ow in cow
au – almost the same as ao, but with a more u sound at the end
ei – like the ay in way
io – like an elision 'ee-yo'
iu – like an elision 'ee-yu'
ue – like an elision 'oo-e'
uo – like an elision 'oo-oh'
When i and u occur in the middle of words, they are sometimes almost silent. For example, *Shitamachi* (Tokyo's 'Low City') is actually pronounced 'sh'ta-machi', while *sukiyaki* sounds more like 's'kiyaki'. A final u is also pronounced so imperceptibly as to be unnoticeable: thus *desu* is always pronounced 'dess'.

Vowels are sometimes elongated (doubled), and this is indicated in Roman letters by a macron (a line over the said vowel), by an extra h (after o), or by writing a double vowel (in the case of i). The spelling in English, however, does not always reflect the double vowel.

Useful Words and Phrases

Hello *Konnichiwa*
Goodbye *Sayonara*
Please *Onegaishimasu*
Thank you *Domo arigato*
Yes *Hai*
No *Lie*
Excuse me *Sumimasen*
I'm sorry *Gomennasai*
Do you speak English?
Eigo o hanasemasuka?
I don't understand
Wakarimasen
Help! *Tasukete!*
My name is ...
Watashi wa ... desu
What is your name? *Anato no namae wa nan desu ka?*

1	*ichi*	**6**	*roku*
2	*ni*	**7**	*nana*
3	*san*	**8**	*hachi*
4	*shi*	**9**	*kyu*
5	*go*	**10**	*ju*

71

Literature

Japanese literature spans two millennia, but for most of that time Tokyo itself was a cultural backwater. Literature in Tokyo dates back only to the 17th-century flowering of the city under the Tokugawa Shogunate. Since Tokyo's emergence as the centre of Japan and the world's largest metropolis, however, it has produced a remarkable stream of literary innovation. Some of its foremost current writers are now worldwide household names. Their works touch contemporary urban audiences often through their use of magical realism or surrealism. And don't forget the hugely popular *manga* comic genre.

Writing in Tokyo

With the rise of a literate middle class in 17th- and 18th-century Tokyo, new forms of writing, including kabuki plays, travel diaries and illustrated fiction arose, many of them influenced by China.

Japanese authors were first exposed to Western influences in the mid-19th century, resulting in the first prose novels. Among those to achieve renown was Edokko (Tokyo-born) novelist Natsume Soseki, whose *Botchan* (1906) takes up the youthful protagonist's struggle to live a moral life.

Fellow Tokyoite Junichiro Tanizaki's sexually frank *Naomi* (1924) depicted the loss of traditional gender roles amid encroaching Westernisation, while Yasunari Kawabata became Japan's first winner of the Nobel Prize for Literature for penetrating works like *Snow Country* (1935–7).

Japan's defeat in World War II produced books by Tokyo-based authors, including Osamu Dazai's account of a returning soldier in *The*

Above: traditional Japanese calligraphy is an art.

Setting Sun (1947). Kenzaburo Oe's *A Personal Matter* (1964) earned Japan a second Nobel Prize.

Tokyo's post-war period also saw the rise of Yukio Mishima, renowned for depictions of tragic love in his *Sea of Fertility* series and avant-garde writers like Kobo Abe, author of *Woman in the Dunes* (1960).

In recent decades Haruki Murakami has become the international face of Japanese literature on the strength of delicate yet fantastical pop fiction works like *Norwegian Wood* (1987).

Another facet of the Tokyo literary scene are the popular women writers including Banana Yoshimoto and Amy Yamada, who both explore the ambiguous benefits of the freedoms accorded to modern Japanese women.

It's also worth noting that manga comic books represent a large chunk of annual publications, covering topics from coming-of-age stories to history and economics.

Further Reading

NON-FICTION

Low City, High City: Tokyo From Edo to the Earthquake, by Edward Seidensticker (Knopf/Tuttle, 1983). The best history of how the city changed from Shogun's capital to a modern metropolis. *My Asakusa: Coming of Age in Pre-War Tokyo*, by Sadako Sawamura (Tuttle Publishing, 2000). A delightful and frank memoir of one of the city's best-loved districts by the late actress-writer Sawamura. *Speed Tribes*, by Karl Taro Greenfeld (HarperCollins, 1994). Profiles of Tokyo's subterranean youth culture.

Left: Japanese literature uses surrealism and magical realism.

Bookshops

Blue Parrot
3F, 2-14-10 Takadanababa, Shinjuku-ku; tel: 3202 3671; www.blueparrottokyo.com; station: Takadanababa; map p.134 C3
An extensive selection of mostly used English books, DVDs and magazines.

Good Day Books
3F, 1-11-2 Ebisu, Shibuya-ku; tel: 5421 0957; www.goodday books.com; Wed–Mon 11am–6pm; station: Ebisu
Tokyo's best selection of used English books, plus several thousand new books. Great bargains.

Kinokuniya Book Store
3-17-7 Shinjuku, Shinjuku-ku; tel: 3354 0131; www. kinokuniya.co.jp; daily 10am–7pm; station: Shinjuku; map p.134 B1
Foreign books on the sixth floor. Another branch in Shinjuku's Times Square.

Manga no Mori
12-10 Udagawa-cho, Shibuya-ku; tel: 5489 0257; www.manga nomori.net; daily 11am–9pm; map p.138 B1
Top manga collection, with just about every post-war Japanese character featured.

Maruzen
1-6-4 Marunouchi, Chiyoda-ku; tel: 5288 8881; www.maruzen. co.jp; daily 9am–9pm; station: Tokyo; map p.141 C3
In the Oazo building, with Japan's largest selection of foreign books. Check first, as the store has plans to move.

Tower Books
1-22-14 Jinnan, Shibuya-ku; tel: 3496 3661; www.tower records.co.jp; daily 10am–10pm; map p.138 B1
On the seventh floor, an imaginative selection of English books and magazines.

The Life and Death of Yukio Mishima, by Henry Scott Stokes (Cooper Square Press, 1999). The standard work on Japan's most controversial writer by the British author and journalist who knew him best.
Tokyo: A View of the City, by Donald Richie (Reaktion Books, 1999). Tokyo through the aesthetic but highly contemporary looking-glass of its foremost expatriate writer.
Nature in Tokyo, by Kevin Short (Kodansha International, 2000). A guide to plants and animals in and around the city.
Tokyo City Atlas (Kodansha International). An essential bilingual guide, with maps covering central and outlying parts of Tokyo.

Ultra-nationalist homosexual writer Yukio Mishima shocked the world by committing suicide by the sword at age 45 in the office of a commander after a failed attempt to spark a nationalist uprising at Japan's Self-Defence Force headquarters in 1970.

LITERATURE
A View from the Chuo Line, by Donald Richie (Printed Matter, 2004). Minimalist stories set in Tokyo from the master observer.
Blind Willow, Sleeping Woman, by Haruki Murakami (Alfred A. Knopf, 2006). Twenty-four stories by Japan's best-known author, several of them set in Tokyo.
Number 9 Dream, by David Mitchell (Sceptre, 2001). A novel set in Tokyo, nominated for the Booker Prize.
Samurai Boogie, by Peter Tasker (Orion, 1999). Private eye Kazuo Mori investigates the underbelly of the city. Check out the more recent *Dragon Dance*, also set in Tokyo.
Scandal, by Shusaku Endo (Tuttle Publishing, 1986). An enigmatic novel of Tokyo characters and places by the late, much-missed master.
Tokyo Stories: A Literary Stroll, translated and edited by Lawrence Rogers (University of California Press, 2002). An anthology of stories by Japanese writers with Tokyo settings.

Museums and Galleries

The opening of the Mori Museum and the National Art Centre, and the renewed vigour of Japan's contemporary art market, make Tokyo ever more compelling for art fans. From the traditional Ueno museum district to the post-Bubble era's cutting-edge contemporary arts and on to its countless galleries, Tokyo is a city steeped in the arts. Beyond the museums and galleries, this is the metropolis that produced artists from *ukiyo-e* master Hokusai to pop-art impresario Takashi Murakami.

Imperial Palace, Yurakucho and Ginza

Bridgestone Museum

1-10-1 Kyobashi, Chuo-ku; tel: 3563 0241; www.bridge stone-museum.gr.jp; Tue–Sat 10am–8pm, Sun and holidays 10am–6pm; entrance charge; station: Nihonbashi; map p.141 C2

The Bridgestone Bijutsukan's collection has mainly Impressionists' works, but there are also early 20th-century painters and post-Meiji-era Japanese artists here, as well as sculptures.

Idemitsu Museum

9F Tei Geki Building, 3-1-1 Marunouchi, Chiyoda-ku; tel: 3213 9402; www.idemitsu.co.jp/museum; Tue–Sun 10am–5pm (Fri until 7pm); entrance charge; station: Yurakucho; map p.140 C3

The Idemitsu showcases Asian art. It features an impressive collection of Chinese ceramics with some fine Japanese pieces too, including Kakiemon, Imari, Kutani and Seto wares. Ancient pottery shards fill a room with a magnificent view of the Imperial Palace. There are also gold-painted screens, Zen calligraphy and *ukiyo-e* prints.

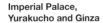

Kite Museum

5F Taimeiken, 1-12-10 Nihonbashi, Chuo-ku; tel: 3275 2704; www.tako.gr.jp; Mon–Sat 11am–5pm; free; station: Nihonbashi; map p.141 D3

Kite-flying has a long tradition in Japan. The Tako no Hakubutsukan's collection exceeds 2,000 kites from around the world. Some resemble birds, squid and Mount Fuji. Others have paintings of samurai warriors, manga characters and *ukiyo-e*-style images.

National Museum of Modern Art

3-1 Kitanomaru Koen, Chiyoda-ku; tel: 5777 8600; www.momat.go.jp; Tue–Sun

Left: entrance to the Mori Art Museum, Roppongi Hills.

10am–5pm (Fri until 8pm); entrance charge; station: Takebashi; map p.136 B1

The Kokuritsu Kindai Bijutsukan displays Japanese art from the Meiji Period to the present day. Three thousand or more pieces, including work by Western artists, are exhibited in rotation. The museum's superb annexe, the **Crafts Gallery** (Kogeikan; Tue–Sun 10am–5pm; admission charge; tel: 5777 8600), is one of only five Meiji-era brick structures left in Tokyo. A fine collection of lacquerware, bamboo, ceramics and textiles.

Science Museum

2-1 Kitanomaru Koen, Chiyoda-ku; tel: 3212 8544; www.jsf.or.jp; daily 9.30am–4.50pm; station: Takebashi; map p.140 B4

A short walk north under the Shoto Expressway, along the paths of Kitanomaru Park, leads to the Kagaku Gijutsukan. Its two floors have interactive displays, space-age exhibits, working models and a robot that lectures on electricity.

Left: the Kite Museum brings colour to a business district.

extraordinary Musée Tomo. With a broad collection of the very best ceramics, from Imari vases to Raku tea bowls, the gallery also features the work of modern pottery masters.

The National Art Centre
7-22-2 Roppongi, Minato-ku; tel: 5777 8600; www.nact.jp; Wed–Mon 10am–6pm, (Fri until 8pm); station: Nogizaka; map p.139 D1
Within walking distance of Roppongi Hills, this centre, designed by architect Kisho Kurokawa, is the largest art space in Japan. With no private collection of its own, it has complete freedom over the exhibitions it mounts.
SEE ALSO ARCHITECTURE, P.30

Okura Shukokan Museum of Fine Arts
Hotel Okura, 2-10-3 Toranomon, Minato-ku; tel: 3583 0781; www.okura.com/tokyo/info/shukokan.html; Tue–Sun 10am–4.30pm; entrance charge; station: Roppongi-Itchome; map p.140 B2
The Okura Shukokan Bijutsukan was set up in 1917. A Chinese-style anomaly, the museum houses a small but intriguing collection of Asian antiquities and Buddhist sculptures.

Suntory Museum of Art
Tokyo Midtown; tel: 3479 8600;

English-language listings of exhibitions in Tokyo can be viewed on *Tokyo Art Beat* (www.tokyoartbeat.com), which also features user reviews, and the exhibition listings section of *Metropolis* magazine (www.metropolis.co.jp) as well as the three English dailies.

Shiseido Gallery
B1F Tokyo Ginza Shiseido Building, 8-8-3 Ginza, Chuo-ku; tel: 3572 3901;www.shiseido.co.jp/gallery/html; Tue–Sat 11am–7pm, Sun and holidays 11am–6pm; free; station: Shimbashi; map p.141 C2
Located in the basement of Shiseido Parlour, the cosmetics boutique, this gallery features experimental art by Japanese and foreign artists. One street east of the gallery, **Shiseido Art House** (Tue–Sun 11am–7pm; free; tel: 3571 0401) has interesting exhibitions. The advertising work for the company, past and present, is especially arresting.

Right: the well-designed Suntory Museum of Art.

Roppongi and Akasaka
Mori Art Museum
Mori Tower, 6-10-1 Roppongi, Minato-ku; tel: 6406 6100; www.mori.art.museum; Wed–Mon 10am–10pm, Tue 10am–5pm; entrance charge; station: Roppongi; map p.140 A1
On the 52nd and 53rd floors of Mori Tower is a first-rate contemporary art gallery with a reputation for some of Tokyo's most daring shows.

Musée Tomo
4-1-35 Toranomon, Minato-ku; tel: 5733 5311; www.musee-tomo.or.jp; Tue–Sun 11am–6pm; station: Kamiyacho; map p.140 B1
Behind the Hotel Okura is the

75

Left: the beautiful Japan Folk Crafts Museum.

www.suntory.co.jp/sma; Wed–Mon 10am–8pm; entrance charge; station: Roppongi; map p.140 A1

This museum's collection of lacquerware, ceramics and paintings from the 17th century to the present is housed in a sleek and light-filled area featuring high ceilings and louvred windows.

21_21 Design Sight
9-7-6 Akasaka, Minato-ku; tel: 3475 2121; www.2121 designsight.jp; Wed–Mon 11am–8pm; entrance charge; station: Roppongi; map p.140 A1

Designed by 'starchitect' Tadao Ando, this edifice sits in 10-hectare grounds. With fashion leader Issey Miyake among its directors, 21_21 has progressive theme-based design exhibitions.

Shibuya, Harajuku and Aoyama

Gallery TOM
2-11-1 Shoto, Shibuya-ku; tel: 3467 8102; www.gallery-tom.co.jp; Tue–Sun 10am–5.30pm; entrance charge; station: Shinsen

Owned by a constructivist sculptor, this concept gallery (the acronym stands for 'Touch Our Museum') is designed for the blind. Broad stairs and handrails lead you to sculptures, which are set at waist level. Visitors are encouraged to touch the forms and let their hands lead them around.

Japan Folk Crafts Museum
4-3-33 Komaba, Meguro-ku; tel: 3467 4527; www.mingeikan.or.jp; Tue–Sun 10am–5pm; entrance charge; station: Komaba-Todaimae; map p.138 A1

The Mingei-kan is one of the best among Tokyo's several hundred museums. The lovely old wood-and-stone building, once owned by master potter Soetsu Yanagi, is a shrine to *mingei*, Japan's folk craft movement. A variety of ceramics, furniture and textiles are exhibited here.

Nezu Institute of Fine Arts
6-5-1 Minami-Aoyama, Minato-ku; tel: 3400 2536; www.nezu-muse.or.jp; Tue–Sun 9.30am–4.30pm; entrance charge; station: Omotesando; map p.139 D1

Concealed behind a sandstone wall, the Nezu Bijutsukan houses the collection of Meiji-era politician and railway tycoon Kaichiro Nezu. The permanent displays feature fine examples of Chinese bronzes, ceramic and lacquerware, calligraphy, textiles and Chinese and Japanese paintings. Its fine-art pieces include objects registered as National Treasures. Among these are a screen painting by Ogata Korin called *Irises*, and a Kamakura Period scroll painting called the *Nanchi Waterfall*. The museum's collection exceeds 7,000 pieces. It is set in a densely wooded and hilly landscape with a small iris pond and a number of teahouses, one of which is open to the public. Closed for renovations until autumn 2009.

Shoto Museum of Art
2-14-14 Shoto, Shibuya-ku; tel: 3465 9421; www.city.shibuya.tokyo.jp/est/museum; Tue–Sun 9am–4.30pm; entrance charge; station: Shinsen; map p.138 B1

The Shoto Bijutsukan features local artists in a cosy setting with a tearoom where pictures can be viewed from the comfort of armchairs.

TEPCO Electric Energy Museum
1-12-10 Jinnan, Shibuya-ku; tel: 3477 1191; www.denryo kukan.com; Thur–Tue 10am–6pm; entrance charge; station: Shibuya; map p.138 B1

Left: the iris pond in the Nezu Institute garden.

Two major art events are the biannual **Design Festa** and the annual **Art Fair Tokyo**. Launched in 1994, Design Festa (www.designfesta.com) is a rollicking convention of youthful artists and performers, open to amateurs and professionals alike. It claims to be the largest art event in Asia. Newcomer the Art Fair Tokyo (www.artfairtokyo.com) is a more highbrow affair, organised by galleries with collectors in mind, intended to help Japan access the booming worldwide contemporary art market.

Located along Fire-dori, two blocks east of the Tobacco and Salt Museum is the Denryokukan. The eight-storey museum can be recognised from its distinctive silver dome. Run by the Tokyo Electric Power Company, its exhibits and interactive displays on every aspect of electricity are especially popular with children.

Tobacco and Salt Museum
1-16-8 Jinnan, Shibuya-ku; tel: 3476 2041; www.jti.co.jp/Culture/museum/; Tue–Sun 10am–5.30pm; entrance charge; station: Shibuya; map p.138 B1

A 10-minute walk south of the NHK complex, along Koen-dori (Koen Avenue), is the Tabako to Shio no Hakubutsukan. Salt and tobacco were a government monopoly until the early 20th century, and remained under strict state control until 1985. The museum traces the history of salt and tobacco production in Japan and overseas through displays that include smoking implements and salt sculptures. The highlight is the fourth-floor special exhibition of *ukiyo-e* woodblock prints of

courtesans and other Edo-period figures relaxing as they prepare their pipes.

Toguri Museum of Art
1-11-3 Shoto, Shibuya-ku; tel: 3465 0070; www.toguri-museum.or.jp; Tue–Sun 9.30am–5pm; entrance charge; station: Shinsen; map p.138 B1

The Toguri Bijutsukan, north of the Shoto Museum, is housed in a yellow-brick building, and features an outstanding collection of fine porcelain. Only a small selection from the Toguri's 3,000-strong collection is shown at any one time. Its Imari, Nabeshima and Hagi pieces, captioned in both Japanese and English, are outstanding.

Ukiyo-e Ota Memorial Museum of Art
1-10-10 Jingumae, Shibuya-ku; tel: 3403 0880; www.ukiyoe-ota-muse.jp; Tue–Sun 10.30am–5pm; entrance charge; station: Harajuku; map p.137 D3

The museum houses the city's finest collection of Edo Period *ukiyo-e* woodblock prints – over 12,000 works in all – including extremely rare prints by artists such as Utamaru, Sharaku and Hiroshige. Remove your shoes before entering the museum.

Watari-um Museum
3-7-6 Jingumae, Shibuya-ku; tel: 3402 3001; www.watarium.co.jp; Tue–Sun 11am–7pm, Wed 11am–9pm; entrance charge; station: Gaienmae; map p.139 C2

A snug yet ultra-modern art space designed by Swiss architect Mario Botta in 1990, the Watari-um features the work of some of today's best Japanese and international avant-garde artists in an intimate setting.

Shinjuku

Bunka Gakuen Costume Museum
3-22-7 Yoyogi, Shibuya-ku; tel: 3299 2387; www.bunka.ac.jp/museum/hakubutsu.htm; Mon–Sat 10am–4pm; entrance charge; station: Shinjuku; map p.138 B3

Part of the Bunka Gakuen fashion institute, the Bunka Gakuen Fukushoku Hakubutsukan has displays of fashions, including Edo Period clothing. Exhibits range from *kosade* dresses and noh drama costumes to the hippy trends of the 1960s.

NTT InterCommunication Centre
4F Tokyo Opera City Tower, 3-20-2 Nishi-Shinjuku,

Below: cutting-edge art at Watari-um Museum.

Left: modern art on show at the Hara Museum.

noon–7pm, Fri–Sat noon–8pm; entrance charge; station: Hatsudai; map p.138 A3
In the same skyscraper complex as the NTT InterCommunication Centre is this sprawling, high-ceilinged, pleasantly uncrowded gallery. Exhibitions focus on contemporary art and design, with an accent on the conceptual.

Ikebukuro and Meijirodai

Ikebukuro Museum of Disaster Prevention
2-37-8 Nishi-Ikebukuro, Toshima-ku; tel: 3590 6565; www.tfd.metro.tokyo.jp/ts/sa/p27.html; Wed–Mon 9am–5pm; free; station: Ikebukuro; map p.134 C4
The Ikebukuro Bosai-Kan is an earthquake simulation centre run by the Tokyo Fire Department. In a city like Tokyo, earthquakes are an ever-present possibility. The experience of being in a room during an earthquake of magnitude six is decidedly weird.

Zoshigaya Missionary Museum
1-25-5 Zoshigaya, Toshima-ku; tel: 3985 4081; daily 10am–5pm; free; station: Higashi-Ikebukuro; map p.135 D4
Another little-visited spot in this older part of the city is the Zoshigaya Kyusenkyoshikan, a lovingly preserved American colonial-style house. It was built in 1907 by an American missionary, John Moody McCaleb, who spent 50 years in Japan.

Shinagawa, Meguro and Ebisu

Hara Museum of Contemporary Art
4-7-25 Kitashinagawa, Shinagawa-ku; tel: 3445 0651;

Shinjuku-ku; tel: 0120 144 199; www.ntticc.or.jp; Tue–Sun 10am–6pm; entrance charge; station: Hatsudai
On the fourth floor of Opera City, this multimedia museum by telecommunications giant NTT hosts innovative exhibitions and interactive displays showing how technology promotes creativity.

Sompo Japan Art Museum
42F Sompo Japan Building, 1-26-1 Nishi-Shinjuku; tel: 3349 3081; www.sompo-japan.co.jp/museum/english; Tue–Sun 10am–5.30pm; free; station: Shinjuku; map p.134 B1
The Sompo Bijutsukan displays works by several Japanese artists. The core of the exhibition are works by Seiji Togo (1897–1978), a skilful but unremarkable painter who specialised in portraits of young women. The highlight of the museum is Van Gogh's *Sunflowers*, which was bought for a whopping ¥6 billion (US$40

million). There is also one work each from Cézanne, Gauguin and Renoir.

Sword Museum
4-25-10 Yoyogi, Shibuya-ku; tel: 3379 1386; Tue–Sun 9am–4pm; entrance charge; station: Sangubashi; map p.138 B3
A few streets northwest of Meiji shrine is the Token Hakubutsukan. Swords were banned during the years of the American occupation, along with mixed bathing in public bathhouses. (In the bewildering double standards of the day, *kabuki* theatres were temporarily closed down at the same time the city's first strip clubs opened.) The museum, run by the Society for the Preservation of Japanese Art Swords, has an astounding collection of 6,000 swords, over 30 of which are registered National Treasures.

Tokyo Opera City Art Gallery
3-20-2 Nishi-Shinjuku, Shinjuku-ku; tel: 5353 0756; www.operacity.jp; Tue–Thur

www.haramuseum.or.jp; Tue–Sun 11am–5pm (Wed until 8pm); entrance charge; station: Shinagawa

Five rooms with connecting corridors display changing exhibitions, which have included works by Yoshitomo Nara and international artists such as Andy Warhol. The grandfather of the museum's founder, Hara Toshio, had the Bauhaus-style home built in 1938. One of Japan's leading architects, Isozaki Arata, recently added an annexe, the Café d'Art, which overlooks a sculpture garden.

Hatakeyama Museum
2-20-12 Shirokanedai, Minato-ku; tel: 3447 5787; www.ebara.co.jp/socialactivity/hatakeyama/english; Tue–Sun 10am–4.30pm; entrance charge; station: Takanawadai

The Hatakeyama Kinen Bijutsukan is located on a wooded hill at the heart of an estate once owned by the Lord of Satsuma in Kyushu. A section of the old garden still remains. The museum reflects the interests of its founder, the industrialist and tea-ceremony master Hatakeyama Issei. Galleries display tea utensils and bowls, hand scrolls and other tea-ceremony objects, but

also lacquerware and noh costumes. There are three tea-ceremony rooms as well.

Tokyo Metropolitan Photography Museum
Ebisu Garden Place, 1-13-3 Mita, Meguro-ku; tel: 3280 0031; www.syabi.com; Tue–Sun 10am–6pm (Thur–Fri until 8pm); entrance charge; station: Ebisu

On the eastern side of the plaza is the superb Tokyo-to Shashin Bijutsukan, the premier exhibition space for notable photography and video art. Major Japanese and Western photographers are featured here.

Tokyo Metropolitan Teien Art Museum
5-21-9 Shirokanedai, Minato-ku; tel: 3443 0201; www.teien-art-museum.ne.jp; daily 10am–5.30pm, closed 2nd and 4th Wed; entrance charge; station: Meguro

The Tokyo-to Teien Bijutsukan is housed in the imposing former villa belonging to Prince Yasuhiko Asaka. This member of the imperial family has the dubious reputation of being the general in charge of Japanese troops during the Nanking Massacre in China. The residence was converted into a museum in 1983, but of more interest is the fact that

Art mavens can top off a day at the Museum of Contemporary Art with a visit to the nearby Shinkawa Gallery Complex. Occupying a former paper warehouse are three of Tokyo's most influential galleries: **ShugoArts** (www.shugarts.com), **Taka Ishii** (www.takaishiigallery) and the **Tomio Koyama Gallery** (www.tomiokoyamagallery.com). They represent some of Japan's top current names, including Yoshitomo Nara and Nobuyuki Araki.

the villa may well be the city's only surviving Art Deco building. The house, surrounded by lovely French-and Japanese-style landscaped gardens, reflects tastes acquired during the prince's three-year sojourn in Paris in the 1920s.

Tokyo Bayside

Museum of Maritime Science
3-1 Higashi-Yashio, Shinagawa-ku; tel: 5500 1111; www.funenokagakukan.or.jp; Tue–Sun 10am–5pm; entrance charge; station: Fune-no-Kagakukan

The Fune-no-Kagakukan, shaped like an ocean liner, has exhibits tracing the history of shipping and commercial transportation. Bringing the whole subject alive are two actual ships, the Soya, once used for expeditions to the Antarctic, and the Yoteimaru, one of a fleet of now almost obsolete ferries that carried passengers between Honshu and Hokkaido islands.

National Museum of Emerging Science and Innovation
2-41 Aomi, Koto-ku; tel: 3570 9151; www.miraikan.jst.go.jp; Wed–Mon 10am–5pm; station: Telecom Centre

Below: attractive and peaceful Zoshigaya Missionary Museum.

Like many of the buildings on the island, the Miraikan also has its own observation lounge. A robot conducts tours of the displays of innovative Japanese design and technology.

Suidobashi, Ochanomizu, Kanda and Akihabara

Museums of Meiji University

1-1 Kanda-Surugadai, Chiyoda-ku; tel: 3296 4432; www.meiji. ac.jp/museum; Mon–Sat 10am–4.30pm (Sat until 12.30pm); entrance charge; station: Ochanomizu

The Meiji Daigaku Kokogaku Hakubutsukan is in the institute's University Hall. The archaeological museum houses objects found on digs around Japan, as well as items from China and Korea. One floor down is the Criminal Museum or Keiji Hakubutsukan, with exhibits relating to the investigation, capture and punishment of criminals during the Edo and Meiji periods. Woodblock prints depicting punishments hang alongside instruments of torture and execution.

Tokyo Wonder Site

2-4-16 Hongo, Bunkyo-ku; tel: 5689 5531; www.tokyo-ws.org; Tue–Sun 11am–7pm; free; station: Suidobashi; map p.136 C2

The Hongo Tokyo Wonder Site was set up by the Tokyo Metropolitan government to encourage and promote exciting new works by young and up-and-coming artists. Three floors of whatever is current, from paintings to video installations.

Ueno and Yanaka

Asakura Choso Sculpture Museum

7-18-10 Yanaka, Taito-ku; tel: 3821 4549; www.taitocity. net/taito/asakura; Tue–Thur and Sat–Sun 9.30am–4.30pm; entrance charge; station: Nippori; map p.137 C4

The Asakura Chosokan is a gallery showing the work of Fumio Asakura. The artist's studio-house and courtyard garden are open to the public.

Drum Museum

2-1-1 Asakusa-Nishi, Taito-ku; tel: 3842 5622; www.tctv.ne.jp/ members/taikokan; Wed–Sun 9am–5pm; entrance charge; station: Asakusa; map p.137 E3

South of Rokku, at the junction of Kaminarimon-dori and Kokusai-dori, the Taiko-kan occupies the second floor above a shop that sells drums and large items like portable shrines used in Shinto festivals. Drums from all over the world are displayed here, and visitors are encouraged to try them out.

National Museum of Western Art

7-7 Ueno Koen, Taito-ku; tel: 3828 5131; www.nmwa.go.jp; Tue–Sun 9.30am–5pm (Fri until 8pm); entrance charge; station: Ueno; map p.137 D3

The Kokuritsu Seiyo Bijutsukan is two different buildings. The original, completed in 1959, is the work of Le Corbusier, while the newer building housing temporary exhibitions is a design by Kunio Maekawa. The permanent collection includes works by Renoir, Degas, Tintoretto, Rubens, as well as Miró, Picasso and Jackson Pollock. The courtyard has 57 Rodin sculptures.

National Science Museum

7-20 Ueno Koen, Taito-ku; tel: 3822 0111; www.kahaku. go.jp; Tue–Sun 9am–4.30pm (Fri until 7.30pm); entrance charge; station: Ueno; map p.137 D3

The Kokuritsu Kahaku Hakubutsukan is devoted to science and technology, engineering, natural history and aerospace research. Its dinosaur displays, exhibits on the oceanography and botany of Japan, and interactive displays and videos are popular with children.

Shitamachi Museum

2-1 Ueno Koen, Taito-ku; tel: 3823 7451; www.taitocity. net/taito/shitamachi; daily 9.30am–4.30pm; entrance charge; station: Ueno; map p.137 D3

The Shitamachi Fuzoku Shiryokan is near the pond in Ueno Park. A transplanted tenement block and merchant house display objects such as kitchenware and children's toys. Demonstrations of handicraft skills are regularly staged, with videos and photographs showing the area up to the 1940s.

Tokyo Metropolitan Art Museum

8-36 Ueno Koen, Taito-ku; tel: 3823 6921; www.tobikan.jp; daily 9am–5pm; entrance charge; station: Ueno; map p.137 D3

The 1975 red-brick Tokyo-to Bijutsukan completes the set of Kunio Maekawa designs in Ueno Park. Over half of the building is below ground to prevent it intruding into the park. Three floors are set aside for its collection of Japanese artists, temporary exhibitions, studio space and an art school. Exhibi-

Left: the National Museum of Western Art's garden.

Left: entrance to the Tokyo Museum of Contemporary Art.

The quaint Tabi Hakubut-sukan is one of several small, often family-run, trade- and crafts-oriented museums in the Sumida Ward area. This museum displays the tools and equipment used in the making of *tabi,* the dainty little split-toe socks worn by women attired in kimono, sumo wrestlers and practi-tioners of certain traditional disciplines like archery.

tions by established painters, calligraphers and promising new artists.

Tokyo National Museum

13-9 Ueno Koen, Taito-ku; tel: 3822 1111; www.tnm.go.jp; Tue–Sun 9.30am–8pm, Dec–Mar until 5pm; entrance charge; station: Ueno; map p.137 D4

The Tokyo Kokuritsu Hakubutsukan houses a per-manent collection of paint-ings, textiles, calligraphy, ceramics and lacquerware in the main Honkan Gallery; archaeological relics from the Jomon Period to the early 19th century can be found in the Heiseikan Gallery; while the Toyokan Gallery has an eclectic mix of Chinese, Cen-tral Asian and Korean art treasures. The Gallery of Horyu-ji Treasures has masks, scrolls, sculpture and treasures from the Horyu-ji Temple in Nara.

Sumida River, Asakusa, Ryogoku and East Tokyo

Edo-Tokyo Museum

1-4-1 Yokoami, Sumida-ku; tel: 3626 9974; www.edo-tokyo-museum.or.jp; Tue–Sun 9.30am–5.30pm (Sat until 7.30pm); entrance charge; station: Ryogoku; map p.137 E1

The museum evokes the

Right: interior of the Edo-Tokyo Museum.

merchant life and culture of people living during the Edo Period, from the common people to samurai. To reach the start of the exhibition, visitors cross a reconstruc-tion of Nihombashi Bridge. Exhibitions not only cover the early life of Edo, but also the years from 1868, through the post-war reconstruction years and the 1964 Tokyo Olympics. The museum shop has a good selection of tradi-tional crafts from the down-town Shitamachi area.

Tabi Museum

1-9-3 Midori, Sumida-ku; tel: 3631 0092; Mon–Sat 9am–5pm; entrance charge; station: Ryogoku; map p.137 E1

Tokyo Museum of Contemporary Art

4-4-1 Miyoshi, Koutou-ku; tel: 5245 4111; www.mot-art-museum.jp; Tue–Sun 10am–5.30pm; entrance charge; station: Kiyosumi-Shirakawa

The Tokyo-to Gendai Bijut-sukan was the first of the recent major contemporary art museums. Located on what was once marshland, this futuristic structure houses art from a collection of over 3,500 items, as well as new work by Japanese and foreign artists. The museum is great fun, with experimental and interactive displays and an extensive database in Japan-ese and English.

Music

Japanese devotion to music is legendary, and as the capital of the world's second-biggest music market, Tokyo is at the centre of it. From its vast stadiums to its concert halls and smoky dives, from ancient sounds to the cutting edge, Tokyo boasts a lifetime's worth of musical experience any night of the week. With an increasing number of bands touring Tokyo and more foreign musicians choosing to make it their home, its music scene is becoming progressively more international. CD and vinyl buffs can also indulge in the world's most diverse market for record-shopping.

Japanese Music

Courtly *gagaku* music is the same today as it was 1,500 years ago. It incorporates not only orchestral music played on wind instruments such as the *shakuhachi* (bamboo flute), string instruments, gongs and drums, but also singing and dancing, when it becomes known as *bugaku*. Most *gagaku* is based on music imported centuries ago from Asian neighbours. Performances are staged at the Imperial Palace, but one needs a connection to gain entrance. Occasional per-formances take place at shrines and the **National Theatre** (see p.121).

Hogaku refers to popular Japanese music in its entirety. This ranges from *minyo* (folk songs) accom-panied on the *shamisen* (a banjo-like instrument) or, in Okinawa, the snake-skinned *sanshin* (a kind of smaller *shamisen*), to the subtle sounds of the harp-like *koto*, to extroverted *matsuri* (festi-val) music played on the massive *taiko* drum, to con-temporary *enka* (ballads) and J-pop, which in turn runs the gamut from rock to hip hop.

Western Classical

Japan opened its doors to classical music in the 19th century, and notwithstanding the frequent presence of over-seas conductors and soloists, now has its own legitimate stars, from conductor Seiji Ozawa to violinist Midori.

Flush with Bubble-era cash, corporate titans and ambitious governors left Tokyo strewn with monu-ments to high culture.

Perhaps less thought was given to how to fill these halls, but Tokyo can claim more classical concerts and venues than any other city.

Greater Tokyo has no fewer than five symphony orchestras, including the Tokyo Symphony Orchestra and the New Japan Philhar-monic Orchestra, while the Fujiwara Opera Company and the New National Theatre stage their own opera pro-ductions.

Left: Tokyo Symphony Orchestra.

Left: Tokyo hosts three major music festivals.

eastern Tokyo, Triphony Hall is the home to the New Japan Philharmonic, established in response to a call by its honorary artistic director Seiji Ozawa.

Suntory Hall
1-13-1 Akasaka, Minato-ku; tel: 3584 3100; www.suntory. com/culture-sports/suntoryhall; station: Roppongi-icchome; map p.139 E1
Renowned for its excellent acoustics, beer-maker Suntory's hall in Akasaka's Ark Hills complex was built with the advice of renowned maestro Herbert von Karajan.

Tokyo Bunka Kaikan
5-45 Ueno Park, Taito-ku; tel: 3828 2111; www.t-bunka.jp; station: Ueno; map p.137 D3
With two halls, this was for decades post-war Japan's premier classical music venue and has recently been refurbished. A wide-ranging programme of symphonic and opera concerts, and home to the Tokyo Ballet.

Tokyo Opera City
3-2-2 Nishi-Shinjuku, Shinjuku-ku; tel: 5353 0770; www.opera city.jp; station: Hatsudai
The home of the superb **New National Theatre**

Concert tickets can be purchased at box offices as well as ticket agency Pia (found in major department stores) and convenience store Lawson. If your Japanese is up to snuff, Pia (http://t.pia.jp) and e+ (http://eplus.jp) both offer online ticketing.

VENUES

Bunkamura Orchard Hall
2-24-1 Dogenzaka, Shibuya-ku; tel: 3477 9150; www.bunka mura.co.jp; station: Shibuya; map p.138 B1
One of Tokyo's first retail and culture complexes, Bunkamura includes Orchard Hall for symphonic concerts, ballets and operas, and the smaller **Theatre Cocoon** for chamber music and theatre.

Muza Kawasaki Symphony Hall
1310 Omiya-cho Saiwai-ku, Kawasaki; tel: 520 0100; www.kawasaki-sym-hall.jp; station: Kawasaki
Home to the Tokyo Symphony Orchestra, Muza Kawasaki, opened in 2004, has an innovative, oblong design that affords good viewing from all seats. The 'Festa Summer Muza Kawasaki' event offers a wide range of programmes at rock-bottom ticket prices.

Sumida Triphony Hall
1-2-3 Kinshi, Sumida-ku; tel: 5608 1212; www.triphony. com; station: Kinshicho; Located in Sumida Ward in

Right: Tokyo Opera City's main Takamitsu Memorial Concert Hall premières works by contemporary Japanese and foreign composers.

Left: despite high entrance fees, the Blue Note is often full.

www.bluenote.co.jp; station: Omotesando; map p.139 C1
Top international acts appear in this sophisticated venue. The ambience is much like that of the original venue in the US, and the performances are top-notch.

Body & Soul
B1F, 6-13-9 Minami-Aoyama, Minato-ku; tel: 5466 3348; www.bodyandsoul.co.jp; station: Omotesando; map p.139 C1
A favourite with music industry folk. The vibes at this 30-year-old club are exclusively jazz.

JZ Brat
2F Cerulean Tower Tokyu Hotel, 26-1 Sakuragaoka-cho, Shibuya-ku; tel: 5728 0168; www.jzbrat.com; station: Shibuya
Top-name international and home-grown acts at this small venue in a posh hotel.

Pit Inn
B1F Accord Building, 2-12-4 Shinjuku, Shinjuku-ku; tel: 3354-2024; www.pit-inn.com; station: Shinjuku Sanchome; map p.138 C4
For over 40 years, Pit Inn has been a temple of jazz for the Tokyo faithful. Avant-garde innovators like Yoshihide Otomo and the occasional overseas act perform in atmospheric confines.

Popular

Tokyo has long been the home of a fevered pop- and rock-music scene. It has offered to the world innovative acts – from the electro-pop of Ryuichi Sakamoto's Yellow Magic Orchestra to the avant-garde noise rock of the Boredoms – to new Japanese-Western hybrid artists like rock group Love Psychedelico and R&B queen Crystal Kay. Also making their mark internationally are the unchal-

(www.nntt.jac.go.jp) and its opera company, which stages Mozart. Smaller adjoining theatres offer ballet and drama.
SEE ALSO THEATRE AND DANCE, P.123

Jazz

Dozens of jazz clubs large and small, featuring all styles from swing to free jazz, cater to a remarkably well-informed audience. Many performers have had great success abroad, notably saxophonist Sadao Watanabe, trumpeter Terumasa Hino and, recently, young pianist Hiromi Uehara. Likewise, many American jazz greats visit Japan regularly, perform at upscale nightclubs. Another highlight are the jazz festivals that liven up torrid Tokyo summers, like Tokyo Jazz.

VENUES
B-Flat Akasaka
Akasaka 6-6-4, Minato-ku; tel: 5563 2563; www.bflat.jp; station: Akasaka; map p.139 E2
A classic jazz club in the nightlife district of Akasaka. Features top, mostly mainstream local acts and the occasional international artist.

Birdland
B2F, 3-10-3 Roppongi, Minato-ku; tel: 3478 3456; www.birdland-tokyo.jp; station: Roppongi; map p.139 E1
One of the older jazz and fusion clubs in town, Birdland may not be as trendy as it was a few years ago, but it manages to put on a good evening's worth of entertainment, with both live acts and DJ spots from some of Tokyo's best-known acts.

Blue Note Tokyo
6-3-16 Minami-Aoyama, Minato-ku; tel: 5485 0088;

The annual **Fuji Rock Festival** is a three-day event held at a ski resort near Tokyo at the end of July that attracts international acts like the Red Hot Chili Peppers. Its rival, **Summer Sonic** targets a younger demographic with headliners like the Arctic Monkeys at a suburban convention centre on the second weekend of August. **Rock in Japan** is the J-rock competitor and is held between the international fests at a seaside park.

lenged *aidoru* (idols) of J-Pop, Hikaru Utada, Kumi Koda and Ayumi Hamazaki.

Akasaka Blitz
5-3-2 Akasaka, Minato-ku; tel: 3584 8811; www.tbs.co.jp/blitz; station: Akasaka; map p.139 E2
The latest 2,000-capacity concert hall in Tokyo boasts the most advanced lighting and sound system. Part of the Tokyo Broadcasting System complex in Akasaka.

Billboard Live
4F Tokyo Midtown, 9-7-4 Akasaka, Minato-ku; tel: 3405 1133; www.billboard-live.com; shows Mon–Fri 7 and 9.30pm; Sat–Sun and hols 6 and 9pm; station: Roppongi; map p.140 A2
Licensed by the American music industry trade magazine *Billboard*, this glistening

international jazz and pop supper club is a centrepiece of Roppongi's new Midtown development.

Club Asia
1-8 Maruyama-cho, Shibuya-ku; tel: 5458 5963; www.clubasia.co.jp; call or see website for schedule; station: Shibuya; map p.138 B1
The dance floors and bars on different levels are an interesting design feature, though the music can get warped in the process. Typical of Tokyo's multi-use spaces, Club Asia might host a punk band in the evening, followed by a night of club jazz, trance or dancehall.

Club Quattro
5F Parco Quattro, 32-13 Udagawacho, Shibuya-ku; tel: 3477 8750; www.net-flyer.com; call or see website for schedule; station: Shibuya; map p.138 B1
Inside the Parco department store – you need to take the lift to reach it. International rock and world music bands as well as local groups play on what is one of Tokyo's most storeyed stages.

Crocodile
B1, 6-18-8 Jingumae, Shibuya-ku; tel: 3499 5205; shows 8pm; station: Shibuya; map p.138 B1
One of the oldest live houses in Tokyo, Crocodile has expanded its repertoire over

the years to include not just rock, but whatever happens to be hip, including rap bands, Latin combos, jazz. etc. Also current home to the Tokyo Comedy Store.

Eggman
1-6-8 Jinnan, Shibuya-ku; tel: 3496 1561; http://eggman.jp/ venue; call or see website for schedule; station: Shibuya; map p.138 B1
Talent-spotters come here to see and sign acts who go on to greater things in the world of Japanese rock and J-Pop.

Gig-antic
2F Sound Forum Building 3-20-15, Shibuya, Shibuya-ku; tel: 5466 9339; www.gig-antic.co.jp; call or see website for schedule; station: Shibuya; map p.138 B1
Tiny venue popular with emerging bands, though older established hardcore rock acts perform here too.

Heaven's Door
B1F, 1-33-19 Sangenjaya, Setagaya-ku; tel: 3410 9581; www.geocities.jp/xxxheavens doorxxx; call or see website for schedule; station: Sangenjaya
A classic rock dive in the heart of studenty Sangenjaya. Cream of the J-indies scene, with the occasional tour by underground international artists.

Below: Tokyo Dome's walk of fame and the trendy Shinjuku district.

La.Mama Shibuya

B1F Premier Dogenzaka Building, 1-15-3, Dogenzaka, Shibuya-ku; tel: 3464 0801; www.lamama.net; call or see website for schedule; station: Shibuya; map p.138 B1

A long-time feature of the vibrant music scene in Shibuya, La.Mama has moved in recent years from hardcore rock and punk acts to the softer world of J-Pop.

Liquid Room

3-16-6 Higashi, Shibuya-ku; tel: 5464 0800; www.liquid-room.net; call or see website for schedule; station: Ebisu

Relocated from seamy Kabuki-cho to trendy Ebisu, Liquid Room is a roomy basement live house with a lounge bar. Upstairs is a Tower Records café that often hosts late-night house parties. The location has changed but the excellent line-up of rock concerts and DJs has not.

Loft

B2F Tatehana Building, 1-12-9 Kabukicho, Shinjuku-ku; tel: 5272 0382; www.loft-prj.co.jp; call or see website for schedule; station: Shinjuku; map p.134 B1

A fixture of Tokyo's domestic rock scene for decades, Loft occupies a sprawling basement in Kabuki-cho. Two stages and a separate bar area afford plenty of room for events from punk to noise to psychedelic rock and beyond. A mostly young but diverse and laid-back crowd parties until the morning at weekends.

Marz

B1F Daiichi Tokiwa Building, 2-45-1 Kabukicho, Shinjuku-ku; tel: 3202 8248; www.marz.jp; call or see website for schedule; station: Kabukicho; map p.134 B1

Some of Japan's most progressive indie rock acts, a smattering of touring bands and even poetry slams make mid-sized Marz one of Tokyo's best bets for the travelling rock fan.

Nippon Budokan

2-3 Kitanomaru-Koen, Chiyoda-ku; tel: 3216 0781; www.nip-ponbudokan.or.jp; station: Kudanshita; map p.136 B1

Built to hold martial arts competitions, this historic venue has welcomed chart-topping acts from The Beatles to Destiny's Child.

O-East

2-14-9 Dogenzaka, Shibuya-ku; tel: 5458 4681; shibuya-o.com; station: Shibuya; map p.138 B1

This new mid-sized hall is part of a two-building, multi-storey venue for live domestic and international concerts in the youth culture mecca of Shibuya. The smaller **West** (tel: 5784 7088), **Nest** (tel: 3462 4420) and **Crest** (tel: 3770 1095) have consistently strong indie-rock line-ups.

Shibuya Ax

2-1-1 Jinnan, Shibuya-ku; tel: 5738-2020; www.shibuya-ax.com; station: Harajuku; map p.138 B1

This purpose-built, medium-sized concert hall next to Yoyogi Park is functional, if lacking in atmosphere. Both domestic and touring acts are featured.

SuperDeluxe

B1F, 3-1-25 Nishi Azabu, Minato-ku; tel: 5412 0515; www.super-deluxe.com; Mon–Sat 6pm–late; station: Roppongi; map p.139 D1

Calling itself 'a place of experimentation/a noisy thing/an intimate ballroom with wholesome food', the

spacious basement assumes a different character depending on the event. A night of cutting-edge electronica may be followed by a contemporary dance performance. An experimental jazz band may give way to an avant-garde fashion show or four-to-the-floor beats. Crowds vary, but the atmosphere is always friendly.

Tokyo Dome (Big Egg)
1-3 Koraku, Bunkyo-ku; tel: 5800 9999; www.tokyo-dome.co.jp; station: Suidobashi; map p.136 B2

Home to baseball's Yomiuri Giants, this vast covered dome is notorious for poor acoustics. Past visitors include the Red Hot Chili Peppers and The Police.

Tokyo International Forum
3-5-1 Marunouchi, Chiyoda-ku; tel: 5221 9000; www.t-i-forum.co.jp; station: Yurakucho; map p.141 C3

An architecturally inspired grouping of elegant concert halls in various sizes that play host to anything from pop to jazz and classical.

Unit
B1F Za HOUSE Building, 1-34-17 Ebisu-Nishi, Shibuya-ku; tel: 5459 8630; www.unit-tokyo.com; days vary, 6–11pm (live events), 11.30pm–5am (club events); station: Daikanyama

A mainstay of youth culture in Daikanyama, Unit sandwiches its medium-sized dance floor and live stage between a mod café above and a lounge bar below. The crowd tends to be serious about its music, and the strength and diversity of its bookings policy speaks for itself. On any given weeknight the cream of Japan's indie and experimental rock

Left: live music at SuperDeluxe in Roppongi.

English-language listings are available in the *Metropolis* (www.metropolis.co.jp) weekly and the daily newspapers, as well as *Tokyo Gig Guide* (www.tokyogigguide.com) and *iFlyer* (www.iflyer.jp/tokyo), but a true picture of everything that's going on requires a look at Japanese entertainment media like *Pia* (www.pia.co.jp) magazine.

scene is on stage. Weekends are given over to heavyweight DJs.

Zepp Tokyo
Daiba, Minato-ku; www.zepp.co.jp; station: Oume

Located on artificial island Odaiba in Tokyo Bay with a Ferris wheel nearby, Zepp Tokyo is a utilitarian hall.

CDs and Vinyl

DJs the world over flock to Tokyo for its unparallelled selection of CDs and vinyl. Huge CD shops and tiny vinyl specialists in Shibuya and Shinjuku are also the best places to pick up flyers for upcoming events, and the free magazine *Metropolis* (www.metropolis.co.jp), has up-to-date information in English.

Dance Music Record
36-2 Udagawa-cho, Shibuya-ku; tel: 3477 1556; www.dmr.co.jp; daily 1–9pm; station: Shibuya; map p.138 B1

One of Japan's largest specialists in vinyl for club DJs, DMR puts the emphasis on hip hop, house, R&B and club jazz.

Disc Union
3-31-4 Shinjuku, Shinjuku-ku; tel: 3352 2691; www.diskunion.co.jp/top.html; daily 11am–9pm, (Sun till 8pm); station: Shinjuku; map p.138 B4

A crowded multi-storey cornucopia of used CDs and vinyls with even more in nearby satellite shops. Every

Above: the well stocked bar at SuperDeluxe.

imaginable genre is catered to, from rock to jazz, world music to electronica.

HMV
1-6F Takagi Building, Udagawa-cho, Shibuya-ku, tel: 5458 3411; www.hmv.co.jp; daily 10am–11pm; station: Shibuya

Its first floor is devoted to new releases and charts; successive floors are divided according to genre. Both HMV and Tower host in-store live music showcases.

Tower
1-22-14 Jinnan, Shibuya-ku; tel: 3496 3661; www.tower-records. jp/store/store03.html; daily 10am–11pm; station: Shibuya

A postmodern monolith with a superb catalogue of Japanese independent releases and international fare.

Vinyl Japan
B1F Hamada Building, 7-4-7 Nishi-Shinjuku, Shinjuku-ku; tel: 3365 0910; www2.odn.ne.jp/vinyl-japan; daily noon–9pm; station: Shinjuku; map p.134 B1

With an astounding selection of imported rare vinyls, covering UK and US rock, new wave, reggae, soul and R&B. Part 2 across the street stocks punk, rockabilly, garage, and pub rock. One of a cluster of rock specialists in the area.

Nightlife

The last but certainly not least hours in Tokyo's 24-hour day are a time when busy urbanites unwind at the city's fathomless horizon of 'live house' music venues, dance clubs and DJ bars. The only challenge is deciding when and where to go. Live-music venues usually start and end early; DJ bars and dance clubs pick up from there until mid-morning at weekends. Tokyo nightlife tends to be a safe and friendly experience; still, the usual caution is advisable. Due to police vigilance over drugs and under-age drinking, many clubs enforce a 20-and-over policy; photo ID is a must.

Clubs and DJ Bars

Ageha
2-2-10 Shin-Kiba, Koto-ku; tel: 5534 1515; www.ageha.com; Fri–Sat 11pm–late; station: Shin-Kiba

Ageha is the name that bayside venue Studio Coast adopts at weekends, when it becomes Tokyo's biggest dance club, with three separate dance rooms and a poolside bar. Hundreds of clubbers bus in from Shibuya for massive hip-hop, house, techno and trance parties.

Air
2-11 Sarugaku, Shibuya-ku; tel: 5784 3386; www.air-tokyo.com; Mon–Sat 10pm–late; station: Shibuya

Between Shibuya and trendy Daikanyama, Air is a comfort-able, mid-sized dance club that competes with Tokyo's leading venues for young, ultra-hip clubbers looking to dance to house, electro, drum 'n' bass and hip hop. Café upstairs for chilling out.

Gas Panic Club
2F Kento's Building, 3-14-11 Roppongi, Minato-ku; tel: 3402 7054; www.gaspanic.co.jp; daily 6pm–5am; station: Roppongi; map p.139 E1

An infamous dance club and pick-up joint with branches in Roppongi and Shibuya; hosts private parties and special events like tattoo nights.

La Fabrique
16-9 Udagawacho, Shibuya-ku; tel: 5428 5100; www.lafabrique.jp; Fri–Sat 11pm–late; station: Shibuya; map p.138 B1

Stylish French-culture outpost that transforms from a chic restaurant into a throbbing house club at weekends.

Module
M&1 Building, 3-4-6 Udagawa-cho, Shibuya-ku; tel: 3464 8432; http://module-tokyo.com/; call or see website for schedule; station: Shibuya; map p.138 B1

The small basement warren and its pitch-black dance floor are the setting for some serious house, techno, electro and drum 'n' bass.

Oto
2F, 1-17-5, Kabukicho, Shinjuku-ku; tel: 5273 8264; www.club-oto.com; daily 10pm–late; station: Shinjuku; map p.134 B1

With a giant wall of speakers and a tiny dance floor, Oto ('sound') is an enduring outpost of house music amid the sleaze of Kabukicho. Expert local DJs deal the beats.

The Room
B1F Daihachi Toto Building, 15-19 Sakuragaoka, Shibuya-ku; tel: 3461 7167; www.theroom.jp; Thur–Sun 10pm–5am; station: Shibuya

Owned by Shuya Okino, one half of famed club jazz DJ collective Kyoto Jazz Massive, The Room is a cosy, welcoming space. Don't miss Okino's Saturday 'Tokyo Jazz Meeting' events.

Salsa Sudada
3F La Pallette Building, 7-13-8 Roppongi, Minato-ku; tel: 5474 8806; daily 6pm–6am; station: Roppongi; map p.139 E1

One of the biggest salsa

Left: Gas Panic Club, Shibuya.

daily noon–4.30pm and 5–9pm;
station: Shinjuku-Sanchome;
map p.138 C4
This atmospheric Japanese-
style theatre features regular
performances of *rakugoh*,
Japan's art of comedic story-
telling, as well as magic and
origami paper-cutting. No
English translation.

Tokyo Comedy Store
www.tokyocomedy.com
Tokyo's leading English-
language comedy group per-
forms at Crocodile (see p.85).

Shows

Kaguwa
5-4-2 Roppongi, Minato-ku; tel:
5414 8818; www.kaguwa.com;
daily 6pm–1am (Fri–Sat until
4am); entrance charge; station:
Roppongi; map p.139 E1
Dinner shows that blend
Meiji-era themes with contemporary song-and-dance.

Tokyo Roppongi
Kingyo Nightclub
3-14-17 Roppongi, Minato-ku;
tel: 3478 3000; Tue–Wed and
Sun 6pm–12.30am, Fri–Sat
6pm–3am; station: Roppongi;
map p.139 E1
Simultaneously titillating and
topical, Kingyo's transvestite/
transsexual shows combine
cabaret, satire and political
theatre. Three shows nightly.

Entry at live houses and clubs
ranges from ¥1,000 for
obscure bands and weeknight
events to ¥5,000 up for overseas acts and superstar DJs.

---

venues in Tokyo and one of
the oldest joints around, its
renovation has helped it to
reclaim its position as the best
salsa spot in town. If you don't
dance, go somewhere else.

Soft
B1F, 3-1-9 Shibuya, Shibuya-ku;
tel: 5467 5817; www.soft-tokyo.
com; Mon–Thur 8pm–3am,
Fri–Sat 9pm–4 or 5am, Sun and
holidays 6–11pm; station:
Shibuya; map p.138 C1
Soft is everything one expects
from a Tokyo club. It is tiny,
tucked out of the way, and has
a futuristic, all-white interior.
Events run from house to
Shibuya kei to electro.

Warehouse 702
B1F Fukao Building, 1-4-5 Azabu-
juban, Minato-ku; tel: 6230 0343;
www.warehouse702.com;
Mon–Sat from 10 or 11pm;
Station: Azabu-juban
Formerly Luners, Warehouse
in the Azabu-juban district
near Roppongi is one of

Tokyo's larger clubs. Reached
via a steep tunnel of a staircase, it is a long and narrow
space with a stage at one end
and a bar at the other.

Womb
2-16 Maruyama-cho, Shibuya-ku;
tel: 5459 0039; www.womb.co.jp;
Fri–Sat 10pm–late, Sun 4–10pm;
station: Shibuya; map p.138 B1
This cavernous, four-floor
club is one of the serious
dance-culture venues in
Tokyo. What it lacks in
atmosphere it makes up for
with excellent music and a
gargantuan sound system.

Comedy

Punchline Comedy Club
Pizza Express, 3F, 4-30-3 Jingumae, Shibuya-ku; tel: 5775 3894;
www.punchlinecomedy.com/
tokyo; station: Harajuku; map
p.138 C2
The Tokyo branch of comedy
entrepreneur John Moorhead's
pan-Asian comedy club hosts
top stand-up comedians from
around the world.

Suehiro-tei
3-6-12 Shinjuku, Shinjuku-ku;
tel: 3351 2974; suehirotei.com;

Otaku Culture

The word *otaku* was originally a derogatory term for people with pathologically obsessive interests in *anime* and *manga*. These days *otaku* has become a hugely popular phenomenon around the world and is now synonymous with Japanese cool, as well as a reportedly US$3.5 billion economy. In Tokyo, *otaku* pilgrims head to Akihabara (*Akiba* to the faithful), home of hundreds of electronics and software shops as well as maid cafés, cosplay hobby outlets and the like. The area ranked among the top five places foreign tourists wanted to visit in 2007.

Akihabara

AKA Comic Tora no Ana 1
4-3-1 Soto-Kanda, Chiyoda-ku; tel: 5294 0123; www.toranoana. jp; daily 10am–10pm; station: Akihabara; map p.137 D2
A palace of *otaku* goods, beginning with *manga* and audiovisual software and extending to *dojinshi – manga* by amateur artists, often with erotic content – as well as *dojin* software. Located on the main Chuo-dori drag.

AKB48 Stage
8F Don Quixote, 4-3-3 Soto-Kanda, Chiyoda-ku; www.akb48.co.jp; station: Akihabara; map p.137 D2
AKB is a revue of *aidoru* (young female singers usually of limited talent) who perform in *seirafuku* schoolgirl outfits for enthusiastic *otaku*, weeknights and weekends on a stage above the Don Quixote discount store. Big queues, and tickets sell out quickly.

AsoBitCity
1-13-3 Soto-Kanda, Chiyoda-ku; tel: 3251 3100; www.akibaaso bit.jp; daily 10am–10pm; station: Akihabara; map p.137 D2
Part of a chain, AsoBit is a multi-storey paradise for *otaku* hobbyists. Each floor features different genres of character figures from hit *anime* shows. The sixth floor is devoted to cosplay wear.

Gamers Head Store
Takarada Building, 1-14-7 Soto-Kanda, Chiyoda-ku; tel: 5298 8720; http://cgi.broccoli. co.jp/gamers/honten2; daily 11am–9pm; station: Akihabara; map p.137 D2
Renowned for its 'DiGi Charat' mascot, this store packs a wide spectrum of game *otaku* goods from CDs and DVDs to books, magazines and trading cards. There are regular events here. The shop is scheduled to relocate in summer 2008.

Heroine Special Effects Research Centre
4-4-9 Soto-Kanda, Chiyoda-ku; tel: 5289 9200; www.heroine tokusatsu.net; Mon–Fri 11am–9pm, Sat 10am–8pm, Sun 10am–7pm; station: Akihabara; map p.137 D2
Next to Don Quixote in a narrow basement space, Heroine Tokusatsu reflects the owner's interest in superhero shows and pornography. A haven for collectors of rare SF movies and other such things.

Below: vending machines in Tokyo Anime Centre

Left: characters and games galore at Tokyo Anime Centre.

giant installations such as *neco basu* (the cat bus from *My Neighbour Totoro*), while for adults there are exhibitions about Miyazaki's creative process. Reservations via the website.

Mandarake
5-52-15 Nakano, Nakano-ku; tel: 3228 0007; www.man darake.co.jp; daily noon–8pm; station: Nakano

The flagship of Japan's leading *manga* speciality store is a temple for *manga* fanatics, with rarities from a range of genres as well as posters, AV software, games and figures.

Suginami Animation Museum
3F Suginami Kaikan, 3-39-5 Kamiogi, Suginami-ku; tel: 3396 1510; www.sam.or.jp; Tue–Sun 10am–5.30pm; station: Ogikubo

Known as '*anime* town', Suginami Ward in western Tokyo opened this museum to its creative industry in 2005. A window into the production of *anime*, as well as workshops.

Events

Comiket
www.comiket.co.jp

Comiket (Comic Market) is the world's biggest *manga* convention, held summer and winter. More than half a million people over three days go to the Tokyo Big Sight convention centre. Comiket is dedicated to *dojinshi* self-publishers, and is notorious for its rowdy Cosplay Square.

Tokyo International Anime Fair
www.tokyoanime.jp

An industry and fan gathering at the Tokyo Big Sight. Hundreds of *anime* production companies exhibit, while *anime*-related performances are staged.

The Japan Travel Bureau (JTB, www.jtbusa.com) and US-based Pop Japan Travel (www.popjapantravel.com) offers *manga*- and *anime*-themed tours of Japan that cater to *otaku* with visits to Akihabara, conventions and maid cafés as well as chances to meet famous *anime* producers.

Nagomi 'Little Sister' Cafe
8-4 Soto-Kanda, Chiyoda-ku; tel: 5256 8001; www.nagomi.tv/ access/index.html; daily 11am–10pm; station: Akihabara; map p.137 D2

Of the many 'maid café' cosplay operations in Akihabara, Nagomi is unusual. Not only do the waitresses dress as maids, they also play the role of your cute (if demanding) little sister. Also in the building are cosplay bars dedicated to the influential *Gundam* series.

Tokyo Anime Centre
4-14-1 Soto-Kanda, Chiyoda-ku; tel: 5298 1188; www.anime center.jp; daily 11am–7pm; station: Akihabara; map p.137 D2

Manga-inspired buildings and sci-fi-lit streets are the perfect setting for the Tokyo Anime Centre in the Akihabara UDX building. A showroom for the newest and best-known *anime* work, with a screening room, exhibition galleries, shop and studio where visitors can listen to actors recording dialogue.

Other Areas

Animate
3-2-1 Higashi-Ikebukuro, Toshima-ku; tel: 3988 1351; www.animate.co.jp; daily 10am–8pm; station: Ikebukuro; map p.135 D4

The main outlet of this nationwide chain is an *anime* megastore, with a vast selection of titles, books, AV software, games and trading cards to satisfy the rabid fan.

Ghibli Museum
1-1-83 Shimorenjaku, Mitaka-shi; tel: 0570-055777; www.ghibli-museum.jp; Wed–Mon 10am–6pm; entrance charge; station: Kichijoji

The parkside Ghibli Museum is a shrine to Hayao Miyazaki *(see Film, p.52)*, the creator of *Spirited Away* and other *anime* classics. There are

Pampering

Tokyo boasts plenty of spas and 'esté' salons (beauty salons) for both men and women. Some aim to replicate the style of the *onsen*, a traditional hot spring in the countryside, with volcanic waters for bathing set in beautiful gardens. However, these urban spas offer a profusion of massage services, oxygen treatments and other beauty regimes. Japanese massage or *shiatsu* is widely available. Of course, there are still some neighbourhood *sento*, or public bath-houses, but here you will find fewer frills. Keep in mind that in general, English will probably not be spoken except in spas at international hotels.

Bathhouses

LaQua
Tel: 5800 9999; www.tokyo-dome.co.jp; daily 11am–9am; admission charge; station: Suidobashi; map p.136 B2
A main attraction of the LaQua water park at Tokyo Dome City is its spa, one of several traditionally styled *onsen* (hot springs) to have opened in Tokyo recently. With its customary Japanese garden design and people strolling around in *yukata* robes, LaQua effectively replicates the *onsen* experience one might have in the countryside. Its waters are piped up from the 1,700m-deep Koishikawa Hot Springs, and are rich in sodium chloride (salt), which is reputed to be effective in aiding poor circulation. Beauty treatments are also available here.

Oedo Onsen Monogatari
2-57 Aomi, Koto-ku; tel: 5500-1126; www.ooedoonsen.jp; daily 11am–9am; admission charge; stations: Telecom Cen-ter, Tokyo Teleport
Edo Monogatari ('Edo Story') is the largest of the new *onsen* resorts in Tokyo. Opened on 1 March, 2003 to celebrate the 400th anniversary of the Shogunate, the spa boasts more than 20 different baths as well as restaurants and an Edo-style main street, through which relaxed, well-soaked patrons can be observed in *yukata*. Filled with water drawn from 1,400m below the ground, the baths include a giant 'Hundred People Bath' as well as a wood-scented 'Barrel Bath'. Massages and beauty treatments are also available at this odd paradox of a traditional hot spring built on top of a futuristic artificial island.

The Sento

The maxim 'cleanliness is next to godliness' certainly holds true for the Japanese public bathhouses or *sento*, which have their origin in the Buddhist temples of India and China. With the widespread diffusion of private baths in recent decades the *sento* is in precipitous decline. Nevertheless, neighbourhood *sento* still remain, and a good scalding at one provides a classic Japanese bathing experience for those unable to make it to an

Right: Oedo Onsen Monogatari.

Left: outdoor luxury.

> Many of the seemingly reputable Chinese massage shops that dot Tokyo's commercial areas also offer sensual massages. The tip off is the addition of the word 'service' to the range of offerings.

TEMOMIN
www.temomin.com

Japan, which has pioneered so much when it comes to convenience, has brought the fast-food concept to massage in the form of Temomin. Recognisable by its brightly coloured signs featuring the image of a hand, Temomin (*te* means hand; *momin* means massage) has reduced the massage to this brilliantly simple formula: 10 minutes for ¥1,000. Its dozens of branches around the country are located in the station areas of key commuter junctions like Shinjuku and Shibuya.

Spas

Aveda Lifestyle Salon and Spa
5-5-21 Minami-Aoyama, Minato-ku; tel: 5468 5800; www.aveda.com; Mon, Wed–Fri 11am–8pm, Sat 10am–8pm, Sun 10am–7pm; station: Omotesando; map p.139 C1

Located on a backstreet in Aoyama, the Tokyo branch of this famous US natural cosmetics brand was opened only after extensive market research, and offers an interesting lesson in how brands localise to Japan. Many of the products were developed to suit Japanese needs, such as all-natural skin whiteners, for a culture in which pale skin is idealised. Treatments in this contemporary yet

> Due to the still-strong association in Japan of tattoos with the *yakuza* underworld, many spas refuse to admit customers with tattoos. At the very least, you may be asked to cover your tattoo with a bandage.

onsen hot-spring resort out in the countryside. The basic layout and procedure of entering a *sento* and *onsen* are the same; the most important etiquette to be observed is to soap up and rinse before one enters the large bath or *ofuro*. To enter unwashed is to invite opprobrium. Men and women bathe separately: the male entry can be identified by a blue curtain and the female by a red. Ask at your hotel front desk for the nearest *sento*. The fee is set at ¥430 for all *sento* in Tokyo.

Massage

SHIATSU

Japan's traditional form of massage, *shiatsu* (*shi* means 'finger'; *atsu* means pressure) grew out of massage forms imported from Asia, but is now a practice licensed by the Ministry of Health and Welfare. Numerous schools exist, such as the Zen school, each with a different approach. As suggested by its name, though, Shiatsu is basically defined by pressure with the fingers and hands to help the body relax and promote good energy flow. Many hotels offer in-house *shiatsu* massage or can direct you to a nearby clinic. *Shiatsu* can be pricey at prestigious hotels' spas, but hourly rates at business hotels or independent massage clinics compare favourably with those overseas, averaging about ¥6,000 per hour.

Left: tranquil surroundings.   **93**

'Keihatsu Enlightenment Massage' among other treatments (four hours for ¥84,000), while basic 50-minute massages start at ¥23,000.

Beauty Treatments

DANDY HOUSE

Thanks to YouTube, it's probably well known that Richard Gere has been the face for Japanese men's esté giant Dandy House for the last few years. Dandy House outlets are complete day spas offering services exclusively for men, ranging from body and facial treatments to electrolysis for hair removal.

Shinjuku Main Shop
2F Shinkuku Sanyou Building, 1-5-11 Nishi-shinjuku, Shinjuku-ku; tel: 5908 4051; www.dandy-house.com; Mon–Fri 11am–9.30pm, Sat–Sun, hols 10am–7pm; station: Shinjuku; map p.134 B1

TAKANO YURI

This national chain of women's beauty salons dominates the field, with 40 branches in the Tokyo area alone. In addition to beauty clinics, Takano Yuri operates spas and resorts, all

earthy structure run from a Hydromat Treatment to the Rosemary Mint Awakening Body Wrap. The vegetarian **Pure Café** is in the building.
SEE ALSO RESTAURANTS, P.104

Mizuki Spa

Conrad Hotel, 1-9-1 Higashi-Shinbashi, Minato-Ku; http://conradhotels1.hilton.com/en/ch/home.do; tel: 6388 8620; daily 10am–10pm; station: Shiodome

Sink into a tub filled with gold flakes at the largest hotel spa in Tokyo, the new 1,400sq m Mizuki Spa, high atop the five-star Conrad. In addition to the usual pool, gym and saunas, Mizuki's unique offerings run from its basic 60-minute 'Energy' massage (¥19,950) to the Marine Caviar Deluxe (¥66,150), a two-hour heaven of massage, body wrap, flower bath and tea ceremony culminating with a spa cuisine of caviar and champagne.

Nagomi Spa and Fitness

Grand Hyatt Tokyo, 6-10-3 Roppongi, Minato-ku; tel: 4333 8823; daily 5am–10pm; station: Roppongi; map p.140 C1

'Nagomi' translates roughly as 'well-being' or 'calm'. With eight private rooms and the 'Nagomi Suite' for two, the sleek, contemporary Japanese-flavoured Nagomi is one of Tokyo's premier spas.

Among its offerings are the 'Nagomi Signature Massage' (¥23,000), a 90-minute full body massage with exfoliation and aroma oils. Facials include the 90-minute 'Nagomi Signature Facial' (¥23,000), which includes a massage and revitalising mask. The menu also runs to body scrubs and all-over mud treatments.

The Peninsula Spa by ESPA

The Peninsula Tokyo, 1-8-1 Yurakucho, Chiyoda-ku; tel: 6270 2888; http://tokyo.peninsula.com; daily 10am–10pm; station: Hibiya; map p.140 C2

Produced by Susan Harmsworth's world-leading ESPA spa franchise, this elegant yet welcoming facility, decorated with Japanese washi-paper light fixtures and earth tones, is part of Tokyo's latest luxury hotel. While not as large as Mizuki or Nagomi, the Peninsula Spa's menu is every bit as fabulous, befitting the hotel's reputation. Treat yourself to one of several half-day spa journeys (two hours for ¥50,000), which run from a 'De-Stress' massage and facial to a 'Bride-to-Be' full-body exfoliation and facial. The ultimate is the 'Tokyo Time-Out', which includes a

---

Japanese barbershops or tokoya offer men the kind of loving attention that has long since fallen by the wayside in Western unisex salons. Immediately recognizable by their old-fashioned barber poles, tokoya treat customers to an expert haircut and shave with a straight-edged razor, complete with a massage and steaming hot towels. All of this often costs only a few thousand yen, although prices at upscale barbershops in international hotels will run higher.

with a similar, gorgeous sense of aesthetics and pampering atmosphere, as well as its Cellcosmet beauty-product line. A vast range of body and facial treatments, weight-loss programmes and the like are available. One of the most convenient branches is the Southeast Asian-themed spa in the Shinjuku Lumine listed here.

Beauty Spa in Bali
8F Lumine 1, 1-1-5 Nishi-shinjuku, Shinjuku-ku; www.takanoyuri.com; tel: 3344-1107; Mon–Fri 11am–10pm, Sat–Sun 10.30am–10pm; station: Shinjuku; map p.138 B4

Cosmetics

KAO
Kao is a venerable skincare conglomerate including such famous brands as Kanebo, Sensai and Sofina, and the more recent Bioré line for men. Based on dermatological research, the approach of these lines is to use innovative technologies to deliver natural amino acids to the 'skin core', which is hard to access. Its lines are sold in department stores and pharmacies nationwide.

POLA
Founded by Shinobu Suzuki in 1929 and something akin

For adventurous fashionistas, the Japanese have taken nail art to new heights, applying their attention to detail and finesse to create nail fashions that boggle the mind and creating a pan-Asian boom in the process. If you wish to glam up your hands like the *gyaru* of Shibuya, the city is dotted with nail art salons that will re-envision your nails as kimonos, flowers, jewels or even Hello Kitty. Ask your hotel for the nearest shop. Having your nails done takes an hour and up and costs ¥3,000–10,000.

to Avon, direct sales market leader Pola is another of Japan's cosmetics giants. Based on a wish for all women to be beautiful, Pola provides sophisticated skin analysis and advice on its lines of cosmetics that include Silfina lotions and Silfique make-up. The Galantom men's skincare line and a health-food line are among Pola's latest ventures. Pola products can be purchased at select Pola the Beauty shops in Tokyo, including Akasaka, listed below, and Kichijoji. (Incidentally, Pola also has a superb museum of modern

art set in the woods of the Hakone hot-spring resort.)

Pola the Beauty
1F Corte, 3-19-9 Asakusa-kotobukicho, Taito-ku; tel: 3845-8171; www.pola.net/pb_asakusatawaramachiekimae; station: Tawaramachi; map p.137 E3

SHISEIDO
Launched by the former head pharmacist to the Japanese Imperial Navy in 1872, Shiseido is the oldest cosmetics firm in the world. The company's make-up and skincare products have a global reputation for quality, and its whiteners are best-sellers throughout Asia. Recently, Shiseido has also brought to the market a full line of men's skincare goods. In addition to the main store listed, there are also Shiseido Beauty Salons at the Tokyu Toyoko department store in Shibuya, Isetan in Shinjuku and other locations. Shiseido products are also available in the cosmetics departments of fine department stores throughout Tokyo.

Shiseido Beauty Salon
7-8F, Shiseido the Ginza Building, 7-8-10 Ginza, Chuo-ku; tel: 3571 4511; www.shiseido.co.jp; Mon–Fri 10am–8pm, Sat 10am–7pm, Sun 10am–6pm; station: Ginza; map p.141 D2

Below: ESPA's Peninsula Spa is a study in understated luxury.

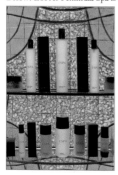

Parks and Gardens

The world's largest urban agglomeration suffers from a lack of green space. But the parks and gardens that do break up Tokyo's concrete tend to be peaceful places where modernity itself gives way. Many of the city's green spaces are finely tended Japanese gardens designed according to ancient principles. Often they were the work of the shogun, feudal lords or Edo-era industrialists. In keeping with this spirit, they are not places for football and sunbathing but for quiet picnics and contemplation of nature.

Imperial Palace, Yurakucho and Ginza

Chidorigafuchi Park

Daily 9am–5pm; free; station: Kudanshita; map p.140 B4

As you exit the Imperial Palace East Garden through the imposing Tayasu Gate (Tayasu-mon), turn left and follow the moat with its dazzling cherry trees to the aquatic Chidorigafuchi Park (Chidorigafuchi-koen). The boathouse rents out skiffs for rowing along the moat.

Imperial Palace

Stations: Hibiya, Nijubashimae, Sakuradamon; map p.140 B3

At the core of Tokyo lies a sublimely empty space: the grounds of the Imperial Palace, or Kokyo. This impregnable embryo of moats and stone walls occupies a 110-hectare expanse of green.

It is possible to visit the outer grounds of the Imperial Palace throughout the year. Most visitors enter by crossing the Babasaki Moat, which leads to the gravel paths of the Imperial Palace Plaza (Kokyomae Hiroba).

Fine stands of pine and a well-manicured lawn lead to Nijubashi (Niju Bridge), a two-tiered construction referred to as the 'Double Bridge'. The elegant arches of the bridge cross the moat into the inner domain of the palace grounds, open only twice a year, when the imperial family assemble on a balcony to greet well-wishers.

Niju Bridge, framed by willow trees, and the water that flows beneath it, stocked with orange carp and gliding swans, is one of the most photographed corners of Tokyo. The image is completed by massive stone ramparts and the graceful outline of the 17th-century Fushimi Tower (Fushimi Yagura), one of the complex's few remaining original buildings.

SEE ALSO ARCHITECTURE, P.30

Imperial Palace East Garden

Tue–Thur, Sat–Sun 9am–4pm; free; stations: Otemachi, Takebashi; map p.140 B4

In its heyday, the main entrance to Edo Castle was via the Otemon Gate. The present gate is a 1967 replica of the original, which was destroyed by a bomb towards

Left: spacious surroundings of the Imperial Palace.

Left: carriage in the surroundings of the Imperial Palace.

develop vertically, leaving some space between tower blocks in which to stroll. Adding to that sense of space is Shinjuku Central Park (Shinjuku Chuo Koen), with its pleasant pathways, trees and hillocks.

In the northwest corner of the park is Kumano-jinja Shrine, a small building founded in the 15th century. The shrine, which had a pond and several teahouses until the 1960s, seems cowed by the wall of skyscrapers that rise on its eastern flank.

Shinjuku Imperial Garden
11 Naito-cho, Shinjuku-ku; tel: 3350 0151; www.env.go.jp; Tue–Sun 9am–4.30pm; daily during April cherry-blossom season; entrance charge; stations: Shinjuku, Shinjuku Gyoenmae; map p.139 C4–D3
Like its district, the Shinjuku Imperial Garden (Shinjuku Gyoen) excels at variety. The former estate of the Naito feudal lords, then owned by the Imperial Household Agency, which used it for receptions and cherry-blossom-viewing parties, before giving it to the state.

Today, the garden is still a popular spot for viewing blooming cherry trees, but what strikes most people is the park's sense of space. The garden is divided into French, English and Japanese sections and has a large botanical garden full of tropical plants in an old, domed greenhouse.

Ikebukuro and Meijirodai

KOMAGOME'S GARDENS
Rikugien Garden
Honkomagome 6-16-3, Bunkyo-ku; tel: 3941 2222; daily 9am–

The Tokyo Metropolitan Park Association's website (www.tokyo-park.or.jp) has an exhaustive list of Tokyo parks as well as a 'Flower Calendar'. Sumiko Enbutsu's *A Flower Lover's Guide to Tokyo* takes one through the city's finest gardens.

the end of World War II. It is one of three entrances to the Imperial Palace East Garden (Kokyo Higashi Gyoen), an immaculately kept ornamental Japanese garden with a pond, stone lanterns, a miniature waterfall, bridges and an authentic tea pavilion.

Shibuya, Harajuku and Aoyama
Yoyogi Park
Daily 24 hours; free; stations: Harajuku, Meijijingumae; map p.138 B2
Fringing the southwestern borders of the Meiji Shrine Inner Gardens at the west end of Omotesando is a generous swath of green, Yoyogi Park (Yoyogi-koen). American military personnel and their families were billeted here for several years after the war,

when the area was known as Washington Heights. The land was handed back to the Japanese government and turned into a village for athletes attending the Tokyo Olympics in 1964. The park is now a gathering place for families as well as young bohemians, with bands and various performers enlivening it at weekends. Tokyo's homeless also make it their habitat.

Shinjuku
Central Park
Daily 24 hours; free; station: Tochomae; map p.138 A4
West Shinjuku has tended to

Left: cherry-blossom-viewing in Yoyogi Park.

Left: expanse of flowers in Hama Rikyu Detached Garden.

from Asakusa, was opened to the public in 1945. The highlight is a large tidal pond, with a small tea pavilion at its centre, and with islets connected by wooden bridges.
Kyu-Shiba Rikyu Garden
1-4-1 Kaigan, Minato-ku; tel: 3434 4029; daily 9am–5pm; entrance charge; station: Hamamatsucho
Arranged around a large pond opposite Hamamatsucho Station, the Kyu-Shiba Rikyu Garden (Kyu-Shiba Rikyu Teien) receives fewer visitors than the Hama Rikyu.

5pm; entrance charge; Station: Komagome
Kyu Furukawa Garden
1 Chome Nisigahara, Kita-ku; tel: 3910 0394; daily 9am–5pm; entrance charge; station: Komagome
Komagome has two excellent gardens. The Rikugien Garden is the closest to the station, created in 1702 by feudal lord Yoshiyasu Yanagisawa. The other is Kyu Furukawa Garden, a 10-minute walk north of the station. The garden and its main building, a charcoal-grey stone residence resembling a Scottish manor house and completed in 1917, are the work of British architect Josiah Conder.

Shinagawa, Meguro and Ebisu

National Park for Nature Study
Tel: 3441 7176; www.ins.kahaku.go.jp; Tue–Sun 9am–4pm, until 5pm during summer; entrance charge; station: Meguro
Near Tokyo's giant Shuto Expressway is a sight you would least expect in a city

like Tokyo: an expanse of deliberately undeveloped land. The National Park for Nature Study (Shizenkyoikuen), an effort to preserve in its original form a section of the Musashino Plain that once covered much of the area Edo was built on, covers 20 hectares. Among the 8,000 or more trees (160 species in all) in the park are moss-covered specimens that were here when Edo was a mere fishing village. Only 300 people are allowed into the park at a time.

Tokyo Bayside

Hama Rikyu Detached Garden
1-1 Hamarikyu-teien, Chuo-ku; tel: 3541 0200; daily 9am–5pm; entrance charge; station: Shimbashi
The expansive Hama Rikyu Teien was developed in the 1650s as grounds for the Hama Palace, and passed into the hands of the sixth shogun, Ienobu, who turned the grounds into landscaped gardens and a duck-shooting site. The present garden, reached by crossing the Nan-mon Bridge, or by waterbus

Suidobashi, Ochanomizu, Kanda and Akihabara

Koishikawa
Korakuen Garden
Koraku 1-6-6, Bunkyo-ku; tel: 3811 3015; daily 9am–5pm; entrance charge; station: Iidabashi, Korakuen; map p.136 B2
Koishikawa Korakuen, one of the city's finest Edo Period stroll gardens, is all that remains of the estate of a powerful Tokugawax clan patriarch. Work began on the garden in 1629, and was finally completed by his heir. Stroll gardens were intended for amusement as much as aesthetic contemplation. The designers of such gardens tried to incorporate scenes from the Chinese classics as well as miniaturised Japanese landscapes.

A small stream passing through the garden, the Oikawa River, symbolises a river of the same name in Arashiyama, near Kyoto, while two small hills, each covered in dwarf bamboo, are said to represent Mount Lu, a Buddhist pilgrimage site in China. The north end of the garden provides a completely different perspec-

Aficionados of *ikebana*, Japan's traditional art of flower arrangement, can take lessons in English with certified instructor Eika Furudate. Info: www.ikebana-eika.com.

tive as paddy, irises and plum trees come into view.

Koishikawa Botanical Garden
Tue–Sun 9am–4.30pm; entrance charge; station: Hakusan; map p136 A–B4

Behind a canopy of trees and the domes of the old greenhouses, one of the first things one notices is a tree with the odd name 'Newton no Ringo'. Grown from a cutting from the actual tree Isaac Newton sat under when the apocryphal apple fell, this ordinary apple tree is the main attraction. The gardens passed into the hands of the Tokyo University faculty in 1877, which grows over 100 species of herbs here.

Ueno and Yanaka

Ueno Park
Daily 24 hours; free; station: Ueno; map p.137 D3

The centrepiece of Ueno is its Ueno Park (Ueno-koen), a fine place for people-watching. In spring, the park is cherished by the Japanese for its cherry-blossom trees.

If you enter the park at the south end, near Keisei-Ueno Station (Keisei-eki), it is a short walk up a slight incline to the modest 1892 statue of Saigo Takamori. Leading the imperial forces to Edo in 1868, Takamori succeeded in taking the Tokugawa castle without battle. The statue shows him walking his dog, wearing a summer kimono, his sword safely sheathed.

To the left is the **Shogitai Tomb**, the resting place of loyal Tokugawa samurai who

refused to accept the shogunate's collapse in 1868 and retreated to Ueno.

Ahead to the left, on the edge of a small bluff, is **Kiyomizu Kannon Hall** (Kiyomizu Kannon-do). Built in 1631 and moved here in 1698, it is a dwarfish imitation of the far grander Kiyomizu-dera Temple in Kyoto.

The temple's location was partly chosen for its fine view of the **Shinobazu Pond** (Shinobazu-no-ike) and its **Benten Hall** (Benten-do). The abbot Tenkai dedicated the temple to Benten, patron of the arts and goddess of beauty. Now a freshwater pond, Shinobazu was once a salty inlet of Tokyo Bay. It is at its best in July and August, when lotus plants bloom each morning.

Sumida River, Asakusa, Ryogoku and East Tokyo

Hundred Flowers Garden
3-18-3 Higashi-mukojima, Sumida-ku; Tue–Sun 9am–4.30pm; admission charge; station: Higashi-Mukojima

The Hundred Flowers Garden (Mukojima Hyakkaen) is one of Tokyo's best-known, though little-visited, Edo Period gardens. Built during the early 19th century, the garden covers little more than a hectare,

but it is intensely planted with trees, deciduous shrubs, flowering bushes and herbaceous perennials, the most notable being a beautiful, 30m- tunnel of bush clover that bursts into a riot of purple-rose flowers in September.

Kiyosumi Garden
1-1 Hamarikyu-teien, Chuo-ku; tel: 3541 0200; daily 9am–4.40pm; entrance charge; tel: 3641 5892; station: Kiyosumi-shirakawa; map p.141 E3

Kiyosumi Garden (Kiyosumi Teien), which is fed by water from the Sumida River, was first built in 1688 by a rich lumber merchant named Kinokuniya Bunzaemon. During the Meiji era, it was bought by another wealthy businessman, Yataro Iwasaki, the founder of the Mitsubishi Group of companies.

The Kiyosumi Garden is a typical *kaiyushiki teien*, or 'pond walk around garden'. Water is the focal point with a beautiful teahouse set serenely on its surface. Stone lanterns, miniature islands, stepping-stones and many species of flower, including Japanese azaleas and hydrangeas, dot the grounds. The garden is surprisingly spacious, a fact that helped to save thousands of lives during the 1923 earthquake.

Below: lanterns strung among the trees in Ueno Park.

Restaurants

Japanese cuisine is justly famous, but at Tokyo restaurants, the more authentic the food, the more difficult the experience can be for the non-native speaker. Visitors who make the effort to resist Western fast food and look beyond the obvious sushi and noodle shops, will be rewarded by the vast range of flavours and styles that define Japanese food. Whether it's lowbrow fare like okonomiyaki pancakes or ancient kaiseki cuisine, Tokyo's restaurants extend beyond the narrow options available at home. They are frequently cheaper than you may have imagined, and offer the culinary adventure of a lifetime.

Imperial Palace, Yurakucho and Ginza

AUSTRALIAN
Salt
5F Shin-Marunouchi Building, 1-5-1 Marunouchi, Chiyoda-ku; tel: 5288 7828; www.pjgroup.jp/salt; daily 11am–3.30pm, 5.30–11pm; ¥¥¥; station: Tokyo; map p.141 C3
Aussie celebrity-chef Luke Mangan's venture features fabulous seafood matched with a fine cellar of Aussie wines in a sleek setting.

FRENCH
Aux Amis des Vins
2-5-6 Ginza, Chuo-ku; tel: 3567 4120; www.auxamis.com/desvins; Mon–Fri 5.30pm–2am, Sat noon–midnight; ¥¥¥; station: Ginza; map p.141 C2
Good French cuisine in the middle ground between bistro and haute, in a casual setting, with an extensive wine cellar. Reservations advised.

Prices for an ¥ average three course meal with wine:
¥ under ¥3000
¥¥ ¥3000–¥6500
¥¥¥ over ¥6500s

Above: Kurosawa's beautiful serene setting.

INDIAN
Dhaba India
2-7-9 Yaesu, Chuo-ku; tel: 3272 7160; www.dhabaindia.com; Mon–Fri 11.15am–3pm, 5–11pm, Sat–Sun from noon; ¥¥; station: Kyobashi; map p.141 C2
Fragrant curries, generous thali meals and masala dhosas. The best South Indian cuisine in the city.
Nair's
4-10-7 Ginza, Chuo-ku; tel: 3541 8246; www.ginza-nair.co.jp; Wed–Mon 11.30am–9.30pm, Sun until 8pm; ¥¥; station: Higashi-Ginza; map p.141 C2
Ever-dependable old-school Indian diner, cramped but always welcoming.

ITALIAN
Locanda Elio
2-5-2 Kojimachi, Chiyoda-ku; tel: 3239 6771; www.elio.co.jp; Mon–Sat 11.45am– 3pm, 5.45–11pm; ¥¥¥; station: Hanzomon; map p.140 A3
Elio Orsara's fresh pasta, Calabrian country soups and excellent southern Italian food. Highly recommended.

JAPANESE
Bird Land
B1F Tsukamoto Sozan Building, 4-2-15 Ginza, Chuo-ku; tel: 5250 1081; Tue–Sat 5–9.30pm; ¥¥; station: Ginza; map p.141 C2
Yakitori (grilled skewers of chicken) of superb quality,

Left: open kitchens reaveal craftsmen at work.

Sakyo Higashiyama

B1F Oak Ginza, 3-7-2 Ginza, Chuo-ku; tel: 3535 3577; www. sakyohigashiyama.com; daily 11am–2pm, 5.30–9pm; ¥¥¥; station: Ginza; map p.141 C2

Sophisticated Kyoto cuisine without airs and graces. Fish and meat dishes prepared over charcoal in a sand pot.

Shin-Hinomoto

2-4-4 Yurakucho, Chiyoda-ku; tel: 3214 8021; Mon–Sat 5pm–midnight; ¥; station: Yurakucho; map p.140 C2

Noisy, friendly no-nonsense *izakaya* (tavern) built under the railway tracks, serving fresh seafood at reasonable prices. English-speaking.

Ten-Ichi Deux

4-1 Ginza, Chuo-ku; tel: 3566 4188; daily 11.30am–10pm; ¥¥; station: Ginza; map p.141 C2

Offshoot of Tokyo's best-known tempura house serves simple meals of deep-fried battered seafood and vegetables in a stylish ambience.

Ten-mo

4-1-3 Nihombashi-Motomachi, Chuo-ku; tel: 3241 7035; Mon–Fri noon–2pm, 5–8pm, Sat noon–2pm; ¥¥¥; station: Nihonbashi; map p.141 D4

This old-style tempura shop prepares exquisite morsels of seafood and vegetables fried

When vaunted food guide Michelin's controversial first Tokyo edition (in 2007) gave eight restaurants including five serving Japanese cuisine the top three-star rating, the number was second only to Paris, which has 10. Tokyo led overall, with 191 stars against Paris's 97. Of course – Tokyo has 160,000 restaurants to Paris's 13,000.

made with free-range chicken grilled with expertise over charcoal. Don't miss the san-sai-yaki (chicken breast grilled with Japanese pepper).

Kurosawa

2-7-9 Nagatacho, Chiyoda-ku; tel: 3580 9638; Mon–Fri 11.30am–3pm, 5–11pm, Sat noon–12pm; ¥–¥¥¥; station: Kokkai-Gijidomae; map p.140 A2

Traditional Japanese food – hand-cut soba noodles and shabu-shabu beef – are the highlights of this classic-look restaurant run by the late, great filmmaker's daughter.

Little Okinawa

8-7-10 Ginza, Chuo-ku; tel: 3572 2930; Mon–Fri 5pm–3am, Sat–Sun 4pm–midnight; ¥¥; station: Shinbashi; map p.140 C2

This cosy bar-restaurant showcases the food of sub-tropical Okinawa. Plenty of pork, stir-fries featuring bitter melon, and Chinese-style noodles, all washed down with potent awamori liquor.

Ohmatsuya

2F, 6-5-8 Ginza, Chuo-ku; tel: 3571 7053; Mon–Fri 5–10pm, Sat 4.30–9pm; ¥¥¥; station: Ginza; map p.140 C2

Refined traditional fare in a rustic setting evoking rural Yamagata. Charcoal-grill beef and seafood at your table.

Otako Honten

5-4-16 Ginza, Chuo-ku; tel: 3571 0057; Mon–Sat 11.30am–10pm; ¥; station: Ginza; map p.140 C2

Sit at the counter, sip sake and nibble on oden (fish, tofu, eggs and vegetables simmered in a savoury broth): blue-collar comfort food.

Rangetsu

3-5-8 Ginza, Chuo-ku; tel: 3567 1021; www.ginza-rangetsu.com; daily 11.30am–10pm; ¥¥¥; station: Ginza; map p.141 C2

Refined Japanese cuisine based around shabu-shabu (hotpot) and sukiyaki (one-pot meal) featuring premium Wagyu beef cooked at table.

Below: fresh is best.

in rich sesame oil. The counter seats just six, so reservations are essential.

Roppongi and Akasaka

CHINESE

Chinese Café Eight

2F, Court Annex, 3-2-13 Nishi-Azabu, Minato-ku; tel: 5414 5708; daily 24 hours; ¥¥; station: Roppongi; map p.139 D1
Budget Chinese diner open round the clock, serving Peking duck (for 3–4 people) dumplings and simple stir-fries at bargain prices. Staff brusque and décor bit risqué.

FRENCH

L'Atelier de Joël Robuchon

2F, Roppongi Hills Hillside, 6-10-1 Roppongi, Minato-ku; tel: 5772 7500; daily 11.30am–2.30pm, 6–11pm; ¥¥¥¥; station: Roppongi; map p.139 E1
Counter seating looking into the open kitchen. Robuchon's tapas-influenced cuisine blends informal and sophisticated, and is quite affordable.

FUSION

Roy's

5F West Walk Roppongi Hills, 6-10-1 Roppongi, Minato-ku; tel: 5413 9571; Mon–Fri 11am–4pm, 5.30–11.30pm, Sat–Sun 11.30am–4pm, 5.30–11.30pm; ¥¥¥¥; station: Roppongi; map p.139 E1

Roy Yamaguchi's (one of Hawaii's top chefs) delectable Asian-American cuisine is beautiful and delicious. A stunning setting, too, with a panorama of Tokyo Tower.

JAPANESE

Butagumi

2-24-9 Nishi-Azabu, Minato-ku; tel: 5466 6775; Tue–Sun 11.30am–3pm, 5.30–11pm; ¥¥; station: Roppongi; map p.139 D1
Traditional setting for Tokyo's finest *tonkatsu* (deep-fried breaded pork cutlets) with premium pork. Choose fatty rosu or lean filet (or Spanish Ibérico). English spoken.

Fukuzushi

5-7-8 Roppongi, Minato-ku; tel: 3402 4116; www.roppongi fukuzushi.com; Mon–Sat 11.30am–2pm, 5.30–11pm; ¥¥¥; station: Roppongi; map p.139 E1
Unfailingly good-quality sushi for the well-heeled Roppongi crowd. Expensive, but not snobbish or exclusive.

Inakaya East

5-3-4 Roppongi, Minato-ku; tel: 3408 5040; www.roppongi inakaya.jp/en; daily 5–11pm; ¥¥¥; station: Roppongi; map p.139 E1
Chefs in traditional garb grill fish, meat and vegetables to order, then pass them on long wooden paddles across to where you're sitting. It's theatrical and fun, but not cheap.

Ninja

1F, Akasaka Tokyu Plaza, 2-14-3 Nagatacho, Chiyoda-ku; tel: 5157 3936; www.ninja akasaka.com; Mon–Sat 5pm–2am, Sun 5–11pm; ¥¥¥; station: Akasaka; map p.139 E3
In this extensive theme-restaurant, black-clad waiters dressed like ninja spies show you to your private room, then entertain you as you nibble on simple Japanese food. Lots of fun for all the family.

Nodaiwa

1-5-4 Higashi-Azabu, Minato-ku; tel: 3583 7852; Mon–Sat 11am–1.30pm, 5–8pm; ¥¥¥; station: Kamiyacho; map p.140 A1
Charcoal-grilled fillets of *unagi* (eel), daubed with a savoury sauce and served with rice: it's one of the great unsung delicacies of Japanese gastronomy, and this is best place in Tokyo to discover it.

Pintokona

B2F, Metrohat, 6-4-1 Roppongi, Minato-ku; tel: 5771 1133; daily 11am–11pm; ¥¥¥; station: Roppongi; map p.139 E1
A stylish conveyor-belt sushi restaurant that stresses quality over quantity. Besides sushi, they also serve a range of light cooked dishes.

Tofuya Ukai

4-4-13 Shiba Koen, Minato-ku; tel: 3436 1028; daily 11am–10pm; ¥¥¥¥; station: Kamiyacho; map p.140 A1
Right below Tokyo Tower, this remarkable restaurant boasts traditional architecture and a beautiful rambling garden with carp ponds. Refined multi-course meals are served in

Prices for an ¥ average three course meal with wine:
¥ under ¥3000
¥¥ ¥3000–¥6500
¥¥¥ over ¥6500

private rooms: fully vegetarian food available by request.

VEGETARIAN
Daigo
2F, Forest Tower, 2-3-1 Atago, Minato-ku; tel: 3431 0811; www.shiba-daigo.com; daily noon–3pm, 5–9pm; ¥¥¥¥; station: Onarimon; map p.140 B1

Buddhist temple cooking elevated to supreme levels of refinement. The extended vegetarian banquets feature 10–15 courses of exquisite complexity, all served in private rooms. Budget plenty of time (and expense). Reservations essential.

Shibuya, Harajuku and Aoyama

AMERICAN
Beacon
1-2-5 Shibuya, Shibuya-ku; tel: 6418 0077; Mon–Fri 11.30am–3pm, 6–10pm, Sat–Sun 11.30am–3pm, 6–9pm; ¥¥¥¥; stations: Shibuya, Omotesando; map p.138 C1

One the best steakhouses in the city, a sleek, 'urban chop house' with good seafood and free-range chicken, and a huge cellar of Californian wines. Perfect for expense account entertaining.

FRENCH
L'Artemis
2-31-7 Jingumae, Shibuya-ku; tel: 5786 0220; Thur–Tue noon–3pm, 6–11pm, closed 2nd Tue of month; ¥¥¥; stations: Harajuku, Meiji-jingumae; map p.138 C2

Excellent, affordable French cuisine worthy of far grander surroundings. Chef Nakada's ¥3,990 three-course dinner menu is a steal. The wine list is less of a bargain.

Benoit
10F La Port Aoyama, 5-51-8 Jingumae, Shibuya-ku; tel: 5468 0881; www.benoit-tokyo.com; daily 11.30am–4pm, 5.30–11.30pm; ¥¥¥; station: Omote-

sando; map p.138 C2

Of French master-chef Alain Ducasse's two restaurants in Tokyo, this one is more informal, concentrating on Mediterranean flavours.

FUSION
Fujimamas
6-3-2 Jingumae, Shibuya-ku; tel: 5485 2262; www.fujimamas.com; daily 11am–11pm; ¥¥¥; stations: Harajuku, Meiji-jingumae; map p.138 C2

American-Asian cuisine with a few Latin flavours in a converted wood-frame house: Tokyo at its eclectic hippest.

INDIAN
Nataraj
B1F Sanwa-Aoyama Building, 2-22-19 Minami-Aoyama, Minato-ku; tel: 5474 0510; www.nataraj.co.jp; Mon–Fri 11.30am–3pm, 5.30–11pm, Sat–Sun 11.30am–11pm; ¥¥; station: Gaienmae; map p.139 D2

Tokyo's foremost Indian vegetarian restaurant serves grills and curries from the tandoor oven. Spice levels are mild but can be raised.

JAPANESE
Maisen
4-8-5 Jingumae, Shibuya-ku; tel: 3470 0071; daily 11am–10pm; ¥¥; station: Omotesando; map p.138 C2

This well-regarded *tonkatsu* (deep-fried breaded pork cut-

lets) restaurant also serves deep-fried chicken and oysters. English menu available.

Sasagin
1-32-15 Yoyogi-Uehara, Shibuya-ku; tel: 5454 3715; Mon–Sat 5–11pm; ¥¥¥; station: Yoyogi-uehara; map p.138 A2

A range of premium sake served with creative modern Japanese cuisine in a casual setting. The master, Narita-san, speaks English and will recommend the best brews.

Soranoniwa
4-17 Sakuragaoka-cho, Shibuya-ku; tel: 5728 5191; daily 5–11.30pm; ¥¥; station: Shibuya

Simple and affordable tofu cuisine. Highlights are tofu shumai dumplings and *yuba* (soya milk 'skin') prepared at the table. English menu.

Sushi Ouchi
2-8-4 Shibuya, Shibuya-ku; tel: 3407 3543; Mon–Sat 11.40am–1.40pm, 5.30–9.30pm; ¥¥¥; stations: Shibuya, Omotesando; map p.138 C1

Chef Ouchi plays classical music and prefers a dark-wood decor. All-natural ingredients: no farmed seafood and absolutely no MSG or other chemicals.

KOREAN
Jap Cho Ok
B1F Alteka Belte Plaza, 4-1-15 Minami-Aoyama, Minato-ku; tel: 5410 3408; Mon–Sat 5.30pm–

Below: fresh fish ready for the grill.

Above: spectacular setting for the New York Grill at the Park Hyatt Hotel.

2am, Sun and holidays 5.30–11pm; ¥¥; station: Gaienmae; map p.139 D1
Stylish yet casual, Jap Cho Ok includes seafood dishes and even Zen Buddhist vegetarian temple cooking alongside the usual Korean barbecue. Great decor.

TURKISH
Ankara
B1F Social Dogenzaka, 1-14-9 Dogenzaka, Shibuya-ku; tel: 3780 1366; www.ankara.jp; Mon–Sat 5–11.15pm, Sun 5–10pm; ¥¥¥; station: Shibuya; map p.138 B1
Excellent down-home cooking, especially the meze, juicy kebabs and *pide* (Turkish 'pizza') topped with meat or cheese. Friendly and casual, plus there's an English menu.

VEGETARIAN
Pure Café
5-5-21 Minami-Aoyama, Minato-ku; tel: 5466 2611; www.pure-cafe.com; daily 8.30am–10.30pm; ¥; station: Omotesando; map p.139 C1
Self-service all-day café serving light additive-free and (almost) entirely vegan meals. Opens early for those looking for a healthy breakfast with organic coffee.

Shinjuku

AMERICAN
New York Grill
52F Park Hyatt Hotel, 3-7-1-2 Nishi-Shinjuku, Shinjuku-ku; tel: 5322 1234; daily 11.30am–2.30pm, 5.30–10.30pm; ¥¥¥¥; stations: Shinjuku, Tochomae; map p.138 B4
Power dining with bravado in a sky-view setting in Shinjuku's Park Hyatt Hotel (the setting for the film *Lost in Translation*). Sunday brunch with cocktails at the adjacent **New York Bar** is an institution for the expat community. SEE ALSO BARS, P.34

FRENCH
Restaurant Le Coupe Chou
1-15-7 Nishi-Shinjuku, Shinjuku-ku; tel: 3348 1610; daily 11.30am–2pm, 5.30pm–midnight, closed 3rd Mon of month; ¥; station: Shinjuku; map p.138 B4
In Shinjuku's electronics district, this retro French bistro offers a great-value ¥1,500 four-course lunch. Popular with the local office crowd.

ITALIAN
Carmine Edochiano
9-13 Arakicho, Shinjuku-ku; tel: 3225 6767; www.carmine.jp; daily 11.30am–3pm, 6–11pm; ¥¥¥; station: Yotsuya-Sanchome; map p.135 D1
Classy Italian fare in a beautiful old house. Dine upstairs on Tuscan cuisine; downstairs serves Neapolitan pizzas from a wood-fired oven.

JAPANESE
Hayashi
2-22-5 Kabuki-cho, Shinjuku-ku; tel: 3209 5672; Mon–Sat 5–11.30pm; ¥¥; station: Shinjuku; map p.134 C1
Around the sand hearth, dine on charcoal-grilled meat, fish or seasonal vegetables in a

Prices for an ¥ average three course meal with wine:
¥ under ¥3000
¥¥ ¥3000–¥6500
¥¥¥ over ¥6500

> Apart from noodle shops, most restaurants close between lunch and dinner. English-language menus are not common, but many eateries have plastic food displays in their windows.

rustic setting. Hard to imagine you're in the heart of sleazy Kabuki-cho.

Kuu
50F Shinjuku Sumitomo Building, 2-6-1 Nishi-Shinjuku, Shinjuku-ku; tel: 3344 6457; daily 11.30am–2pm, 5–11pm; ¥¥; station: Shinjuku; map p.134 B1
This casual *izakaya* (tavern) gives panoramic views. The core of the menu is charcoal-grilled seafood, chicken and seasonal vegetables. This is also an affordable place to explore some different types of premium sake.

Tsunahachi
3-31-8 Shinjuku, Shinjuku-ku; tel: 3352 1012; daily 11am–10.30pm; ¥¥¥; station: Shinjuku; map p.134 C1
Hearty tempura (deep-fried battered seafood and vegetables) in large portions in an atmospheric wooden building. Good value and busy.

KOREAN
Matsuya
1-1-17 Okubo, Shinjuku-ku; tel: 3200 5733; Mon–Sat 11am–5am, Sun 11am–2am; ¥; station: Shin-Okubo; map p.134 B1
Long-established restaurant in Little Seoul, where you sit on the floor at low tables. The speciality is fiery, meat-laden stews cooked at the table.

Tokaien
1-6-3 Kabuki-cho, Shinjuku-ku; tel: 3200 2934; daily 11.30am–3.30pm, 4pm–4am; ¥¥; station: Shinjuku; map p.134 B1
Nine floors of *yakiniku* (Korean barbecue) and other

Korean meat dishes. Sign up for all-you-can-eat meals if you have a large appetite.

SOUTHEAST ASIAN
Hyakunincho Yataimura
2-20-25 Hyakunin-cho, Shinjuku-ku; tel: 5386 3320; Sun–Thur 11.30am–2.30pm, 5pm–2am, Fri–Sat 11.30am–2.30pm, 5pm–4am; ¥; station: Shin-Okubo; map p.134 B2
Low-budget street food: choose from Indonesian, Thai, Korean and others. It's fun and open until the wee hours.

Restaurant Mahathir Malaysia
1-17-10 Hyakunin-cho, ST Building, Shinjuku-ku; tel: 3367 3125; daily 11.30am–1am; ¥; stations: Okubo, Shin-Okubo; map p.134 B2
Cheerful basement diner offering Malaysian classics, including *laksa* and *nasi goreng*. Buffet lunch is ¥750.

Ikebukuro and Meijirodai
CHINESE
Chion Shokudo
B1F Miyakawa Building, 1-24-1 Ikebukuro, Toshima-ku; tel: 5951 8288; daily 11am–2pm, 6pm–4.30am, Sat–Sun 6pm–4.30am; ¥; station: Ikebukuro
Fiery Sichuan fare such as *mabo-dofu* (ground pork and tofu) and spicy hotpots, as authentic (and almost as cheap) as you'd find in China.

JAPANESE
Goemon
1-1-26 Hon-Komagome, Toshima-ku; tel: 3811 2015; Tue–Fri noon–2pm, 5–10pm, Sat–Sun noon–8pm; ¥¥; station: Hakusan; map p.136 B4
Goemon serves multi-course Kyoto-style cuisine featuring tofu, in a traditional setting overlooking a tranquil garden.

Sasashu
2-2-6 Ikebukuro, Toshima-ku; tel: 3971 6796; Mon–Sat 5–11pm; ¥¥; station: Ikebukuro
Long-established tavern serves premium sake, with a range of traditional food. Try the excellent duck noodles.

SOUTHEAST ASIAN
Malaychan
3-22-6 Nishi-Ikebukuro, Toshima-ku; tel: 5391 7638; www.malaychan.jp; Tue–Sat 11am–2.30pm, 5–11pm, Sun 11am–11pm, Mon 5–11pm; ¥¥; station: Ikebukuro
Chinese-Malay cuisine such as shark's fin soup and *nasi lemak* (rice with coconut milk and spicy toppings), with Thai influences.

Saigon
3F, Torikoma Dai-ichi Building, 1-7-10 Higashi-Ikebukuro, Toshima-ku; tel: 3989 0255; Mon–Fri 11.30am–2.30pm, 5–10.30pm, Sat–Sun and holidays 11.30am–10.30pm; ¥¥; station: Ikebukuro

Right: bento boxes and other light fare.

Down-to-earth Vietnamese fare, including spring rolls, hot pancakes with spicy sauce and beef noodle soup. Set lunches for under ¥1000.

Shinagawa, Meguro and Ebisu

AMERICAN
T.Y. Harbor Brewery
2-1-3 Higashi-Shinagawa, Shingawa-ku; tel: 5479 4555; www.tyharborbrewing.co.jp; daily 11.30–2pm, 5.30–10pm; ¥¥; stations: Tennozu Isle, Shinagawa

Microbrewed ales and high-quality American bar food – canalside. English menu.

JAPANESE
Buri
1-14-1 Ebisu-Nishi, Shibuya-ku; tel: 3496 7744; daily 5pm–3am; ¥¥; station: Ebisu

Great sake and tasty food at this standing-only bar that's open until the wee hours.

Chibo
38F Yebisu Garden Place Tower, 4-20-3 Ebisu, Shibuya-ku; tel: 5424 1011; Mon–Fri 11.30am–2.30pm, 5–10pm, Sat–Sun 11.30am–10pm; ¥¥; station: Ebisu

Okonomiyaki (savoury pancakes) made before your eyes on grills set in the table. Fun food and never expensive, plus a brilliant view.

Ebisu Imaiya Sohonten
1-7-11 Ebisu-Nishi, Shibuya-ku; tel: 5456 0255; Sat–Thur 5pm–2am, Fri 5pm–4am; ¥¥; station: Ebisu

The speciality is delectable free-range chicken, served either as yakitori (charcoal grilled) or in warming hot-pots before you. Spotless and efficient, and everything is explained in English.

SOUTHEAST ASIAN
Keawjai
B1, 2-14-9 Kami-Osaki, Shinagawa-ku; tel: 5420 7727; www.keawjai.com; Tue–Sun 11.30am– 9.30pm; ¥¥; station: Meguro

Authentic and refined Thai cuisine, with the chili levels kept in check. Mostly Thai staff and customers, as the Thai embassy is nearby.

Tokyo Bayside

INDIAN
Khazana
5F Deck's Tokyo Beach, 1-6-1 Daiba, Minato-ku; tel: 3599 6551; www.maharaja-group.com; daily 11am–11pm; ¥¥; station: Odaiba Kaihin Koen

All-you-can-eat lunches (until 5pm) and good curries, plus outside tables giving views of the Rainbow Bridge.

JAPANESE
Edogin
4-5-1 Tsukiji, Chuo-ku; tel: 3543 4401; Mon–Sat 11am–9.30pm; ¥¥¥; station: Tsukiji; map p.141 D1

An old-school sushi emporium, cavernous but packed. The fish is fresh, portions generous, and the location close to Tsukiji Fish Market ensures honest prices.

Icho
Hotel Nikko Tokyo, 1-9-1 Daiba, Minato-ku; tel: 5500 5500; daily 11.30am–2.30pm, 5.30–9.30pm; ¥¥¥; station: Daiba

Teppanyaki — meat, fish and vegetables prepared on the griddle in front of you — in a romantic setting that over-looks the Rainbow Bridge.

Sushi-Bun
Chuo Shijo Building, No.8, 5-2-1 Tsukiji, Chuo-ku; tel: 3541 3860; www.sushibun.com; Mon–Sat 6am–2.30pm; ¥¥; station: Tsukiji; map p.141 C1

One of a handful of sushi counters in the heart of the Tsukiji Fish Market. Squeeze in at the counter and order the sushi set platter: you won't find fresher fish or cheaper prices anywhere else in Tokyo. English menu available.

Suidobashi, Ochanomizu, Kanda and Akihabara

ITALIAN
Stefano
6-47 Kagurazaka, Shinjuku-ku; tel: 5228 7575; www.stefano-jp.com; Tue–Sat 11.30am–2pm, 6–11.30pm, Sun noon–3pm, 5.30–9pm; ¥¥¥; station: Kagu-razaka; map p.135 E2

Chef Stefano Fastro serves excellent Italian food, special-ising in the cuisine of Venice and the northeast. Home-made pasta and gnocchi.

JAPANESE
Botan
1-15 Kanda-Sudacho, Chiyoda-ku; tel: 3251 0577; Mon–Sat 11.30am–9pm; ¥¥; station: Aki-habara; map p.137 D1

Old-style wooden restaurant serving, sukiyaki casserole with chicken (not the more usual beef) only. The wait-resses explain everything.

Kanda Yabu Soba
2-10 Kanda-Awajicho, Chiyoda-ku; tel: 3251 0287; www.yabu soba.net; daily 11.30am–8pm; ¥; stations: Awajicho, Ogawa-machi; map p.137 C1

Left: sample microbrews at T.Y. Harbor Brewery.

Illustrious noodle shop serving Edo-style handmade soba in a classic, tranquil setting.

Seigetsu

2F, Kamuya Building, 6-77-1 Kagurazaka, Shinjuku-ku; tel: 3269 4320; Mon–Sat 5–11.30pm, Sun 5–11pm; ¥¥¥; stations: Kagurazaka, Ushigome-kagurazaka; map p.135 E2

A casual, modern *izakaya* (tavern) serving above-average Japanese food. Great sake list (in English), with brews from all over Japan.

Ueno and Yanaka

JAPANESE
Hantei

2-12-15 Nezu, Bunkyo-ku; tel: 3828 1440; Tue–Sat noon–2.30pm, 5–10pm, Sun noon–2.30pm, 5–9.30pm; ¥¥; station: Nezu

Kushiage (deep-fried skewers of fish, meat and vegetables) served in an old wooden building in one of Tokyo's best-preserved areas. English menu available.

Ikenohata Yabu Soba

3-44-7 Yushima, Bunkyo-ku; tel: 3831 8977; Thur–Sat, Mon–Tue 11.30am–2pm, 4.30–8pm, Sun 11.30am–8pm; ¥¥; station: Yushima

Prices for an¥ average three course meal with wine:
¥ under ¥3000
¥¥ ¥3000–¥6500
¥¥¥ over ¥6500

Simple, filling and affordable light meals of soba noodles. English menu available.

Nezu Club

2-30-2 Nezu, Bunkyo-ku; tel: 3828 4004; Thur–Sun 6–10pm; ¥¥¥; station: Nezu; map p.136 C4

Delightful place in one of Tokyo's most traditional neighbourhoods. Contemporary Japanese cuisine midway between formal and home cooking.

Sasanoyuki

2-15-10 Negishi, Taito-ku; tel: 3873 1145; www.sasanoyuki.com; Tue–Sun 11.30am–10pm; ¥¥¥; station: Uguisudani; map p.137 D4

Tokyo's most historic tofu restaurant is simple and relaxed, with reasonable prices. The set courses can be quite filling.

Sumida River, Asakusa, Ryogoku and East Tokyo

JAPANESE
Bon

1-2-11 Ryusen, Taito-ku; tel: 3872 0375; Mon–Fri noon–3pm, 5–9pm, Sat noon–9pm, Sun noon–8pm; ¥¥¥¥; station: Iriya; map p.137 E4

Memorable multi-course fucha ryori (Buddhist vegetarian cuisine) featuring exquisitely prepared seasonal foods in a serene setting. Set menu changes with the seasons.

Chanko Kawasaki

2-13-1 Ryogoku, Sumida; tel: 3631 2529; Mon–Sat

Left: Yabusoba Noodle Restaurant.

5–10pm; ¥¥; station: Ryogoku; map p.137 E1

Quaint old restaurant specialising in chanko-nabe, the hearty stew of sumo wrestlers, which you cook at your table. This is winter fare, and always popular when sumo tournaments are on.

Ichimon

3-12-6 Asakusa, Taito-ku; tel: 3875 6800; Mon–Fri 6–11pm, Sat–Sun noon–2pm, 5–10pm; ¥¥; station: Asakusa; map p.137 E4

Atmospheric old-world restaurant close to the sights. Excellent sake to accompany the good selection of Japanese dishes.

Namiki Yabu Soba

2-11-9 Kaminarimon, Taito-ku; tel: 3841 1340; Fri–Wed 11am–7.30pm; ¥; station: Asakusa; map p.137 E3

This small soba (buckwheat noodle) shop makes a convenient and cheap stop for visitors to Senso-ji Temple.

Sometaro

2-2-2 Nishi-Asakusa, Taito-ku; tel: 3844 9502; daily noon–10.30pm; ¥; station: Tawaramachi; map p.137 E3

The speciality at this rustic eatery is okonomiyaki, eggy pancakes stuffed with vegetables, shrimp, etc. covered with lashings of soy sauce and mayonnaise. Great atmosphere.

PUB GRUB
Beer Station Ryogoku

2-18-7 Ryogoku, Sumida; tel: 3633 2120; www.40beersontap.com; Mon–Fri 5–11.30pm; ¥¥; station: Ryogoku; map p.137 E1

Explore Japanese microbrewed ales, with 40 different beers on draught. A good range of affordable pub grub. Always popular, especially when there are beer events.

Shopping

Unsurprisingly, Tokyo is not a cheap place to shop for anything, but recently increased competition helps it to compare favourably with other large cities. Products are of high quality, the range is staggering and the courteous staff make shopping a pleasure. 'The customer is always right,' in Japan becomes: 'The customer is God.' Most shops operate on a fixed-price system. In Akihabara, however, discounts can be had on electronics: try to compare prices, as these will vary. Traditional crafts – textiles, paper, ceramics, lacquerware and woodblock prints – are also available in Tokyo.

Shopping Areas

Akihabara: A high-tech bazaar of electronics and computers, with many competitively priced stores.
Aoyama: High-class fashion and designer boutiques.
Asakusa: Traditional toys, snacks and souvenirs.
Daikanyama: Upmarket fashion district for young people. Lots of small boutiques and some name designers. **Nakameguro** and **Jiyugaoka**, the next stops down on the Tokyu Den-en Toshi Line from Shibuya, continue the theme.
Ginza: The most expensive shopping district. Several major department stores are located here, such as Matsuya, Matsuzakaya, Mitsukoshi, Seibu and Wako, fashion stores and many exclusive boutiques. Also traditional Japanese goods stores and high-quality art galleries.
Harajuku/Omotesando: Another fashion area, blending youth tastes in the Urahara backstreets with European designer brands in the striking buildings fronting

Omotesando. There are several antique shops, plus Kiddy Land's four storeys of toys.
Ikebukuro: Dominated by giant department stores Seibu and Tobu; also many boutiques in the Sunshine City complex, plus the Amlux Toyota showroom.
Kanda-Jimbocho: New and second-hand bookstores. The area also specialises in musical-instrument shops and ski-equipment retailers.
Kappabashi: Restaurant and kitchen hardware, especially plastic models of foods for restaurant window displays.

Left: Mitsukoshi department store.

Nihombashi: A good place to pick up traditional crafts. Two of Japan's oldest department stores, Mitsukoshi and Takashimaya, are here.
Shibuya: Has a little of everything: designer clothes, hip-hop fashion and the most complete DIY department store at Tokyu Hands. Also the Seibu, Tokyu and Marui department stores, the Parco 'fashion' malls, plus numerous boutiques and record stores aimed at young shoppers.
Shimo Kitazawa: A charming mass of small fashion, novelty and thrift shops in a district of narrow lanes near the station of the same name.
Shinjuku (East): Big camera and electronics stores, such as Yodobashi and Sakuraya. Northwest of the station are backstreets with small shops selling CDs and rare vinyl.
Shinjuku (West): Isetan, Marui and Takashimaya department stores; Kinokuniya bookshop.
Ueno: Ameyoko-cho, one of Tokyo's open market areas, is

Left: high-quality and attractive glassware for sale.

station: Mitsukoshi-mae; map p.141 D4
Elegant Japanese department store Mitsukoshi began life as a dry-goods store in 1673, and was the first to display goods in glass cabinets, employ women sales assistants, sell imported wares and install an escalator.

Seibu
1-28-1 Minami-Ikebukuro, Toshima-ku; tel: 3981 0111; www2.seibu.co.jp/ikebukuro; daily 10am–9pm, Sun until 8pm; station: Ikebukuro; map p.135 C4
Goes head to head with Parco in aiming its products at a young demographic.

Takashimaya
2-4-1 Nihombashi, Chuo-ku; tel: 3211 4111; www.takashimaya. co.jp; daily 10am–8pm; station: Nihombashi; map p.141 D3
One of the most revered Japanese department stores, along with Mitsukoshi. Takashimaya also has lines for the youth market, with its gargantuan Times Square branch in Shinjuku.

Tokyu
2-24-1 Dogenzaka, Shibuya-ku; tel: 3477 3111; www.tokyu-dept. co.jp/honten; daily 11am–7pm; station: Shibuya; map p.138 B1
An upscale and uncrowded edifice for the wealthy matrons of the Shoto district. Chanel, Cartier and Lanvin.

Shopping Malls
Caretta Shiodome
1-8-2, Higashi-Shinbashi, Minato-ku; tel: 6218 2100; www.caretta.jp/english; station: Shiodome
Part of the Shiodome complex, this mall is strong on fashion; also excellent cafés, restaurants and bakeries.

Department stores listed here are mostly main stores, or *honten*. Smaller branches can be found at disparate locations around Tokyo, usually near large stations.

good for cheap food, cosmetics, clothing and toys. Shops selling traditional Japanese goods in the backstreets.

Department Stores
Isetan
3-14-1 Shinjuku, Shinjuku-ku; tel: 3352 1111; www.isetan.co.jp; daily 10am–8pm; station: Shinjuku San-chome; map p.138 C4
One of Japan's most successful department stores has a winning formula of elegance and youth fashions.
SEE ALSO FASHION, P.47

Loft
21-1 Udagawa-cho, Shibuya-ku; tel: 3462 3807; www.loft.co.jp; daily 10am–9pm; station: Shibuya; map p.138 B1
Furnish your trendy downtown apartment at this multi-storey upmarket home centre.

Matsuya
3-6-1 Ginza, Chuo-ku; tel: 3567 1211; www.matsuya.com; daily 10am–8pm; station: Ginza; map p.141 C2
A classy department store with a good selection of traditional Japanese souvenirs on the fifth floor. Clothing by designers like Issey Miyake.

Matsuzakaya
3-29-5 Ueno, Taito-ku; tel: 3832 1111; www.matsuzakaya.co.jp; daily 10am–7.30pm; station: Ueno; map p.137 D2
This 300-year-old establishment appeals to more traditional female shoppers.

Mitsukoshi
1-7-4 Nihombashi-Muromachi, Chuo-ku; tel: 3241 3311; www.mitsukoshi.co.jp; daily 10am–8pm, Sun until 7.30pm;

Left: Takashimaya department store.

Above: expect a themed shopping experience at Decks.

PingMag (http://pingmag.jp), the Tokyo-based bilingual design magazine, is a hip, articulate source of up-to-date info and interviews that goes beyond design to fashion, *manga* and technology.

Hotel, a beer museum, Mitsukoshi department store, and numerous stylish cafés.

What to Buy

ANTIQUES

Daikanyama Address
17 Daikanyamacho, Shibuya-ku; tel: 3461 6492; www.17dixsept. jp; station: Daikanyama
A small but stylish retail complex of the Tokyo fashion scene. An open plaza into overhead bridges link sections of the complex.

Decks
1-6-1 Daiba, Minato-ku; tel: 3599 6500; www.odaiba-decks.com; station: Odaiba-Kaihin Kouen
Prime beachside location on Odaiba island with two themed sections: Chinatown and a re-created 1950s shopping street.

Glassarea Aoyama
5-4-41, Minami-Aoyama, Minato-ku; tel: 5485 3466; www.glassarea.com; station: Omotesando; map p.139 C1
This medium-sized mall emphasises quality and novelty. Run by Tokyu Hands, expect intriguing household goods alongside trendy boutiques.

Mark City
1-12-1, Dogenzaka, Shibuya-ku; tel: 3780 6503; www.s-mark city.co.jp; station: Shibuya; map p.138 B1
Expect boutiques, fashion-accessory stores, cafés and restaurants – all-in-one.

Marunouchi Building
2-4-1, Marunouchi, Chiyoda-ku; tel: 5218 5100; www. marubiru.jp; station: Tokyo; map p.141 C3
Very upmarket complex, even for Tokyo. Vanish into designer fashion stores, a gourmet food hall, cafés and restaurants.

Roppongi Hills
6-10 Roppongi, Minato-ku; tel: 6406 6000; www.roppongi-hills. com; daily 11am–9pm; station: Roppongi; map p.139 E1
A 16-hectare shopping, housing and entertainment centre in a crowded part of town. Cinemas, a contemporary art museum, restaurants, cafés and three shopping areas.

SEE ALSO ARCHITECTURE, P.31; FASHION, P.48

Venus Fort
Palette Town, Aomi, Koto-ku; www.venusfort.co.jp; tel: 3599 0700; station: Aomi
A windowless indoor complex, complete with artificial sky. Mainly for women, with good patisseries and cafés.

Yebisu Garden Place
4-20, Ebisu, Shibuya-ku; http://gardenplace.jp/english/; tel: 5423 7111; station: Ebisu
Contains a major photography museum, the Westin

Akariya
4-8-1 Yoyogi, Shibuya-ku; tel: 3465 5578; Mon–Sat 11am–7pm; www.akariya.co.jp; station: Yoyogikoen; map p.138 B2
Antique *tansu* chests and furniture. Second outlet called **Akariya II** (2F, 5-58-1 Yoyogi; tel: 3467 0580), has high-quality antique kimono and other fabrics from the Edo, Meiji and Taisho eras.

Fuji-Tori
6-1-10 Jingumae, Shibuya-ku; tel: 3400 2777; Wed–Mon 11am–6pm; station: Omotesando; map p.139 C1
Traditional screens and Imari porcelain, but also simple artifacts and art souvenirs.

Hasegawa Ginza
1-7-1 Ginza, Chuo-ku; tel: 5524 7576; daily 11am–7pm; station: Ginza; map p.141 C2
Multi-storey emporium with a selection of expensive but exquisite Buddhist ceremonial objects and ornaments. The sixth floor houses a museum of arts and crafts.

Oriental Bazaar
5-9-13 Jingumae, Shibuya-ku; tel: 3400 3933; Fri–Wed 9.30am– 6.30pm; stations: Meijijingumae, Omotesando; map p.138 C2
Not antiques, but interesting pieces at reasonable prices. No bargaining. A certificate of age is given. Traditional toys, *washi* paper and kimono.

ARTS AND CRAFTS

Bingoya
69 Wakamatsucho, Shinjuku-ku, tel: 3202 8778; www.quasar.nu/bingoya; Tue–Sun 10am–7pm; station: Waka-matsu-kawada
Six floors of folk crafts in a narrow building.

Japan Traditional Craft Centre
Metropolitan Plaza, 1F–2F, 1-11-1 Nishi-Ikebukuro, Toshima-ku, tel: 5954 6066; www.kougei.or.jp; daily 11am–7pm; station: Ikebukuro; map p.135 C4
Information and a gallery for Japan's traditional crafts and producers. Ceramics, lacquer, glass, *washi* paper and dolls.

Yoshitoku
1-9-14 Asakusabashi, Taito-ku, tel: 3863 4419; www.yoshi-toku.co.jp; daily 9.30am–5.30pm; station: Asakusabashi; map p.137 D1
Doll-makers since 1711; prices are moderate.

CAMERAS AND ELECTRONICS

Laox
1-2-9 Soto-Kanda, Chiyoda-ku, tel: 3255 9041; www.laox.co.jp; daily 10am–7.30pm; station: Akihabara; map p.137 C2
Massive discount chain store with staff who speak English.

Sakuraya Camera
3-17-2 Shinjuku, Shinjuku-ku; tel: 3354 3636; www.sakuraya.co.jp; daily 10am–8pm; station: Shinjuku; map p.138 B4
Giant retailer with similar prices and selection to Yodo-bashi Camera *(see below)*.

Yodobashi Camera
1-11-1 Nishi-Shinjuku, Shinjuku-ku; tel: 3346 1010; www.yodobashi.com; daily 9.30am–9pm; station: Shinjuku; map p.138 B4
A second, newer store has opened in Akihabara, north of the station.

JAPANESE PAPER

Isetasu
2-18-9 Yanaka, Taito-ku, tel: 3823 1453; daily 10am–6pm; station: Sendagi; map p.137 C4
A tiny shop worth browsing even if you don't buy.

Ito-ya
2-7-15 Ginza, Chuo-ku, tel: 3561 8311; www.ito-ya.co.jp; Mon–Sat 10am–7pm, Sun 10.30am–7pm; station: Ginza; map p.141 C2
Nine floors of stationery and traditional Japanese paper.

Tsutsumo Factory
137-15 Udagawacho, Shibuya-ku, tel: 5478 1330; www.tsutsumu.co.jp; daily 10.30am–8pm; station: Shibuya; map p.138 B1
Wide range of wrapping paper in traditional and mod-ern designs.

JEWELLERY AND PEARLS

Mikimoto
4-5-5 Ginza, Chuo-ku; tel: 3535 4611; www.mikimoto.com; daily 11am–7pm; station: Ginza; map p.141 C2
Flagship branch of this famous pearl jewellery store. A newer store, the eye-catching **Mikimoto Ginza 2**, is in a backstreet northwest.

Uyeda Jeweller
Imperial Hotel Arcade, 1-1-1, Uchisaiwai-cho, Chiyoda-ku; tel:

3503 2587; www.uyedajeweller.com; Mon–Fri 10am–7pm, Sat 11am–7pm, Sun 11am–6pm; station: Hibiya; map p.140 C2
Uyeda's classic designs bring Japanese elegance to modern Western jewellery.

Wako
4-5-11 Ginza, Chuo-ku; tel: 3562 2111; http://shop.wako.co.jp; Mon–Sat 10am–6pm; station: Ginza; map p.141 C2
A sophisticated selection of watches and clocks as well as pearls, jewellery, table-ware and interior decor, all at equally refined prices.

NOVELTIES

Don Quixote
1-16-5 Kabukicho, Shinjuku-ku; tel: 5291 9211; www.donki.com; daily 24 hours; station: Shin-juku; map p.138 B4
By Shinjuku Station, a chain-store outlet crammed with cheap character goods, toys, kitchenware and booze.

Tokyu Hands
12-18 Udagawa-cho, Shibuya-ku; tel: 5489 5111; www.tokyu-hands.co.jp; daily 10am–8pm; station: Shibuya; map p.138 B1
Hardware store stocking all sorts of goods and novelties.

WOODBLOCK PRINTS

Hara Shobo
2-3 Kanda-Jimbocho, Chiyoda-ku; tel: 3261 7444; www.harashobo.com; station: Jimbocho; map p.136 C1
Selection of old and new prints, with a good range of prices. English spoken.

Tolman Collection
2-2-18 Shiba-Daimon, Minato-ku; tel: 3434 1300; www.tolmantokyo.com; Wed–Mon 11am–7pm; sta-tion: Daimon
Finest stocks of modern Japanese prints, with Japan-ese themed work by resident foreign artists.

Left: elegance and quality indicates Japanese style.

Sport

Sports demonstrate the remarkable, if sometimes uneasy coexistence in Japan of antiquity with modernity. Sumo and Japanese martial arts are ritualistic practices that emphasise ancient spiritual codes as much as physical prowess. On the other hand, sports like baseball, football and even more recent inventions such as K-1 fighting have plenty of the brash commercialism that one expects from modern big business sports entertainment. Japan has hosted the Olympics twice, the World Cup once, and is determined to bring more international events to the country, including the 2016 Olympics.

Sumo

The 150kg-plus giants of sumo fascinate visiting sports fans. Steeped in Shinto rituals, sumo has been around for at least 2,000 years. Matches were traditionally held at shrines. They are punctuated by ritual stomping to drive evil spirits from the ring, and salt-throwing for purification.

The training involves harsh days and a long apprenticeship. Only when a rikishi, or wrestler, makes it to the ranks of ozeki or yokozuna (grand champion, the highest rank and rarely achieved) does life become easier. Those in the lower ranks become the ozeki's or yokozuna's servants, running errands and scrubbing backs.

Mongolian *yokozuna* Asashoryu and Hakuha are currently lording it over the domestic competition. Three of sumo's six annual 15-day tournaments take place at Tokyo's National Sumo Stadium or Ryogoku Kokugikan *(See Sumida River, Asakusa, Ryogoku and East Tokyo, p.25)* in January, May and September. In downtimes it's possible to visit sumo stables to observe wrestlers' morning practice sessions.

National Sumo Stadium
1-3-28 Yokoami, Sumida-ku; tel: 3623 5111; www.sumo.or.jp/eng; station: Ryogoku; map p.137 E1

Tickets for the Tokyo tournaments are sold at the office of the Nihon Sumo Kyokai at the National Sumo Stadium and at ticket agencies. Box seats are usually monopolised by corporate season-ticket-holders, but a limited number of unreserved seats go on sale each day of a tournament at 8am (one per person). Tickets are priced ¥2,100–10,500.

Martial Arts

Judo, karate, aikido, kyudo (archery) and kendo (fencing) all have regular championships or demonstration events, which are usually held at the Nippon Budokan.

All-Japan Judo Federation
1-16-30 Kasuga, Bunkyo-ku; tel: 3818 4199; www.judo.or.jp; station: Kasuga; map p.136 B2

International Aikido Federation
17-18 Wakamatsucho, Shinjuku-ku; tel: 3203 9236; www.aikido-international.org; station: Wakamatsu-Kawada; map p.135 C2

Nippon Budokan
2-3 Kitanomaru-Koen, Chiyoda-ku; tel: 3216 5100; www.nippon budokan.or.jp; station: Kudanshita; map p.140 B4

World Union of Karate-do Organisation
4F Sempaku Shinkokaikan Building, 1-15-16 Toranomon, Minato-ku; tel: 3503 6640; www.wuko-karate.org; station: Toranamon; map p.140 B2

Baseball

Some of Japan's top *yakkyu* (baseball) stars have moved to the US Major Leagues, but a game at either the Tokyo Dome or Jingu Stadium

---

Some sports are also the outlet for Japan's only legal gambling. Horse-racing, in particular, has become fashionable in recent years. Schedules in English are available from the National Association of Racing, at www.jair.jrao.ne.jp.

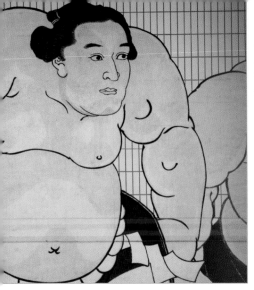

Left: mural at the National Sumo Stadium.

Football and Rugby

The J-League football season runs from March to October, with a special Emperor's Cup event in December. Regular J-League games are played at the National Stadium, as well as international fixtures. The capital's two top teams, Tokyo FC and Verdy, play at the new Ajinomoto Stadium, in Chofu City, western Tokyo. Check www.j-league.or.jn for the latest fixtures and information.

As the strongest rugby nation in Asia, Japan regularly qualifies for the Rugby World Cup. There is an enthusiastic following for the sport at the universities as well as a thriving corporate league.

National Stadium
Kasumigaoka, Shinjuku-ku; tel: 3403 1151; www.naash. go.jp/kokuritu; station: Sendagaya; map p.139 C3

Ajinomoto Stadium
376-3, Nishimachi, Chofu City; tel: 0424-400555; www.ajinomo tostadium.com; station: Tobitakyu

Chichibu-no-miya Rugby Stadium
2-8-35 Kita-Aoyame, Minato-Ku; tel: 3401 3881; station: Gaien-mae; map p.139 D2

demonstrates how the Japanese have made the sport their own.

Japan's 'second national sport' maintains its appeal among the older generation. Younger Japanese seem less keen, although the Major League success of Ichiro Suzuki, Daisuke Matsuzaka and others may change that.

Tokyo has three teams: the Yomiuri Giants (in the Central League), the Nippon Ham Fighters (Pacific League) and the Yakult Swallows (Central League). The Giants and Ham Fighters are based at the Tokyo Dome, while the Yakult Swallows share the Jingu Stadium. The season is April–October, culminating in the best-of-seven Japan Series between the pennant winners of the two leagues.

Jingu Stadium
13 Kasumigaoka, Shinjuku-ku; tel: 3404 8999; www.jingu-stadium.com; station: Sendagaya; map p.139 D2

Most baseball fans prefer the atmosphere at the Jingu ballpark (built as part of the 1964 Olympic complex) to the Big

Egg. It is the home ground of the Swallows, and draws big crowds for the games against the Giants and the Hanshin Tigers (from Osaka).

Tokyo Dome
1-3-61 Koraku, Bunkyo-ku; tel: 5800 9999; www.tokyo-dome. co.jp; station: Suidobashi; map p.136 B2

Japan's first sports dome, nicknamed the Big Egg, is home to both the Giants and the Fighters, who play there alternately. The US Major League 2008 season opener was held here.

Below: the Big Egg, home to the Giants and the Fighters.

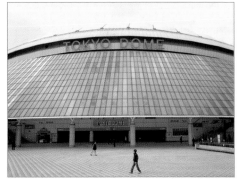

Temples and Shrines

Japan has two major religions, Buddhism and Shinto, but contemporary Japanese people are strikingly free of strongly held religious beliefs. Funerals tend to be Buddhist; weddings Shinto and Christian. Despite the fact that many of Tokyo's temples and shrines were destroyed in the Great Kanto Earthquake or World War II, Japan's custom of rebuilding means that they continue to offer venues for contemplation and worship in the midst of Tokyo's hustle and bustle, as well as providing a much-needed link to the past.

Buddhism and Shinto

Buddhism came to the archipelago by way of mainland Asia. Making its way from India through China via the Silk Road, and then on to Korea, Buddhism is believed to have reached Japan and become widespread when Empress Suiko encouraged its universal acceptance towards the end of the fifth century. In Tokyo, numerous temples are devoted to various sects of Buddhism. In particular, the teachings and aesthetics that emerged out of the great Zen centres of Kamakura have had a profound impact on Japanese culture, particularly in the subtle designs of its Buddhist temples and gardens.

Shinto is Japan's indigenous religion, an animist faith that involves the worship of spirits, or *kami*. *Kami* can be resident in a river or mountain, but also take the form of gods, such as Japan's founding sun goddess Amaterasu. In the period leading up to and during World War II, Shinto also became a state religion, with the emperor worshipped as a living god descended from Amaterasu. At Shinto shrines, the most noticable feature is the ever-present torii gate, which symbolises a door between the earthly realm and that of the *kami*.

Buddhism and Shinto have become interwoven along with other belief systems from Asia including Confucianism and Taoism. This is reflected both positively, in Japanese people's open-minded approach to religion and negatively, in creepy syncretic cults such as Aum Shinrikyo, that have brought rudderless people under their sway, with murderous results like the 1995 gassing of the Tokyo subway system.

Imperial Palace, Yurakucho and Ginza

Yasukuni-jinja Shrine

3-1-1 Kudanshita, Chiyoda-ku; tel: 3261 8326; www.yasukuni. or.jp; daily 6am–5pm; station: Kudanshita; map p.140 A4
One of Tokyo's favourite cherry-blossom-viewing spots is Yasukuni-jinja, entered by the grand Tayasu

Gate just off Yasukuni-dori (Yasukuni Street) from Kudanshita Station. Founded in 1869 as a memorial to combatants who died in the battles preceding the Meiji Restoration, the names of 2.5 million soldiers and others, including war criminals, are among those commemorated.

The shrine attracts right-wingers who view Japan's activities during World War II as a campaign to free Asia from Western imperialism. The shrine's notorious **Military Museum** (Yushukan) displays torn uniforms, letters from soldiers, a curious human torpedo and a suicide glider. Given the lack of information on the atrocities wrought by the Japanese military in Asia, it gives the

Left: Yushima-Tenjin Shrine.

one of Tokyo's most impressive temples, Zojo-ji. Founded in 1393, the site was chosen by the Tokugawa clan in the late 1600s as their ancestral temple. Close to the bay and the Tokaido Road, it also served as a post station for travellers. Most of the temple buildings, once numbering over 100, were destroyed, but its main entrance, the 1612 red-lacquered **Sanmon Gate**, an Important Cultural Treasure, is original.

The large bell here was made from melted down hairpins donated by ladies of the shogun's court. The **Main Hall** (Taiden) contains ancient sutras and statuary. The new leaders of the Meiji government confiscated the temple, turning it into a park and removing six of the mummified shogun to the rear of the Main Hall.

Shibuya, Harajuku and Aoyama

Meiji-jingu Shrine and Gardens

1-1 Yoyogi-Kamizonocho, Shibuya-ku; tel: 3379 5511; hours vary according to season; www.meijijingu.or.jp; station: Harajuku; map p.138 B2

One of Tokyo's chief sights is Meiji-jingu. To reach the shrine, cross an open plaza

troubling impression of a shrine to valour.

Exhibits in the glass annexe include a Zero fighter plane used in World War II. Behind the main hall is a garden with a pond, a teahouse, and a ring for sumo wrestling and performances of court music and dance, noh dramas and kendo martial art.

Roppongi and Akasaka

Hie-jinja Shrine

2-10-5 Nagatacho, Chiyoda-ku; tel: 3581 2471; www.hiejinja.net; daily, Apr–Sept: 5am–6pm; Oct–Mar: 6am–5pm; station: Tameiki-sanno; map p.139 E2

Transplanted to the borders of the Akasaka and Nagatacho districts in the 17th century in the belief that it would help to deflect evil from Edo Castle, a massive stone torii gate leads uphill through an avenue of smaller gates to the current buildings, erected in 1967. The shrine's role as protector is still evident today; look carefully at a carving to the left of the main

shrine and you will see a monkey cradling its baby. Pregnant women come here to pay homage to the image.

Every two years in June, the shrine is the stage for the massive Sanno Matsuri festival. Participants in period costumes take part in an impressive parade, which includes the carrying of heavy *mikoshi* (portable shrines) on the shoulders of local residents.

Zojo-ji Temple

4-7-35 Shiba Koen, Minato-ku; tel: 3432 1413; www.zozoji.or.jp; daily 6am–5.30pm; station: Shiba-koen; map p.140 B1

Adjacent to Tokyo Tower in Shiba Park (Shiba Koen) sits

Right: Sanmon Gate at Zojo-ji Temple in Shiba Park.

Left: the Meiji-Jingu Shrine.

Shinjuku

Hanazono-jinja Shrine

5-17-3 Shinjuku, Shinjuku-ku; tel: 3209 5265; www.hanazono-jinja.or.jp; station: Shinjuku; map p.138 C4

Hanazono-jinja, set back from busy Yasukuni-dori, is best approached by entering under a torii gate and walking along a stone path lined with red- and white-paper lanterns that are lit at night. Although the structure, with its vermilion walls and wood rails, is a post-war creation, the site has a long history. The shrine's principal deity is Yamato-taeru-no-Mikoto, a 4th-century warrior prince. It is also a venue for flea markets and festivals.

above the railway tracks in front of Harajuku Station, a popular spot at weekends for Tokyo's fashion tribes, buskers and street performers, and through the **Ichi-no-torii**, a massive gate made from 1,700-year-old cypress trees from Mount Alishan in Taiwan.

The shrine, dedicated to the Meiji emperor and his wife, Empress Shoken, is in the centre of the **Meiji Shrine Inner Gardens** (Meiji-Jingu Gyoen), an area of forest. The park's famous **Iris Garden** (Jingu Naien), where over 100 varieties bloom in mid-June, was designed by the emperor for his wife.

The shrine is a beautiful example of Shinto architecture, completed in 1920, with a sweeping copper roof and a white-gravel forecourt. The original shrine burnt down, so the present building is a 1958 reconstruction. The compound, with its shrine maidens in white kimonos, plays host to events including formal Japanese weddings.

As many as 3 million people come here to pray during the days following New Year. And on the second Monday in January, young women dressed in their best kimono come to celebrate Coming-of-Age Day. Spring, in late April and early May, is marked with horseback

archery, traditional dances and court music.

In the northern section of the park, the **Imperial Treasure House** (Meiji-jingu Hakubut-sukan; Mar–Oct daily 9am–4.30pm, Nov–Feb daily 9am–4pm; entrance charge; tel: 3261 8326) displays a modest collection of sacred objects, garments and personal effects of the Imperial family.

Nogi-jinja Shrine

8-11-27 Akasaka, Minato-ku; tel: 3478 3001; www.nogi jinja.or.jp; daily 8.30am–5pm; station: Nogizaka; map p.139 D2

The remains of General Nogi Maresuke, a hero of military campaigns in China and Russia during the Meiji Period, and those of his wife, are interred in Aoyama Cemetery. The couple were so devoted to the Meiji emperor that, on 13 September 1912, when the emperor's body was removed from the Imperial Palace for burial in Kyoto, the general (like ancient samurai following their lord into death) performed *seppuku* (ritual disembowelment) while his wife slit her throat.

The Nogi-jinja is along Gaien Higashi-dori, east of Aoyama Cemetery. The house and the bloodstained clothes can be viewed as they were on the eve and day of the suicides. On an upbeat note, there is a fine Sunday flea market here.

Ikebukuro and Meijirodai

Gokoku-ji Temple

5-40-1 Otsuka; Bunkyo-ku; tel: 3941 0764; www.gokokuji.or.jp; station: Otsuka; map p.135 D4

On the east side of atmospheric Zoshigaya cemetery is Gokoku-ji. The main hall of this temple dates from 1681. The buildings are approached up steps lined with zelkova trees, to the main compound. The Nio-mon Gate is flanked by beautiful Nio statues. This temple is known as the centre for Japan's tea ceremony.

Shinagawa, Meguro and Ebisu

Sengaku-ji Temple

2-11-1 Takanawa, Minato-ku; tel: 3441 5560; www.sengoku ji.or.jp; station: Sengakuji

A stroll west of Sengakuji Station near Shinagawa is Sengaku-ji. This temple, played a part in a well-known Edo event, enacted countless times in kabuki.

Lord Asano, scorned by his teacher Lord Kira, caused

offence by drawing his sword in anger within the castle grounds and was obliged to perform *seppuku* (ritual disembowlment). In revenge, on 1 December 1702, Asano's 47 retainers decapitated Kira and carried the head through the streets of Edo to their lord's grave at Sengaku-ji. As retribution, the 47 ronin (masterless samurai) were also ordered to commit *seppuku*.

This act is admired by the Japanese as an example of the highest samurai ideal, and incense is placed every day on the graves of the 47 retainers and Lord Asano, who are buried together at Sengaku-ji. The temple's entrance gate is carved with a dragon motif from 1836. A side building, the **Gishiken** (Hall of Loyal Retainers), contains some of the personal effects of the 47 ronin.

Suidobashi, Ochanomizu, Kanda and Akihabara

Kanda Myojin Shrine
2-16-2 Soto-Kanda, Chiyoda-ku; tel: 3254 0753; www.kanda myoujin.or.jp; station: Ochanomizu; map p.137 C2

In the Soto-Kanda district north of Ochanomizu Station is one of Tokyo's great centres of religious devotion, Kanda Myojin. It is dedicated to rebel general Taira no Masakado, who led subjugated Kantoites against imperial forces. There is a *taiko* (drum) troupe attached to Kanda Myojin called Masakado Taiko. The troupe's main themes celebrate the life

of Masakado. They are one of the few all-women *taiko* groups in Japan.

The temple, a concrete reconstruction of a 1616 original, enshrines two other deities besides Masakado: Ebisu, the god of commerce, family prosperity and good marriages; and Daikoku, entrusted with the care of farmers and fishermen. Side stores sell *mikoshi* (portable shrines) used during the Kanda Matsuri, one of the city's three great festivals marked by a magnificent street procession.

Takuzosu-Inari Shrine
3-17-12 Koishikawa, Bunkyo-ku; tel: 3811 1327; http://takuzosu inari.com; station: Kasuga; map p.136 B3

In the middle of a narrow backstreet five minutes from Kasuga Station is an old tree said to be visited by an Inari fox deity. The tree indicates the presence a few steps away of Takuzosu-Inari, one of the creepiest locales in Tokyo. Squeezed into the precincts of the shrine are rows of torii gates, Jizo and Kannon statues, and fierce-looking fox messengers. This is not a place to venture after twilight.

Stone steps descend under damp, blackened trees to an eerie cave called the **Oana**, its dank rock face the

home, it is believed, of the white fox. Credence of this comes from author Nagai Kafu who, in his short story 'Kitsune' (The Fox), relates how his father spotted the bushy-tailed messenger here one afternoon.

Yushima Tenjin Shrine
3-30-1 Yushima, Bunkyo-ku; tel: 3836 0753; www.yushima tenjin.or.jp; station: Yushima; map p.137 C2

Yushima Tenjin is the city's great shrine of learning. Yushima's 'Shrine of Literature' was erected in memory of the 9th-century statesman and poet Sugawara no Michizane, deified here in the form of Tenjin, patron of learning and the arts. A regular stream of students come here to worship all year, but spring, the traditional time for entrance exams, sees high numbers flocking to the shrine to seek Tenjin's help on their behalf.

The shrine holds its annual Plum Festival in February (its

Below: votive papers at Yushima Tenjin Shrine

tiny garden is said to be one of the best spots in Tokyo for plum-viewing). This is also a good time of the year to see open-air performances of the tea ceremony. In late October, admirers of the imperial chrysanthemum throng to the shrine to see clever tableaux made from petals.

Ueno and Yanaka
Tosho-gu Shrine
1-2 Ueno Kouen, Taito-ku; tel: 3822 3455; daily 9am–5pm; admission charge; station: Ueno; map p.137 D3

Situated on a rise in Ueno Park *(see p.99)*, Tosho-gu was built in 1627 (the present buildings date from a 1651 renovation) by a warlord to pay respects to the first Tokugawa shogun, Tokugawa Ieyasu. The walkway to Tosho-gu ('Illuminator of the East') is lined with dozens of large symbolic stone or copper free-standing lanterns; the tallest is 6m, and was donated by warlords to cultivate merit with the shogun.

The main shrine building is a superb structure; its outer hall features murals by the famous Edo artist Kano Tanyu. Another fascinating point is the Chinese-style **Kara-mon**, a gate adorned with dragons that are meant to be ascending to heaven.

According to local superstition, the dragons slide over to Shinobazu Pond at midnight to quench their thirst.

The 36m- high **Five-Storey Pagoda** (Gojuno-to), visible from the grounds of the shrine, was originally a part of the Kan'ei-ji complex, much of which was burnt down. You have to be in the precincts of the Ueno Zoo for a close-up look.

Sumida River, Asakusa, Ryogoku and East Tokyo
Asakusa Kannon Temple
2-3-1 Asakusa, Taito-ku; tel: 3842 0181; www.asakusa jinja.jp (shrine); daily 6am–5pm (temple), 24 hours (grounds); station: Asakusa; map p.137 E3

To reach Asakusa's main temple compound, pass under the **Kaminarimon** (Thunder Gate), a wooden entrance flanked by statues of meteorological gods (Fujin, the wind god, on the right; Raijin, the thunder god, on the left) and a huge red paper lantern with the character for 'thunder'.

Asakusa became an important pilgrimage site after three fishermen discovered a tiny golden statue of Kannon (the Buddhist goddess of mercy) in their nets in the Sumida River. According to legend, when the statue

Many Japanese maintain shrines at home. There are Buddhist shrines called Butsudan ('Butsu'=Buddha, 'dan'=house) for the worship of ancestors, and Shinto shrines known as Kamidana ('kami shelf') for making obeisance to a range of spirits.

appeared, a golden dragon descended to earth from the heavens. The temple became a favourite with samurai and shogun, and prospered economically and politically.

Founded in AD 628, the Asakusa Kannon Temple, also known as Senso-ji, is still the sacred heart of the quarter. The great pilgrimage site at one time also became a place of entertainment, including theatres, archery galleries, circuses and brothels. The current temple is a replica of a building from 1692, destroyed in an air raid.

The temple's *hondo* (main hall) sells souvenirs and fortunes. On busy days, it is noisy with clapping and bell-ringing. The statue of Kannon, just 6cm high, is believed to be in a fireproof box behind the golden altar. It has never been seen by the public. Three times a day, the temple's monks chant sutras in its honour. The hall contains votive paintings from the 18th and 19th centuries, while the altar is packed with religious objects.

The 17th-century **Asakusa-jinja Shrine**, just to the right of the main temple, is dedicated to the three fishermen and one of few buildings in its original state. Behind the shrine is **Nitenmon**. The gate, built in 1618 and a designated Important Cultural Treasure, is usually covered with votive papers.

Below: Kaminarimon (Thunder Gate), Asakusa Kannon Temple.

Left: Narita-san Temple.

22,000kg stone, is engraved with the names of sumo wrestlers who have reached the exalted rank of *ozeki*, the highest in the sumo world.

The shrine is also the focus of the Fukagawa Matsuri, one of Tokyo's greatest festivals, which is held every third year in mid-August. Portable shrines and palanquins are carried through the streets on the shoulders of some 30,000 bearers, local geisha lead a procession, and teams of chanting, hollering men heave gigantic logs through the streets. More than half a million spectators turn up for the event. If you are lucky enough to catch it, be prepared to get wet, as the festival involves much splashing of water.

Tokyo's Surroundings

Narita-san Temple

1 Narita, Narita-shi, Chiba-ken; tel: 0476 22 2111; www.narita san.or.jp; station: Narita
A 10-minute walk from Narita stations, Narita-san or Shinshoji, as it's also known, makes a convenient sightseeing stop-off before leaving from Narita Airport. One of the most important in the Kanto area, the temple has 2 million visitors who come to pray in the first three days of the year. It is dedicated to an image of the deity of mercy, Fudomyoo, said to be carved by the founder of the Buddhist Shingon sect, Kukai, in the 10th century. The imposing main temple is accessed by a steep stairwell, and in its grounds there are five-storey pagodas and a garden. The atmospheric streets around play host to the Kanto region's largest *taiko* drum festival in spring.

The western section of the Asakusa complex is dominated by the **Five-Storey Pagoda** (Gojuno-to), a reconstruction standing beside the **Denbo-in Monastery**. The building is closed to the public but its peaceful garden, created in the 17th century by the Zen gardener Kobori Enshu, can be visited. A pass is obtainable on request from the booth left of the pagoda.

Every year in May, Asakusa is the setting for one of Tokyo's most dynamic street events: the Sanja Matsuri (Three Shrines Festival). Senso-ji and the roads around it are the centre of this mammoth four-day spectacle, an important spring event for Tokyo families.

Dozens of portable shrines are carried through the streets by young jostling men and women. You will spot geisha and men sporting full-body tattoos, rare sights in Tokyo these days.

Tomioka Hachiman-gu-jinja Shrine

1-20-3 Tomioka, Edo-ku; tel: 3642 1315; www.tomioka hachimangu; station: Monzen-Nakacho
The important Tomioka Hachiman-gu-jinja lies near the Sumida River along Kasaibashi-dori.

Founded in 1627, the current building, impressive with its towering copper-tiled green roof, prayer and spirit halls, was constructed in 1968. The shrine is dedicated to eight deities, including the goddess Benten, Ebisu, the god of commerce, and to the spirit of Emperor Ojin who is credited with founding the ancient city of Nara.

The shrine is strongly associated with sumo wrestling. In the Edo era, the shrine was the official venue for the sport. Some interesting stone monuments at the back of the shrine commemorate the link. One of the most important, the **Yokozuna Monument**, a

Theatre and Dance

Tokyo offers an interesting range of performing arts. From Japanese antiquity there is the entrancing masked stillness of noh, the masterful puppetry of bunraku, and the garish stylisation of kabuki. Or there are outstanding performance halls for top-notch musicals, ballet and contemporary dance. Then there is avant-garde butoh or experimental theatre at one of Tokyo's tiny black-box venues. Locating performance information, tickets and venues can be a challenge, but it's all part of the experience.

Traditional

BUNRAKU

These puppeteers trace their art back to the 7th century, when itinerant Chinese and Korean performers presented semi-religious puppet plays. Bunraku is adult theatre and deals with themes such as revenge and sacrifice, love and rejection, reincarnation and futility.

Each major puppet is manipulated by three operators, a logistic marvel in itself. In theory, the audience does not notice all the shuffling of the professional puppeteers, concentrating instead on the puppets, which are roughly one-third human size. The real tour de force, though, are the narrators, the *gidayu* performers, who speak, gesture and weep from a kneeling position at stage left. Tokyo's **National Theatre** *(see p.121)* is the best venue for bunraku.

KABUKI

Japan's most splendid theatre form is kabuki, a performance that resembles

opera and ballet. In Japanese, kabuki translates as 'song-dance skill', with no mention of theatre. The word 'kabuki', in the early 16th century, meant 'avant-garde', and referred to all-female performances, often of a licentious nature. The Tokugawa shogunate banned female performers in 1629. This started the all-male tradition that continues today; actresses are allowed only for certain special events.

Kabuki developed into its present form during the 17th and 18th centuries when it was theatre for the Edo masses. The actors were the rock stars of feudal Japan.

Left: a traditional Noh mask.

The older plays began as puppet performances with social comment and satire. English programmes are sometimes available.

The main kabuki theatres are the **Kabuki-za** *(see p.121)*, the **National Theatre** *(see p.121)*, and the **Shimbashi Embujo** *(see p.123)*. Most programmes span 10 hours, with generous intervals for tea-drinking and socialising. The Kabuki-za is the most tourist-friendly, and allows the choice of seeing only one act or part of an act.

KYOGEN

Many people much prefer kyogen, comic interludes designed to provide light relief between noh performances. Some last only 10 minutes and present amusing situations based on folk tales and Buddhist parables. Much like Shakespeare, they represent universal human foibles. There are occasional performances in English, which is not as bizarre as it sounds.

Left: elaborate costumes for kabuki productions.

For a taste of the art form, buy a fourth-floor ticket for just one act. If you like what you see, get a seat in the main auditorium: the most expensive are those near the stage or the *hana-michi* (walkway), where the actors can be seen close up. English programme and earphone guides available. Shows at 11am–4pm and 5–9pm.

National Noh Theatre
4-18-1 Sendagaya, Shibuya-ku; tel: 3423 1331; www.ntj.jac.go.jp/english; station: Sendagaya; map p.138 C3
Noh performances are given about once a week. A short English programme is available. Shows are usually during the afternoon (call for details).

National Theatre
4-1 Hayabusa-cho, Chiyoda-ku; tel: 3265 7411 (enquiries); tel: 3230 3000 (reservations); www.ntj.jac.go.jp/english; station: Hanzamon; map p.140 A3
The Large Hall stages kabuki for eight months of the year. Bunraku performances are given in the Small Hall for the remaining months. English-language summaries are included in the programmes; earphone guide available.

Performance festivals for stage and dance buffs include the Tokyo International Arts Festival (http://tif.anj.or.jp/en/), the Tokyo Performing Arts Market (www.tpam.or.jp), and the Dance Triennale at the Aoyama Theatre.

NOH
This minimalist theatre is a development from early temple plays. Aristocratic patronage demanded esoteric poetry, sophisticated language and a refined simplicity of movement, precisely what you see six centuries later. It is difficult to describe noh – words like 'ethereal', 'inaccessible' and 'subtle' spring to mind. Fortunately, some English translations are available. Catch noh performances at the **National Noh Theatre** *(see right)* and the new **Cerulean Tower Noh Theatre** *(see below)*.

VENUES
Cerulean Tower Noh Theatre
26-1 Sakuragaoka-Cho, Shibuya-ku; tel: 3476 3000; www.ceruleantower.com/noh theater.html; station: Shibuya
This beautiful noh theatre hosts professional as well as amateur noh and kyogen performances (without English translations).

Kabuki Theatre (Kabuki-za)
4-12-15 Ginza, Chuo-ku; tel: 3541 3131 (information); tel: 5565 6000 (tickets); www.shochiku.co.jp/play/kabuki za/theater; station: Ginza; map p.141 C2
The most accessible place to watch kabuki. Performances can last up to five hours (with intermissions).

Below: the splendid entrance to the Kabuki Theatre.

Left: a Bunraku puppet.

Western

Translations of foreign plays and musicals are very popular, and range from Chekhov to *Cats*. Musicals are imported from London or New York, though most are performed in Japanese by Japanese dancers and singers. Lyrics are sung in English, and performances can be a mixed experience. The group **Yumeno Yuminsha** has a large and devoted following, while **Gekidan Shiki** is now exporting localised musicals across Asia.

Tokyo also offers a lively experimental theatre scene, known as the shogekijo ('little theatre') movement, which first flourished in the 1980s. Much of the activity centres on the counterculture district of Shimokitazawa, with directors like **Yoji Sakate** and his Rinkogun troupe taking on a variety of difficult social and political subjects.

A handful of amateur drama and comedy groups performing in English call Tokyo their home. The **Tokyo International Players**' season runs from late September till late May.

TAKARAZUKA

The takarazuka revue is an all-female song and dance extravaganza. It is unashamedly flamboyant and romantic, with gorgeous costumes. Watched mainly by middle-aged housewives and young women. Catch it at Yurakucho's **Takarazuka Theatre**.

Dance

BALLET

A dedicated following exists for classical ballet, with performances by domestic companies the **Tokyo Ballet** and **Asami Maki Ballet** at the **Tokyo Bunka Kaikan** *(see p.123)* and **New National Theatre** *(see p.123)*, respectively. There are visits by overseas companies, notably a month-long tour by the Leningrad Ballet in winter. Japan has its own ballet stars, including Tetsuya Kumakawa, with a loyal audience for his **K-Ballet Company**.

BUTOH

Originally called a 'dance of darkness', butoh strives not for beauty and physical grace, but to depict the inhumanity and discord of existence, with cathartic results for the audience. This internationally renowned avant-garde dance form is becoming more widely accepted in its home country. The best places for viewing the ghostly white dancers of butoh are the **Die Pratze theatre** *(see right)*, and butoh company **Dairakudakan's Studio Kochuten** in Kichijoji (www.dairakudakan.com); performances by **Sankai Juku** should also not be missed.

CONTEMPORARY DANCE

Tokyo has a fervent audience for boldly experimental dance performances, which often combine butoh and theatre with innovative multimedia. Performances are at **Session House** *(see p.123)*, **Aoyama Theatre** *(see below)* and the **New National Theatre** *(see right)*. Some of the more intriguing companies are **Ikuyo Kuroda's Batik**, **Kim Itoh's Glorious Future**, Kakuya Ohashi and Dancers, and Gekidan Kaitaisha.

VENUES

Aoyama Theatre
5-53-1 Jingumae, Shibuya-ku; tel: 3797 5678; www.aoyama. org; station: Omotesando; map p.138 C1
Two theatres including the Aoyama Round Theatre, an unusual and intimate venue that often plays host to challenging contemporary dance performances.

Bunkamura Theatre Cocoon
2-24-1 Dogenzaka, Shibuya-ku; tel: 3477 9999; www.bunkamura. co.jp; station: Shibuya; map p.138 B1
A highly regarded dance venue, the Cocoon stages lively international acts from flamenco to modern experimental dance.

Die Pratze
2-12 Nishi-gokencho Shinjuku-ku; tel: 3235 7990; station: Kagurazaka; map p.135 E2
This storeyed black-box theatre for avant-garde performances and butoh also hosts the annual, experimental Die Pratze Dance Festival.

Imperial Theatre
3-1-1 Marunouchi, Chiyoda-ku; tel: 3213 7221; www.tohostage. com; station: Hibiya
Long-established venue for everything from Ibsen to Yukio Mishima's noh dramas.

Meiji Theatre (Meiji-za)
2-31-1 Nihombashi-Hamacho, Chuo-ku; tel: 3660 3939; www. meijiza.co.jp; station: Nihonbashi
Modern plays as well as samurai costume dramas.

New National Theatre
1-1-1 Honmachi, Shibuya-ku; tel: 5351 3011; www.nntt.jac.go. jp/english; station: Hatsudai
Divided into the Opera House, Playhouse and Pit. The first is for opera, the other two are theatre and modern dance venues.

Session House
158 Yaraicho, Shinjuku-ku; tel: 3266 0461; www.session-house.net; station: Kagurazaka; map p.135 E2
This Spartan performance space launched by dancer Naoko Itoh hosts contemporary dance pieces without complex staging and lighting.

Shimbashi Embujo
6-12-2 Ginza, Chuo-ku; tel: 3541 2600; station: Shimbashi
Lowbrow, swashbuckling samurai dramas, but also performances of 'Super-Kabuki', by star performer Ichikawa Enosuke – a high-octane version of the original.

The Suzunari
1-45-15 Kitazawa, Setagaya-ku; tel: 3469 0511; www.honda-geki.com/suzunari; station: Shimokitazawa
This cramped venue in bohemian Shimokitazawa is a storeyed venue for experimental, alternative-style theatre.

Takarazuka Theatre
1-1-3 Yurakucho, Chiyoda-ku; tel: 5251 2001; station: Yuraku-cho; map p.141 C2
Camp dramas and musicals from an all-women troupe who cross-dress to extraordinary effect.

Tokyo Bunka Kaikan
5-45 Ueno Park, Taito-ku; tel: 3828 2111; www.t-bunka.jp; station: Ueno; map p.137 D3
Home to the prestigious Tokyo Ballet, which has premièred pieces by choreographers Bejart and Neumeier.

Tokyo International Forum
3-5-1 Marunouchi, Chiyoda-ku; tel: 5221 9000; www.t-i-forum. co.jp; station: Yurakucho; map p.141 C3
A collection of soaring contemporary halls offering theatre, musicals and dance, as well as music.

Tokyo International Players
Tel: 090-6009 4171; www.toky-oplayers.org
Very professional performances in English from foreign and Japanese communities. Venues change regularly. Check the website for listings.

The Art of the Geisha
Geisha sing, dance, play silly games and serve sake with finesse. There are very

Information on upcoming events can be found in city magazines like *Metropolis* and *JSelect*, as well as the daily newspapers' arts sections. Online sources include the Japan Contemporary Dance Network (www.jcdn.org) and Performing Arts Network Japan (performingarts.jp). Tickets can be purchased at agencies such as Pia.

few true geisha left, and one has to pay a lot (in cash) for their company. Few foreigners really derive much pleasure from a geisha evening as the entertainment is designed for Japan's middle-aged businessmen and politicians.

There are occasional chances to see the geisha: at the Sanja Matsuri in May, and at special performances of Japanese dancing, or *buyo*, at theatres such as Shimbashi Embujo and the Meiji-za.

The **Hato Bus Tour** offers a 'Mukojima Geisha Tour'.
SEE ALSO TRANSPORT, P.127

Below: it is rare to see a geisha performer these days.

Transport

With flights of 10 or more hours the norm from most Western cities, getting to Tokyo requires commitment. Add to that the fact that Narita airport is located far outside the city. However, once you've recovered in your hotel and set out to explore, you'll find the world's finest public transport system: a miraculous integrated circuit board of interlocking subway, train, monorail and bus lines that function safely, efficiently and on time. With little order in the city's layout, finding your way around at street level can be a challenge, though sometimes getting lost can be half the fun.

Getting There

BY AIR

Tokyo is served by two main airports: New Tokyo International Airport (Narita), about 66km east of the city, and the Tokyo International Airport (Haneda), 15km to the south. The airports are usually referred to as Narita and Haneda. Most international flights arrive at Narita, but with the opening of a new runway, Haneda will see more flights to neighbouring countries.

Narita Airport

Tel (general and flight info): 0476-348000, (tourist info, terminal 2): 0476-346251, (terminal 1): 0476-303383; www.narita-airport.jp/en/index.html

Although inconveniently located, Narita has been recently renewed and extended. It has two terminals, both with exchange counters, restaurants, cafés, Internet facilities, post offices, health clinics and a range of shops including duty free. Terminal 2 has a children's playroom, rooms for taking a nap and showers.

Haneda Airport

Tel: 5757 8111; www.tokyo-airport-bldg.co.jp/fl/english Haneda airport is Tokyo's main domestic hub. Both domestic airlines, Japan Air Lines (JAL) and All Nippon Airways (ANA), operate flights throughout Japan from here. Haneda's two terminals are well designed, with Japanese, Western and Chinese restaurants, cafés, shops, post office and information desks.

Flying From the UK and US

Four big airlines serve Tokyo from the UK: British Airways, JAL, ANA and Virgin Atlantic. From the US or Canada, JAL

Left: Tokyo's Narita airport is well outside the city.

and ANA, Northwest, American Airlines, Delta, Continental and United Airlines all have routes. Tokyo is also an increasingly important hub for flights to Asian destinations. April, August and December tend to be the most expensive times to fly to Japan, as they coincide with the country's Golden Week, O-bon and Christmas-New Year holidays. Flying a few days either side of these peak periods can result in huge savings.

BY ROAD

Expressways are of extraordinarily high quality. Like Britain, the Japanese drive on the left. Highway tolls are high, so trains and buses are more affordable.

Japan has an excellent system of inter-city buses. They are a comfortable and cheaper alternative to the bullet train. Buses include destinations not covered by trains, and many services are direct. Night buses are the

Left: Tokyo has a very efficient subway system.

where between one-and-a-half to three hours.

By Limousine Bus
Tel (info): 3665 7220; www.limousinebus.co.jp

Frequent and comfortable airport 'limousine' buses are much cheaper than taxis. These connect Narita Airport with most parts of the city, including major hotels, railway stations and Tokyo City Air Terminal (a pre-boarding check-in facility), as well as Haneda Airport and Tokyo Disneyland. Tickets (around ¥3,000, depending upon destination) can be bought in the arrivals lobby after clearing immigration and customs. Buses are boarded outside the terminal.

By Train
Tel: 3423 0111; www.jreast.co.jp/e/index.html

This is the fastest way to reach Tokyo. JR Narita Express and Keisei Skyliner stations are found on the basement level of both terminal buildings.

Narita Express connects with the JR railway network at Tokyo, Shinagawa, Shinjuku, Ikebukuro, Omiya, Yokohama and Ofuna stations. It takes one hour to travel to Tokyo Station, and the price is ¥2,940 for standard class.

The Keisei Skyliner runs to Tokyo's Ueno Station, stopping first at nearby Nippori. The connection to JR lines or the subway at Ueno is not as convenient as the Narita Express, but the Skyliner is usually less crowded. It takes one hour to Ueno and costs ¥1,920.

There is no need to touch the doors at all when getting in or out of a taxi. The doors are opened and closed by the driver, who operates a lever at the front. After hailing a taxi, wait for the door to open; at your destination the door will be opened for you.

cheapest, but leave late and arrive early. These are operated by Japan Railway; buy tickets at the Green Window offices at JR stations.

The main JR bus office is on the south side of Tokyo Station (tel: 3215 0498). The **Tokyo Bus Association** (tel: 5360 7111) has information on departures and arrivals.

BY TRAIN
The majority of train lines entering Tokyo from major Japanese cities, whether JR or *shinkansen* (bullet train), stop at Tokyo Station on the JR Yamanote Line. Day trips to places like Hakone usually involve taking a private line. Most of these connect with major JR terminals like Shibuya and Shinjuku stations.

Getting Around
FROM NARITA AIRPORT
Because of its distance from Tokyo, you should allow at least one-and-a-half to two hours to reach the city centre. There are four ways to get into Tokyo: taxi, limousine bus, Japan Railways Narita Express (N'EX) or the private Keisei Railway Skyliner train.

By Taxi
This is the most expensive option, and usually the slowest. The fare to Tokyo is ¥20,000–30,000, and the roads are often jammed. Expect the 66km ride to central Tokyo to take anywhere

Left: there is no need to tip the taxi driver.

Left: subway ticket
machine and train.

FROM HANEDA AIRPORT
By Taxi
It should take about 30 minutes to central Tokyo by taxi, and cost around ¥5,000, but beware of traffic congestion.

By Train
Most people opt for the cheaper trains. Frequent services run from the Keihin Kyuko Railway Station in the airport basement. The train takes about 20 minutes to Shinagawa Station, and costs ¥400.

By Monorail
The Tokyo Monorail connects Haneda with Hamamatsucho Station on the JR Yamanote line. It takes only 17 minutes and costs ¥470, but can be very crowded.

By Limousine Bus
An airport limousine bus service connects Haneda with central Tokyo. Fares start at ¥1,000, depending on which part of the city you're heading to. There is also a service from Haneda to Narita that takes about 75 minutes and costs ¥3,000.

ORIENTATION
Tokyo Prefecture covers 2,168 sq km. Besides the 23 central wards of the inner city (616 sq km), it also incorporates 27 smaller cities, plus 14 towns.

Tokyo is divided into 23 *ku* (wards), which are subdivided into *cho* (districts), then numbered *chome* (blocks). Japanese people think in terms of city blocks, often finding their way from one to the next using landmarks. Even taxi drivers get confused away from the main thoroughfares. Maps are essential for getting around.

Exits at train stations are usually clearly marked. Landmarks like museums, department stores and government offices are marked in English on yellow boards. Train stations usually have maps near their exits. Though often in Japanese, they can help with orientation. For more information on Tokyo's eccentric address system, *see Essentials, p.44*.

PUBLIC TRANSPORT
The public transport system in Tokyo is unrivalled anywhere. The city is served by a sophisticated network of railway lines, subways and bus routes. During rush hour, services run every 1–2 minutes on some lines, at a degree of reliability inconceivable elsewhere.

Both trains and subways are notoriously crowded during rush hour, and sometimes run at 300 percent of seating capacity. The roads are even more congested. For that reason, taxis are only useful at night or if you are travelling routes not served by a subway.

Metro
The Tokyo Metro is clean, safe and convenient. Its 13 lines are also the fastest and most economical means of getting across town. Subways run to precise schedules, indicated on timetables posted at each station. Services run from 5am to 12.30am at intervals of 2–3 minutes during rush hours, with frequencies dropping to around every 5–10 minutes in off-peak periods. The frequency is slightly reduced on weekends. All stations have a route map indicating fares for each stop near the ticket machines, usually in English.

Fares are regulated on a station-to-station basis, so if you cannot determine the fare required, just purchase the cheapest ticket available (¥160 for Teito lines, ¥180 for Toei lines) at the ticket machine. Fare correction can be done on arrival.

Pasmo magnetic smart cards good on any public transportation line in Tokyo can be bought at subway stations (¥500 deposit), and recharged when depleted. These are simply passed over sensors of the automated ticket gates as you

> If you are planning to travel around Japan, buying a rail pass makes sense. The Japan Rail Pass comes in 7-, 14- and 21-day versions, and can be bought online from www.japan-railpass.net. You must buy it before you arrive in Japan.

Active sightseers should buy a Tokyo Combination Ticket, a one-day pass good on all JR, subway and bus lines in the Tokyo region. Pass offices at major stations sell the tickets for ¥1580.

enter, with the fare deducted at your destination.

Train

Above ground, Japan Railways (JR) operates an equally efficient service, with equivalent frequency and operating hours (5am–1am) on commuter lines. Like the subways, the lines are colour-coded.

The Yamanote Line (green) makes a long, 35km oval loop around central Tokyo, with JR and private lines branching out to the suburbs. JR fares start at ¥150. Prepaid Orange Cards can be used instead of cash at ticket machines. There are also automated IO Cards that can be inserted directly into the ticket slots as you enter and exit the stations. Both cards are available in ¥1,000, ¥3,000 and ¥5,000 denominations. A one-day ticket for unlimited train travel in central Tokyo sells for ¥730. JR's latest system, the chargeable Suica cards, operate just like the **Pasmo** cards.

Taxis

Taxis are a convenient but pricey way of getting around. The standard flagfall in Tokyo is ¥700; anything other than short trips can run from ¥3,000 to ¥5,000. No tipping is expected.

Taxis are readily available on the streets, and at every major hotel and railway station. A red light in the front window signifies that the taxi is available. Roads are narrow and traffic congestion is appalling at rush hour.

Most taxi drivers speak only Japanese, so it helps to have your destination written down in Japanese. Do not be surprised if taxis fail to stop when you hail them, particularly at night. Drivers will be looking for profitable runs to the suburbs rather than foreigners wanting to return to their hotels. Recommended taxi operators are:

Hinomaru: tel: 3814 1111
Nihon Kotsu: tel: 5755 2151

Buses

Buses are plentiful in Tokyo, and are often packed well beyond seating capacity. Buses are not as easy to use as the trains, as their routes are often written only in Japanese kanji characters.

The famous **Hato Bus** (tel: 3435-6081; www.hatobus.com) tours are synonymous with Tokyo tourism and offer well-organised half-day and full-day highlight itineraries with English-speaking guides. Hato provides pick-up services at most major hotels.

RIVER BUSES
Tokyo River Buses
Tel: 5733 4812; www.suijobus.co.jp/english
The most popular river cruise itinerary is the trip up the Sumida River to Asakusa (40

minutes). Other routes include a 45-minute cruise around Tokyo Harbour, past Rainbow Bridge to Kasai Sealife Park (55 minutes), and to the Shinagawa Aquarium (35 minutes). All boats depart from Hinode Pier, near Takeshiba Station on the Yurikamome Line. The Sumidagawa River Bus can also be boarded at the Hama Rikyu Garden (near Shimbashi Station). Look out for the striking, *manga*-esque Himiko vessel, designed by cartoonist Reiji Matsumoto.

DRIVING
Tokyo is not an easy place in which to drive. Except on the crowded expressways, there are few road signs in Romanised Japanese. For getting out of town, it is usually faster to take public transport.
Avis: tel: 5550 1011
Hertz: tel: 5401 7651

BICYCLES
Intrepid travellers may want to try cycling around Tokyo. Roads are perilous and narrow, but bikes offer a great way to get intimate with the city at surface level. Bicycle rentals:
Tokyo Bike!! (rental and guide): tel: 3215 0008
Extremo (rental): tel: 5610 0638

Below: sleek and efficient – Japanese bullet trains are an expensive but very fast way of getting around the country.

Walks and Views

Situated on the great Kanto Plain sandwiched between mountains and the sea, the Tokyo area offers a number of superb destinations for walks, many of them within convenient reach of downtown. This section provides a more detailed look at some of the places described in the chapter Tokyo's Surroundings; together they comprise the most significant historic and geographic destinations in the region. As you walk around Tokyo and its environs it's worth bearing in mind that Japan largely lacks sidewalks. Be careful not to make your first visit to the country your last!

Hakone

The closest major hot-spring resort to Tokyo, Hakone, set against the backdrop of Mount Fuji, is one of Tokyo's most beloved getaways. Tours start an hour from Tokyo at Odawara Station (Odakyu and JR lines), where the Hakone Tozan Railway begins its 9km zigzag route up to the terminus at Gora, or take the Odakyu Line's Romance Car express service direct from Shinjuku.

Hakone-Yumoto is the first stop on the line and the gateway to Hakone's 16 hot springs. It nestles in a shallow ravine where two rivers join. On a day trip, the Tenzan public bath provides an exquisite hot-spring treat. **Miyanoshita**, the oldest and most thriving of the spa towns, is 20 minutes from Hakone-Yumoto. Miyanoshita is home to the famous **Fujiya Hotel**. Opened in 1878, it is one of Japan's first Western-style inns, with a fabulous, 1930s-style dining room, a library and waitresses in 1930s uniforms. The guest book has comments from

Above: the great Buddha statue at Kamakura.

Margaret Thatcher, John Lennon and Yoko Ono.

The Hakone Tozan train also stops at **Hakone Open-Air Museum** (Chokoku no Mori Bijutsukan) a stunning outdoor sculpture garden. The works of Picasso, Rodin, Leger, Takamura Kotaro and many others are on display.

At the Gora terminal, change to the funicular to Mount Sounzan, and transfer to the cable car for Togendai Station on the shore of **Lake Ashino**, a beautiful caldera lake. On the way up is **Owakudani** ('Valley of the Greater Boiling') in the old

crater of Mount Kami. The views from the ropeway offer stunning panoramas of Mount Fuji against its foothills.

From Togendai either return the way you came, or take the sightseeing boat to Hakone and then a bus.

Kamakura

Under an hour from Tokyo by the JR Yokosuka or Shonan-Shinjuku lines, Kamakura lies cradled in a stunning natural amphitheatre, edged by mountains and the Pacific. For roughly 150 years from 1192, Kamakura was the heart of power in Japan. At its height, the warrior administration built imposing temples and Zen works of art.

Kamakura's 65 Buddhist temples, 19 Shinto shrines and the surrounding hills make a fine walk, but are busy at weekends. Many tourists start at Kita-Kamakura Station, close to the grand Zen temples of **Engaku-ji**, **Tokei-ji** and **Kencho-ji**.

The Enoden Line to Hase Station is nearest to the **Daibutsu** (Great Buddha). In the hills to the left is Hase-

Left: entrance to Wakamiya-dori boulevard, Kamakura.

sure Hall (Kamakura Kokuhokan), displaying the 2,000 treasures from Kamakura's temples.

Continuing up the avenue, cross a dirt track, along which, every 16 September, mounted archers gallop and fire arrows at targets in an ancient samurai ritual. Then you reach an open area below the steps to the Main Hall of the Tsurugaoka Hachiman-gu Shrine, the geographical as well as sacred heart of Kamakura.

From the shrine the closest station for your return trip is Kamakura Station.

Kawagoe

The historic former castle town of Kawagoe northwest of Tokyo is under an hour from Shinjuku or Ikebukuro on the Seibu-Shinjuku, JR Saikyo or Tobu Tojo lines to either Kawagoe or Hon-Kawagoe Station.

From Kawagoe Station walk for another 15 minutes to reach the core of antique merchant buildings and weather-beaten temples that give Kawagoe its nickname, 'Little Edo'.

Cross over the walkway on the left in front of Kawagoe Station to the Atre Department Store, walk down the steps and across the traffic lights to **Sun Road**, a busy pedestrian shopping mall. Cross the next set of traffic lights until you reach a T-junction where on the right is the first *kurazukuri* (a traditional, black warehouse), now a liquor and teashop called **Kameya**. It specialises in *sayama-cha*, a leaf from the hills of Sayama. Exiting the shop, turn right and walk a few steps to the next inter-

---

Public toilets are widely available in Japan, making walks an unhurried pleasure. They are uniformly safe and clean, but often lack toilet paper. It is advisable to bring toilet paper, which can often be obtained at station kiosks or free on the streets as part of promotion campaigns.

---

dera Temple, with its 9m 11-headed Hase Kannon statue, thousands of small Jizo statues in colourful bibs, and also Kosoku-ji Temple, known for its association with the famous priest Nichiren.

On a knoll to the right of the approach to the Great Buddha is the 1,200-year-old **Amanawa Myojin Shrine**. Dedicated to the sun goddess, the shrine offers a majestic view to the sea.

At 11m in height and weighing 94,000kg, the Daibutsu is striking. Cast in 1252, the statue has survived typhoons, tsunami, and earthquakes.

To the east of Kamakura Station is the wide Wakamiya-dori road. Parallel is pedestrian-only Kamachi-dori, a lane of shops and eateries.

Kamakura is known for Kamakura-bori (lacquerware), dating from the 13th century and used as utensils for religious ceremonies.

The approach to the **Tsurugaoka Hachiman-gu Shrine** at the end of Wakamiya-dori crosses a steep, half-moon bridge. Behind the Heike Pond is the **Kanagawa Prefectural Museum of Modern Art** (Kanagawa Keritsu Kindai Bijutsukan).

A little way past the Genji Pond is the **National Trea-**

Below: old godowns of Kawagoe, now shops and restaurants.

129

Above: gilded rooftop of Toshogu-jinja Shrine, Nikko.

section. Turn right onto **Ichiban-gai**, Kawagoe's famous street, with the largest concentration of *kurazukuri*.

During the Edo Period, the walls of the warehouses were covered with charcoal powder mixed with plaster and buffed to a mirror-like shine.

The **Hattori Folk Museum** (Hattori Minzoku Shiryokan) along this street has maps in English. Across the street is Yamawa, a beautiful ceramic shop in a warehouse. Its stylish café serves green tea and sweet-potato delicacies.

One block from the Hattori Folk Museum, down a lane to the right is the **Toki no Kane**, a wooden bell tower that is synonymous with Kawagoe. The current structure was built after a fire in 1893.

On the main street, **Osawa House**, dating from 1792, is Kawagoe's oldest *kurazukuri*. The house is now a handicraft shop selling traditional products like masks and Kawagoe dolls.

Two blocks up and across the street, the narrow lane on the left is **Kashi-ya Yokocho**, or Confectioners' Row, lined with shops selling old-fashioned sweets and purple sweet-potato ice cream. Returning to the bell tower, a 10-minute walk east leads to

the ruins of Kawagoe Castle. Exquisite **Honmaru-goten Palace**, built by a local lord, Ota Dokan, and his son, houses beautifully painted screens and archaeological artefacts.

A 10-minute walk south takes you to **Kita-in Temple**, a Buddhist temple-museum with a traditional Japanese garden. Kita-in's main draw is the **Gohyaku Rakan stones**, 540 statues depicting disciples of the Buddha in different poses – one scratches his head, a couple get drunk on wine, others meditate, rub a sore foot or beat drums.

Travellers should retrace their steps to Kawagoe or Hon-Kawagoe station for the trip back into town.

Nikko

The jewel in the crown of the Tokugawa Shogunate, Nikko is reached in less than two hours via the Tobu Nikko Line from Asakusa.

From Tobu Nikko Station, approach the shrine complex, nestled amid soaring cedar trees, via the steps opposite the vermillion **Shinkyo** (Sacred Bridge), spanning the Daiya River at the top of the main street. Follow the cedar avenue to **Rinno-ji Temple**, where you

can buy a combination ticket that includes Futarasan Shrine and Nikko's main sight, the **Toshogu-jinja Shrine** and mausoleum.

Rinno-ji's Sanbutsudo Hall houses three gigantic images: Bato Kannon (protector of horses), Amida and the thousand-armed Kannon, goddess of mercy. Continue along the main Omote-sando path towards the **Five Storey Pagoda** (Gojuno-to). Just before the main entrance to the Toshogu-jinja Shrine, the Buddhist-style gate **Omotemon** is guarded by two mythical kings. The adjacent **Sacred Horse Stable** is carved with scenes illustrating the life cycle of humanity.

Past the torii gate at the top of the stone steps is Toshogu's most famous feature, the **Yomei-mon**, beyond which only the highest-ranking samurai could pass. Standing 11m high, this gate is covered with intricate carvings – children at play, clouds, pine trees and animals – all painted in brilliant colours.

More treasures await inside: the east and west corridors surrounding the main building are also covered with carvings, among them the celebrated but difficult-to-find **Nemuri-Neko**, or Sleeping Cat, on the side of the **Sakashita-mon** gate. Beyond this gate are the 200-odd steps to the mausoleum of Tokugawa Ieyasu. The next point of interest is the **Toshogu Treasure House**, which houses a collection of Tokugawa portraits, samurai armour and swords.

The second path to the left takes you to the **Futarasan-jinja Shrine**, the oldest of the buildings in the complex, dating back to 1617.

Return to Tokyo from Tobu Nikko Station.

Yokohama

West of the capital is Yokohama, an integral part of Greater Tokyo and an urban centre in its own right, as well as a major Asian seaport.

Yokohama ranks second after Tokyo, with a population of more than 3 million. It is easily covered on foot, with a more open layout and relaxed atmosphere than Tokyo.

A convenient place to begin your trip to Yokohama is Minato Mirai Station on the private Tokyu Toyoko Line from Shibuya (connecting to the Minato Mirai subway line), but Yokohama can also be reached using JR.

Yokohama Bay was recently overhauled with the creation of the Minato Mirai 21 complex. It includes the 73-storey **Landmark Tower**, nearby **Nippon Maru**, a sailing ship, and **Maritime Museum**, as well as the **Yokohama Museum of Art** (Yokohama Bijutsukan), with its excellent collection of modernist sculpture.

A short walk from here, through the Nippon-Maru Memorial Park and across the Kisha-Michi Promenade, takes you to **Shinkocho**, a man-made island housing Akarenga Park. The island's old red-brick custom houses have been recently renovated

and now accommodate boutiques, restaurants, a jazz club and performance space.

The other side of the Okagawa River from Sakuragicho Station is an area of old government buildings and banks. Further on is a charming tree-lined street with red-brick pavements called **Basha Michi-dori** (Street of Horse Carriages). **Kanagawa Prefectural Museum** (Kanagawa Kenritsu Kindai Bijutsukan) is a good example of the city's old commercial architecture.

The wide street **Honchodori** was the centre of commercial activities in the early days, and it retains buildings like the stately **Yokohama Banker's Club** and, on the right, four blocks down, the lovely red-brick Yokohama Port Opening Memorial Hall (Yokohama-shi Kaiko Kinen Kaikan), which survived the 1923 earthquake and World War II. Near the waterfront is the **Yokohama Custom House** (Yokohama Zeikan). **The Yokohama Archives of History** (Yokohama Kaiko Shiriokan), on the site of the former British consulate, now a museum.

Opposite is the **Yokohama Port Opening Square**, where Japan and the US signed the Treaty of Peace and Amity in 1854. A bit fur-

For comfortable rides to destinations out of town, many lines offer reserved seating. Some lines also have 'Green Car' first-class sections, which are often just marginally more expensive than regular seats.

ther down the same road are the somewhat garish 106m **Marine Tower** and the **Yokohama Doll Museum** (Ningyo no Ie), with almost a thousand dolls on display. **Yamashita Park** (Yamashita-koen) along the waterfront is worth a visit. The former passenger liner and hospital ship **Hikawa-Maru** can be visited.

Most visitors feast in **Chinatown** (Chukagai), further back from the waterfront. The dozen or so blocks are the biggest Chinatown in Japan, and nearly as old as the port.

East of the waterfront is **Yamate**, where foreign merchants lived in palatial homes. Pause for a spectacular view of the bay from **Harbour View Park** (Minato no Mieru Oka Koen) at the top of France Yama Hill. In the park's rose garden visit the **British House Yokohama**, home to the city's first British legation. Cross the road opposite the gates for the Foreigners' Cemetery (Gaijin Bochi), where 4,200 are buried. The adjacent **Yamate Museum** (Yamate Shiriokan) has displays on early foreign residents.

A short walk east leads to Sankeien Garden, a traditional Japanese garden from 1906 with extensive grounds, including a farmhouse and three-storey pagoda. Back in Yamate, descend to the lively shopping street of **Motomachi**.

The station for the return trip is Motomachi-chukagai on the Minato Mirai line.

Below: Yokohama's waterfront seen from the Landmark Tower.

Atlas

The following streetplan of Tokyo
makes it easy to find the attractions
listed in our A–Z section. A
selective index to streets and sights
will help you find other locations
throughout the city

Map Legend

Motorway		Ⓜ	Metro Station
Main road		🚌	Bus station
Other road		✈	Airport
Footpath		❶	Tourist information
Railway		✉	Main post office
Ward boundary		★	Sight of interest
District boundary		⚓	Beach
Pedestrian area		卍 ▲	Temple
Notable building		⛪	Cathedral / church
Park		☾	Mosque
Hotel		✡	Synagogue
Urban area		1	Statue / monument
Non urban area		✚	Hospital
Cemetery			

p134	p135	p136	p137
p138	p139	p140	p141

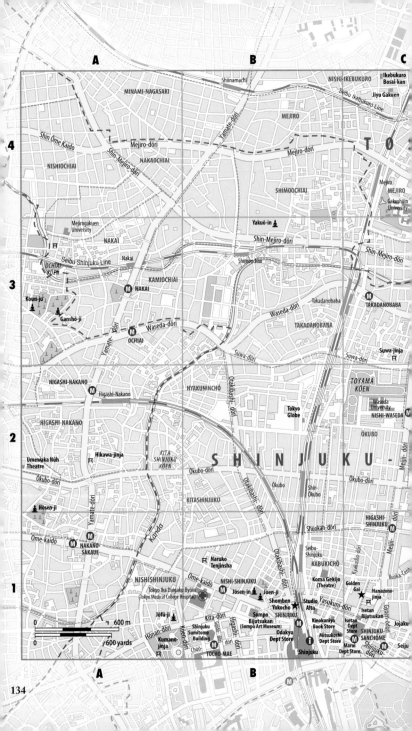

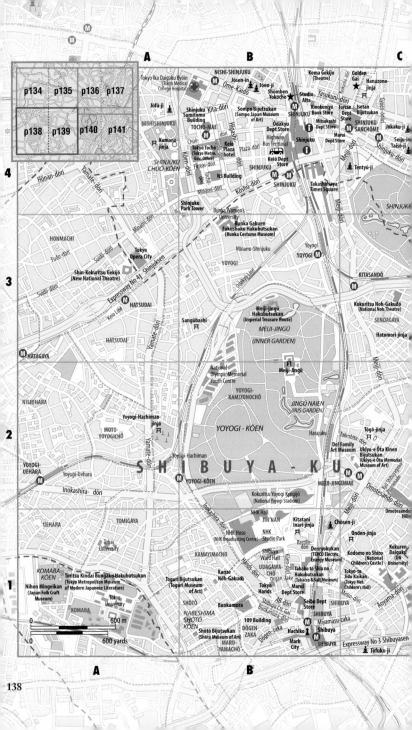

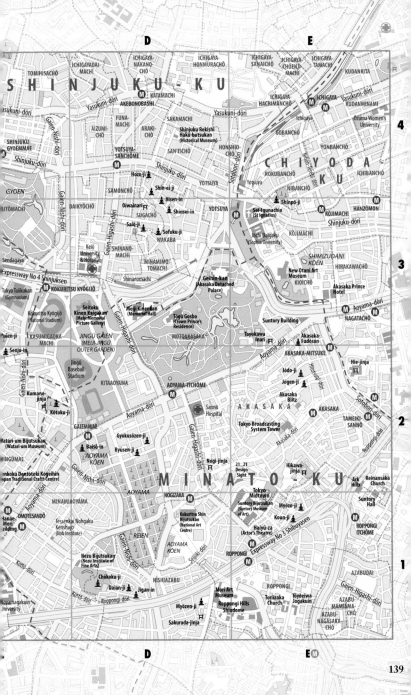

D

E

TOMIHISACHŌ

ICHIGAYADAI-MACHI

ICHIGAYA-NAKANO-CHŌ

ICHIGAYA-HONMURACHŌ

ICHIGAYA-SANAICHŌ

ICHIGAYA-CHŌEN-MACHI

ICHIGAYA-TAMACHI

KUDANKITA

S H I N J U K U - K U

KATAMACHI

Yasukuni-dōri

AKEBONOBASHI

Yasukuni-dōri

ICHIGAYA-HACHIMANCHŌ

GOBANCHŌ

ICHIGAYA

Yasukuni-dōri

KUDANMINAMI

asukuni-dōri

SHINJUKU-GYOEMMAE

AIZUMI-CHŌ

FUNA-MACHI

ARAKI-CHŌ

SAKAMACHI

Ichigaya

Ōzuma Women's University

Shinjuku-dōri

YOTSUYA-SANCHŌME

SAN'EICHŌ

Shinjuku Rekishi Hakō-butsukan (Historical Museum)

HONSHIO-CHŌ

YONBANCHŌ

GYOEN

Hozo-ji

Shinjuku-dōri

YOTSUYA

C H I Y O D A - K U

ROKUBANCHŌ

ICHIBANCHŌ

AITŌMACHI

DAIKYŌCHŌ

Shin-ei-ji

Yotsuya

NIBANCHŌ

Galen-Higashi-dōri

Oiwainari

Aisen-in

Sei-Ignachio (St Ignatius)

Shinpō-ji

KŌJIMACHI

HANZŌMON

SUGACHŌ

Shinsei-in

Shinjuku-dōri

Sendagaya

Keiō University & Hospital

Saiō-ji

SHINANO-MACHI

WAKABA

Sofuku-ji

Jōchi Daigaku (Sophia University)

KŌJIMACHI

SHIMIZUDANI KŌEN

HIRAKAWACHŌ

Expressway No 4 Shinjuksen

MINAMIMO-TOMACHI

New Otani Art Museum

KIOICHŌ

Akasaka Prince Hotel

Tokyo Taiikukan (Gymnasium)

KOKURITSU KYŌGIJŌ

Shinanomachi

Geihin-kan Akasaka Detached Palace

Suntory Building

Aoyama-dōri

NAGATACHŌ

Kokuritsu Kyōgijō (National Stadium)

Seitoku Kinen Kaigakan (Meiji Memorial Picture Gallery)

Meiji Kinenkan (Memorial Hall)

Tōgu Gosho (Crown Prince's Residence)

MOTOAKASAKA

Toyokawa Inari

Akasaka-Fudōson

uien-ji

KASUMIGAOKA-MACHI

JINGŪ GAIEN (MEIJI JINGŪ OUTER GARDEN)

Hie-jinja

Senju-in

AKASAKA-MITSUKE

Galen-Nishi-dōri

Jingū Baseball Stadium

KITAAOYAMA

AOYAMA-ITCHŌME

Jōdo-ji

Jōgen-ji

Kumano-jinja

Akasaka Blitz

Kōtoku-ji

Aoyama-dōri

Sannō Hospital

A K A S A K A

AKASAKA

GAIEMMAE

Gyokusōzen-ji

Tokyo Broadcasting System Tower

Akasaka-dōri

TAMEIKI-SANNŌ

Watari-um Bijutsukan (Watari-um Museum)

Baisō-in

AOYAMA KŌEN

Ryūsen-ji

Nogi-jinja

21_21 Design Sight

Hikawa-jinja

Ark Hills

Reinansaka Church

INGŪMAE

M I N A T O - K U

enkoku Dentōteki Kōgeihin apan Traditional Crafts Centre)

MINAMIAOYAMA

NOGIZAKA

AOYAMA

Tokyo Midtown

Myozo-ji

Suntory Hall

anae Mori uilding

OMOTESANDŌ

Tessenkai Nohgaku Kenshujo (Noh Institute)

REIEN

Kokuritsu Shin Bijutsukan (National Art Centre)

Suntory Bijutsukan (Suntory Museum of Art)

Koun-ji

ROPPONGI ITCHŌME

AZABUDAI

Nezu Bijutsukan (Nezu Institute of Fine Arts)

AOYAMA KŌEN

Seijiki-dōri

Haiyū-za (Actor's Theatre)

ROPPONGI

Expressway No 3 Shibuyasen

oyamagakuin University

Chōkoku-ji

Daian-ji

Jigan-in

NISHIAZABU

Roppongi-dōri

Mori Art Museum

ROPPONGI

Torizaka Church

Tōyōeiwa Jogakuin

AZABU-MAMIANA-CHŌ

Myōzen-ji

Roppongi Hills Shiodome

AZABU-NAGASAKA-CHŌ

Sakurada-jinja

D

E

139

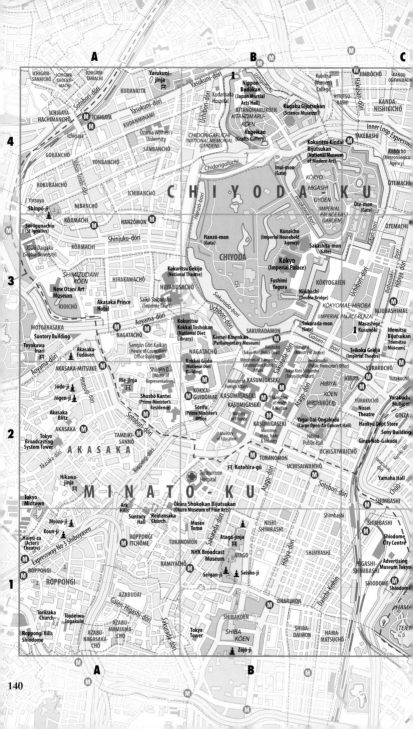

ICHIGAYA-SANAICHO
ICHIGAYA-CHOENJI-MACHI
ICHIGAYA-TAMACHI
Yasukuni-jinja
Kudanshita Hospital
Nippon Budokan (Japan Martial Arts Hall)
Kagaku Gijutsukan (Science Museum)
Kyoritsu Women's College
JIMBOCHO
KANDA-OGAWAMACHI

KUDANKITA
Yasukuni-dōri
KITANOMARUKŌEN
KITANOMARU-KŌEN
NITOTSU-BASHI
KANDA-NISHIKICHŌ

ICHIGAYA-HACHIMANCHŌ
Ōzuma Women's University
CHIDORIGAFUCHI (NATIONAL MEMORIAL GARDEN)
Kōeikan (Crafts Gallery)
Kokuritsu Kindai Bijutsukan (National Museum of Modern Art)
Inner Loop Expressway
TAKEBASHI

4

ICHIGAYA
KUDANMINAMI
Ichigaya
Kishōchō (Meteorological Agency)
ŌTEMACHI

GOBANCHŌ
SANBANCHŌ
Inui-mon (Gate)

Mitsuki-tetsu-dōri
Sotobori-dōri
Yasukuni-dōri
KŌKYO HIGASHI GYOEN
(IMPERIAL PALACE EAST GARDEN)
Ōte-mon (Gate)
ŌTEMACHI

ROKUBANCHŌ
YONBANCHŌ
Chidorigafuchi

ICHIBANCHŌ
CHIYODA-KU

Yotsuya
Shinpō-ji
NIBANCHŌ

Sei-Ignachio (St Ignatius)
KŌJIMACHI
HANZŌMON
Hanzō-mon (Gate)
Kūnaichō (Imperial Household Agency)
Sakashita-mon (Gate)

Jōchi Daigaku (Sophia University)
KŌJIMACHI
Shinjuku-dōri
CHIYODA
Kōkyo (Imperial Palace)

3

SHIMIZUDANI KŌEN
HIRAKAWACHŌ
Kokuritsu Gekijo (National Theatre)
HAYABUSACHŌ
Fushimi Yagura
KŌKYOGAIEN

New Otani Art Museum
KIOICHŌ
Saikō Saibansho (Supreme Court)
Nijūbashi (Double Bridge)
KŌKYOMAE-HIROBA (IMPERIAL PALACE PLAZA)
NIJUBASHIMAE

Akasaka Prince Hotel
Hanzō-bori
Uchibori-dōri

MOTOAKASAKA
Aoyama-dōri
Kokuritsu Kokkai Toshokan (National Diet Library)
SAKURADAMON
Sakurada-mon (Gate)
Masashige Kusunoki
Idemitsu Bijutsukan (Idemitsu Museum)

Suntory Building
Sangiin Giin Kaikan (House of Councillors' Office Building)
Kensei Kinenkan (Parliamentary Museum)
Keishichō (Tokyo Met. Police Dept)
Hōmushō (Ministry of Justice)
Teikoku Gekijo (Imperial Theatre)

Toyokawa Inari
Akasaka-Fudōson
NAGATACHŌ
Kokkai Gijidō (National Diet Building)
KASUMIGASEKI
Ministries of Transport, Construction, Home Affairs
Kōsatsuchō (Public Prosecutor's Office)
Tokyo Kōtō Saibansho (Tokyo High Court)
YŪRAKUCHŌ
Yūrakuchō

Jōdo-ji
Hitotsugi-dōri
Hie-jinja
Shūgiin Dai (House of Representatives)
Ministry of Foreign Affairs
HIBIYA
HIBIYA KŌEN
YŪRAKUCHŌ Mullion

Jōgen-ji
Shushō Kantei (Prime Minister's Residence)
KOKKAI GIJIDŌMAE
Ministry of Finance
Ministries of Health & Welfare
Nissei Theatre
GINZA

Akasaka Blitz
Sōrifu (Prime Minister's Office)
KASUMIGASEKI
Yagai Dai-Ongakudō (Large Open-Air Concert Hall)
Hankyu Dept Store
Sony Building

2

Tokyo Broadcasting System Tower
TAMEIKE-SANNŌ
Ministry of Education
KASUMIGASEKI
Ministries of Int. Trade & Industry
Hibiya Public Hall
UCHISAIWAICHŌ
Ginza Nob-Gakudo

AKASAKA
Sotobori-dōri
Roppongi-dōri
UCHISAIWAICHŌ
Yamaha Hall

Hikawa-jinja
TORANOMON
Toranomon Hospital
Kotohira-gū
Sotobori-dōri
SHIMBASHI

MINATO-KU

Tokyo Midtown
Ark Hills
Suntory Hall
Reinanzaka Church
Ōkura Shokakan Bijutsukan (Ōkura Museum of Fine Arts)
Shimbashi
SHIMBASHI
Shiodome City Centre

Myozo-ji
Musée Tomo
NISHI-SHIMBASHI
HIGASHI-SHIMBASHI

Kōun-ji
ROPPONGI ITCHŌME
TORANOMON
Atago-jinja
SHIMBASHI
Advertising Museum Tokyo

Haiyū-za (Actor's Theatre)
NHK Broadcast Museum
ATAGO
Shiodome

1

ROPPONGI
KAMIYACHŌ
Seigan-ji
Seisho-ji
ŌNARIMON

ROPPONGI
Gaien-Higashi-dōri
AZABUDAI
SHIBAKŌEN
SHIBA-DAIMON
HAMA-MATSUCHO

Toriizaka Church
Tōyōeiwa Jogakuin
AZABU-NAGASAKA-CHŌ
AZABU-MAMIAMA-CHŌ
Tokyo Tower
SHIBA KŌEN
TEIEI

Roppongi Hills Shiodome
Sakaedo-dōri
Zōjō-ji
Daichi-Keihin

Selective Index for Street Atlas

PLACES OF INTEREST

Advertising Museum Tokyo *140 C1*
Aka-mon (Red Gate) *136 C3*
Akasaka-Fudōson *140 A3*
Ark Hills *139 E2*
Asakura Chosokan (Sculpture Museum) *137 C4*
Asakusa Kōgel-kan (Handicraft Museum) *137 E3*
Asakusa-Toei Theatre *137 E3*
Asakusabashi *137 E1*
Atago-jinja *140 B1*
Bakurochō *137 D1*
Benten-dō *137 D3*
Bridgestone Museum *141 C2*
Bunka Costume Museum *138 B3*
Currency Museum *141 D4*
Daimyo Tokei Hakubutsukan (Clock Museum) *137 C4*
Denryokukan (TEPCO Electric Energy Museum) *138 B1*
Do! Family Art Museum *138 B2*
Edo-Tokyo Hakubutsukan *137 E1*
Fushimi Yagura *140 B3*
Ganshō-ji *134 A3*
Geihin-kan (Akasaka Detached Palace) *139 D3*
Genkaku-ji *136 B3*
Gōjūnō-to (Five-Storey Pagoda) *137 D3, E3*
Gokoku-ji *135 D4*
Golden Gai *134 C1*
Hachiko *134 B1*
Hachiman-jinja *137 E3*
Haiyū-za (Actor's Theatre) *139 E1*
Hakusan-jinja *136 B4*
Hanae Mori Building *139 C1*
Hanazono-jinja *134 C1*
Hanzō-mon (Gate) *140 B3*
Harajuku *138 B2*
Hatchōbori *141 D2*
Hatomori-jinja *138 C3*
Hie-jinja *139 E2*
Higashi-Ikebukuro *135 D4*
Higashi-Nakano *134 A2*
Higashien *137 C3*
Hikawa-jinja *134 A2, 139 E2*
Hōmyō-in *135 C4*
Hongōkan *137 C3*
Idemitsu Bijutsukan (Idemitsu Museum) *140 C2*
Iidabashi *136 B2*
Ikebukuro Bosai-kan *134 C4*
Inui-mon (Gate) *140 B4*
Isetan Bijutsukan *134 C1*
Isetan Dept Store *134 C1*
Jingū Baseball Stadium *139 D2*
Kabuki-za *141 C2*
Kabuto-jinja *141 D3*
Kagaku Gijutsukan (Science Museum) *136 B1*
Kaminarimon *137 E3*
Kan'ei-ji *137 D4*
Kanda Myōjin *137 C2*
Kanda-ji *137 C2*
Kanju-in *135 D4*
Kanze Nōh-Gakudō *138 B1*
Kaya-dera *137 C4*
Keidanren Hall *141 C4*
Kensei Kinenkan (Parliamentary Museum) *140 B3*
Kinryū-ji *137 E3*
Kishimojinmae *135 C3, C4*
Kitatani Inari-jinja *138 B1*
Kiyomizu Kannon-dō *137 D3*
Kōdōkan (Judo Hall) *136 B2*
Kodomo no Shiro (National Children's Castle) *138 C1*

Kokugikan (National Sumo Stadium) *137 E1*
Kokuritsu Gekijo *140 A3*
Kokuritsu Kahaku Hakubutsukan (National Science Museum) *137 D3*
Kokuritsu Kindai Bijutsukan (National Museum of Modern Art) *136 B1*
Kōkyo (Imperial Palace) *140 B3*
Koma Gekijo (Theatre) *134 B1*
Kōtoku-ji *139 C2*
Koun-ji *139 E1*
Koun-ju *134 A3*
Kurofune-jinja *137 E2*
Meiji Daigaku Kokogaku Hakubutsukan (Archaeological Museum) *136 C1*
Meiji Kinenkan (Memorial Hall) *139 D3*
Meiji-jingū Hakubutsukan (Imperial Treasure House) *138 B3*
Musée Tomo *140 B1*
Myōzo-ji *139 E1*
Namiyoke-jinja *141 D1*
National Olympic Memorial Youth Center *138 B3*
Nensonu-ji *136 B3*
New Otani Art Museum *139 E3*
Nezu Bijutsukan (Nezu Institute of Fine Arts) *139 D1*
Nihon Mingeikan (Japan Folk Craft Museum) *138 A1*
Nijūbashi (Double Bridge) *140 B3*
Nikolai-do (Cathedral) *137 C1*
Nippon Budōkan *136 B1*
Nissei Theatre *140 C2*
Ochanowizu University *135 E4*
Okūra Shukokan Bijutsukan (Okura Museum of Fine Arts) *140 A2*
Onoterusaki-jinja *137 E4*
Osakana Shiryōkan *141 D1*
Roppongi Hills Shiodome *139 D1–E1*
Saigō Takamori *137 D3*
Sangūbashi *138 B3*
Sei-Ignachio (St Ignatius) *139 E3*
Seibu Dept Store *138 B1*
Seigan-ji *140 B1*
Seisho-ji *140 B1*
Seitoku Kinen Kaigakan (Meiji Memorial Picture Gallery) *139 D3*
Shōtō Bijutsukan (Shōtō Museum of Art) *138 B1*
Shin Maru Building *141 C3*
Shin-ei-ji *139 D4*
Shin-Kokuritsu Gekijō (New National Theatre) *138 A3*
Shinjuku Rekishi Haku-butsukan (Historical Museum) *139 D4*
Shinko-ji *135 E3*
Shiodome City Centre *140 C1*
Sompo Bijutsukan (Sompo Art Museum) *134 B1*
Sony Building *140 C2*
Sōrifu (Prime Minister's Office) *140 B2*
Sumo Hakubutsukan *137 E1*
Suntory Building *139 E3*
Suntory Hall *139 E1*
Tabako to Shio no Hakubutsukan (Tobacco & Salt Museum) *138 B1*
Taiko-kan (Drum Museum) *137 E3*
Taitō Traditional Crafts Museum *137 E3*
Takarazuka 1000 Gekijo *141 C2*
Tako no Hakubutsukan *141 D1*
Takuzosu-Inari *136 B3*
Teikoku Gekijō *140 C3*
Teishin Sōgō Hakubutsukan (Communications Museum) *141 C4*
Tōfuku-ji *138 C1*
Tōgō-jinja *138 C2*
Tōgū Gosho (Crown Prince's Residence) *139 D3*
Toguri Bijutsukan (Toguri Museum of Art) *138 B1*
Tokudai-ji *137 D3*
Tokyo Anime Centre *137 D2*

Tokyo Bunka Kaikan (Tokyo Metropolitan Festival Hall) *137 D3*
Tōkyō Chūō Oroshiurishijo *141 C1*
Tokyo Domu (Tokyo Dome City) *136 B2*
Tokyo-eki *141 C3*
Tokyo Honganji *137 E3*
Tokyo Katedoraru Sei-Maria Daiseidō (St Mary's Cathedral) *135 D3*
Tokyo Kokuritsu Hakubutsukan (Tokyo National Museum) *137 D4*
Tokyo Kokuritsu Kindai Bijutsukan (National Film Centre) *141 D2*
Tokyo Kokusai Forum (Tokyo International Forum) *141 C3*
Tokyo Kōtō Saibansho (Tokyo High Court) *140 B2*
Tokyo Opera *138 A3*
Tōkyō Shoken Tōvrihikijo (Tokyo Stock Exchange) *141 D3*
Tokyo-to Bijutsukan (Tokyo Metropolitan Art Museum) *137 D3*
Tōkyo University *138 A1*
Tōkyō Wonder Site *136 C2*
Tōkyū Dept Store *138 B1*
Toritsu Chūō Bungaku Hakubutsukan (Tokyo Metropolitan Museum of Modern Japanese Literature) *138 A1*
Uenomori Art Museum *137 D3*
Ukiyo-e ōta Kinen Bijutsukan (Ukiyo-e ōta Memorial Museum of Art) *138 C2*
Umewaka Nōh Theatre *134 A2*
Waseda Memorial Hall *135 D2*
Watari-um Museum *139 C2*
Yakuō-in *134 B3*
Yasukuni-jinja *136 B1*
Yōgen-ji *136 B4*
Yokoyama Taikan Kinenkan *137 C3*
Yoshin-ji *137 E3*
Yūshūkan (Military Museum) *136 B1*
Zenkoku Dentōteki Kogeihin (Japan Traditional Crafts Centre) *139 C2*
Zōjō-ji *140 B1*
Zuien-ji *139 C3*
Zuirin-ji *137 C4*

STREETS

AB-dōri *138 B1*
Akasaka-dōri *139 E2*
Ameya Yokocho *137 D3*
Aoyama-dōri *138 C1, 139 C1–D2–E2–E3*
Asakusa-dōri *137 E3*
Asashio-bashi *141 E1*
Atago-dōri *140 B2*
Bastille-dōri *138 B1*
Bunka-Centre-dōri *134 C1*
Bunkamura-dōri *138 B1*
Chūō-dōri *134 B1, 137 D1–D2–D3, 140 C2, 141 D3–D4*
Dōgen-zaka *138 B1*
Daiichi-Keihin *140 B1*
Denboin-dōri *137 E3*
Edo-dōri *137 D1 - E1 - E2*
Eitai-bashi *141 D3*
Eitai-dōri *141 D3*
Expwy No 1 - Uenosen *137 D1–D2–D3, 141 C1–C2–D3*
Expwy No 3 Shibuyasen *138 C1, 139 E3*
Expwy No 4 Shinjuksen *138 A3, 139 C3*
Expwy No 5 *136 A2*
Expwy No 5 - Ikebukurosen *135 D4–D3*
Expwy No 6 Mukojimasen *137 E1–E2*
Expwy No 7 Komatsugawasen *141 E4*
Fudo-dōri *138 A3*
Fureai-dōri *138 B1*
Gaien-Higashi-dōri *139 D2–D3–E1, 135 D1–D2*
Gaien-Nishi-dōri *139 C4–C3–C2–D1*
Gyoen-dōri *134 C1*
Hakusan-dōri *136 B4–B3–B2–B1–C1*
Hanatsubaki-dōri *140 C2*

Harumi-bashi *141 E1*
Harumi-dōri *141 C2–D1*
Hibiya-dōri *140 B1–C3*
Higashi-dōri *134 B1*
Hitotsugi-dōri *139 E2*
Hongō-dōri *136 B4–C3, 137 C1–C2*
Ikebukurosen *136 B2*
Inner Loop Expressway *140 C4*
Inokashira-dōri *134 A2–B1*
Kachidoki-bashi *141 D1*
Kaminarimon-dōri *137 E3*
Kandaheisei-dōri *137 C1–D1*
Kaooaashi-dōri *137 E3*
Kasuga-dōri *136 A4–B3–C2, 137 D2–E2*
Keiyō-dōri *138 B1*
Kiyosubashi *141 E3*
Kiyosubashi-dōri *137 D2–D3*
Kiyosumi-dōri *141, E2*
Kōen-dōri *134 A1–B1, B4*
Kokusai-dōri *137 E4–E3*
Kōshū-dōri *138 B4*
Kōsokutoshinkanjōsen *141 C4*
Kototoi-dōri *137 C4–D4–E4*
Kottō-dōri *139 C1–D1*
Kuramaebashi-dōri *137 C2–D2–E2*
Kyū Shibuyagawa Promenade *138 C2*
Kyū-Hakusan-dōri *136 B4*
Matsuya-dōri *141 C2*
Meiji-dōri *138 C1–C2–C3–C4*
Meiji-dōri *134 C1–C2, 135 C3*
Mejiro-dōri *134 A4–B4, 135 C4–D3*
Metro-dōri *138 C1*
Minami-dōri *138 A3–B4*
Miyamasu-zaka *138 B1–C1*
Namiki-dōri *140 C2*
Nichi-idai-Tsutsuji-dōri *136 C4*
Nihon-Terebi-dōri *139 E4*
Ningyōchō-dōri *141 D4*
Nishinaka-dōri *141 D1*
Ōkubo-dōri *134 A2–B2–C2, 135 C2–D2–E2*
Okura-dōri *141 C2*
Ome-kaidō *134 A1–B1*
Omotesando-dōri *138 C2*
Organ-zake *138 B1*
Otakibashi-dōri *134 B2–B1*
Plaza-dōri *138 B4*
Reimei-bashi *141 D1*
Roppongi-dōri *139 D1–E2*
Ryogoku-bashi *137 E1*
Sakura-dōri *136 B1*
Sakurada-dōri *140 A1–B1–C1*
Sansaikizaka *137 C4*
Seijōki-dōri *139 D1*
Shōwa-dōri *137 E4*
Shibuya Ctr. Gai *138 B1*
Shin Ome Kaidō *134 A4*
Shin-Mejiro-dōri *134 A4–B2–C2, 135 D2–E2*
Shin-Ōhashi-dōri *141 C1–D2–E3–E4*
Shinjuku-dōri *138 C4, 139 C4–D4–E3*
Shinobazu-dōri *136 A4, 137 C2–C3–C4*
Shuokan-dōri *134 B1, 135 D1–D2*
Sotobori-dōri *136 A1–B2–C2, 137 C1, 139 E2–E4, 140 A2–B3, 141 C3–C4*
Suidō-dōri *138 A3*
Sumidagawa-ōhashi *141 E3*
Suwa-dōri *134 B3–C3, 135 C2*
Suzuran-dōri *136 C1*
Takeshita-dōri *138 C2*
Tochō-dōri *138 B4*
Tsukishima-bashi *141 D1*
Tsukuda-ōhashi *141 D2*
Uchibori-dōri *140 B4–B3–C3*
Waseda-dōri *134 A3–B3, 135 C3–D2–E2*
Yaesu-dōri *141 D3*
Yamate-dōri *134 A1–A2–A3–B4, 138 A2–A3*
Yasukuni-dōri *134 B1–C1, 135 C1–E1, 136 A1–B1–C1, 137 D1*

Index

A

addresses 44
air quality 42
Akasaka 8, 9
  hotels 63–5
  restaurants 102–3
Akihabara 21, 69, 90–91
Ancient Orient Museum 15
Aoyama 10, 11
  hotels 65–6
  restaurants 103–4
Asakura Choso Sculpture Museum 23, 80
Asakusa 24–5
  hotels 69
  restaurants 107
Asakusa Kannon Temple 24, 30, 118–19
Ashino, Lake 27, 128

B

Bayside 18–19
  hotels 68
  restaurants 106
Beer Museum Yebisu 17
Boso Peninsula 26
Bridgestone Museum 7, 74
Buddhism 114
Bunka Gakuen Costume Museum 77

C, D

Chiba 26
cinemas 52–3
customs requirements 44
Daien-ji Temple 16
Daikanyama 17
Disney Resort 5, 26, 41
DisneySea 26, 41
drinking etiquette 34
'drinking shops' (izakaya) 35
Drum Museum 80

E

earthquakes 43
East Tokyo 25
  restaurants 107
Ebisu 16, 17
  hotels 67–8
  restaurants 106
Edo-Tokyo Museum 25, 81
embassies and consulates 44
emergency numbers 44
Engaku-ji Temple 27, 128

F

Fukagawa Matsuri festival 25
Fuji, Mount 4, 27
Fuji TV Building 19
further reading 72–3

G

Gallery TOM 76
Ginza 7
  restaurants 100–102
Ginza 4-chome 7
Gokoku-ji Temple 15, 116
Golden Gai area 13
grocery markets 57

H

Hakone 27, 128
Hama Rikyu Detached Garden 18, 98
Hanazono-jinja Shrine 13, 116
Harajuku 10, 11
  hotels 65–6
  restaurants 103–4
Hara Museum of Contemporary Art 16, 78–9
Hatakeyama Museum 79
health 44
Hie-jinja Shrine 9, 115
Higashi-Ikebukuro 15
Hongo 23

I

Idemitsu Museum 7, 74
Iidabashi 20
Ikebukuro 14–15
  hotels 67
  restaurants 105–6
Ikebukuro Museum of Disaster Prevention 78
Imperial Palace 5, 6, 30, 96
Imperial Palace area 6
  hotels 62–3
  restaurants 100–102
Isetan department store 13, 47, 109
Ito-ya 7, 111

J

Japanese cuisine 54–6
Japanese designers 46–7
Japanese films 52
Japanese music 82
Japanese sweets 57
Japan Folk Crafts Museum 76
Japan Traditional Craft Centre 15, 111
jazz 84

K

Kabuki Theatre 7, 121
Kabuki-cho 13
Kamakura 5, 27, 128–9
Kanda Myojin Shrine 21, 117
Kawagoe 26, 129–30
Kencho-ji Temple 27, 128
Kite Museum 7, 74
Kiyomizu Kannon Hall 22
Kiyosumi Garden 25, 99
Koishikawa Botanical Garden 20, 98–9
Komagome 15

Kume Museum 17

Kyu Furukawa Garden 15, 98
Kyu-Shiba Rikyu Garden 18–19, 98
Kyu Yasuda Garden 25

L, M

Loft department store 10, 109
Mark City shopping mall 10, 110
Marui department store 47–8
Marunouchi 6–7
Matsuya department store 7, 109
Matsuzakaya department store 7, 109
Meguro 16–17
  hotels 67–8
  restaurants 106
Meiji-jingu Shrine 11, 30, 115–16
Meijirodai 14, 15
  hotels 67
  restaurants 105–6
Mikimoto Pearls 7, 111
Mitsukoshi department store 7, 13, 109
money 44
Mori Art Museum 8, 75
Musée Tomo 9, 75
Museum of Maritime Science 19, 79
Museums of Meiji University 80

N

Nakameguro 17
Namco Namja Town 15
Narita-san Temple 26, 119
National Art Centre 8–9, 30–31, 75
National Children's Castle 11, 38
National Diet Building 6, 31
National Museum of Emerging Science and Innovation 19, 79
National Museum of Modern Art 6, 74
National Museum of Western Art 22–3, 80
National Park for Nature Study 17, 98
National Science Museum 23, 80
National Sumo Stadium 25, 112
National Theatre 6, 121
New National Theatre 12, 123
Nezu Institute of Fine Arts 76
Nezu-jinja Shrine 23
Nikko 27, 130
Nogi-jinja Shrine 116
Nokogiriyama, Mount 26
NTT Intercommunication Centre 77

O

Ochanomizu 21
  hotels 69
  restaurants 106–7
Odaiba Island 19
Odaiba Marine Park 19
Oedo Onsen Monogatari hot-spring bath 19
Okura Shukokan Museum of Fine Arts 9, 75

Omotesando Hills **11, 108**
109 Building **10, 47**

P, R, S

public holidays **50**
Rikugien Garden **15, 97**
Roppongi Hills **8–9, 31**
  hotels **63–5**
  restaurants **102–3**
Ryogoku **25**
St Mary's Cathedral **15**
Sanja Matsuri festival **24–5, 51**
Sanno Matsuri festival **9, 51**
Science Museum **74**
Seibu department store **10, 14, 109**
Sengaku-ji Temple **16, 116–17**
Shiba **9**
Shibuya **5, 10 –11**
  hotels **65–6**
  restaurants **103–4**
Shinagawa **16**
Shinjuku **12–13**
  hotels **66–7**
  restaurants **104–5**
Shinjuku Imperial Garden **13, 97**
Shinjuku ni-chome **13, 58–9**
Shomben Yokocho **12–13**
Shinto **114**
Shiodome City Centre **19**
Shiseido Gallery **75**
Shitamachi Museum **80**
Shoto Museum of Art **76**
Sompo Japan Art Museum **78**
Stream of Starlight Ferris wheel **19**
Suidobashi **20**
Sumo Museum **25**

Sunshine City **14**
Suntory Hall **9, 83**
Suntory Museum of Art **8, 31, 75**
Sword Museum **78**

T

Tabi Museum **81**
Takashimaya department store **7, 109**
Takashimaya Times Square **13**
Takuzosu-Inari Shrine **20, 117**
TEPCO electric Energy Museum **76**
telephones **4, 45**
Tenjin Shrine **21, 117**
Tobacco and Salt Museum **77**
Toguri Museum of Art **77**
Tokei-ji Temple **27, 128**
Tokyo Broadcasting System Tower **8, 9**
Tokyo Dome and City **20, 40**
Tokyo Disneyland **5, 26, 41**
Tokyo International Forum **7, 123**
Tokyo Metropolitan Art Museum **23, 80**
Tokyo Metropolitan Children's Hall **11, 38**
Tokyo Metropolitan Festival Hall **22**
Tokyo Metropolitan Photography Museum **17, 79**
Tokyo Metropolitan Teien Art Museum **17, 79**
Tokyo Museum of Contemporary Art **25, 81**
Tokyo National Museum **23, 81**
Tokyo Opera City **12, 78**
Tokyo Tower **9, 31**

Tokyo Wonder Site **20, 80**
Tomioka Hachiman-gu-jinja Shrine **25, 119**
Tosho-gu Shrine **22, 118**
tourist offices **45**
Tsukiji Fish Market **5, 18**
Tsukudajima **18**
Tsurugaoka Hachiman-gu Shrine **27**
21_21 Design Sight **8, 76**

U, V, W

Ueno **22–3**
Ueno Park **22, 99**
Ueno Zoo **22, 40**
Ukiyo-e Ota Memorial Museum of Art **11, 77**
Venus Fort **19, 110**
Wako Building **7, 111**
Watari-um Museum **11, 77**
water quality **42–3**
Western classical music **82–4**

Y, Z

Yanaka **22, 23**
Yanaka Cemetery **23**
Yanaka Ginza **23**
Yasukuni-jinja Shrine **6, 114–15**
Yebisu Garden Place **17**
Yokohama **26, 131**
Yokohama Museum of Art **26**
Yurakucho **7**
Yushima **20–21**
Yushima Tenjin Shrine **117**
Zojo-ji Temple **9, 115**
Zoshigaya Cemetery **15**
Zoshigaya Museum **15, 78**

Insight Smart Guide: Tokyo

Text by: Dan Grunebaum

Edited by: Jet Leng, Scarlett O'hara, Sarah Sweeney and Joanna Potts

Proofread and indexed by: Neil Titman

Photography by: Alamy 53B; Beezer 89; Corbis 53T, 59B&T, 60BL&BR, 61TL,TR,M, 83T; Click Chicago/APA 27B, 50; Francis Dorai/APA 4B, 5BL; Fotolibra 2T; Hara Museum of Contemporary Art 78; Istock-photo 43T, 73T, 120, 122; Japan National Tourist Organisation 27T, 56B&T, 70, 71, 72, 81B, 93B&T, 101B, 103,105; Jean Kuggler 119; Stephen Mansfield/APA 5TR, 55T, 128, 129B&T, 130, 131; National Museum of Western Art 80, 81T; Ming Tang-Evans/APA 2B, 3B, 4T,5TL&ML&B, 6, 7B&T, 9B, 10, 11B&T, 13B&T, 14, 15, 17B, 20, 21T, 22, 24, 25B, 29, 31B, 33B, 33T, 34, 35, 36, 37T&B, 42, 43B, 45B, 445T, 46, 47BL&BR, 47T, 48B&T, 49, 54, 57, 58, 75B&T, 85L&R, 86, 87T, 89, 90, 91, 92, 96, 97B&T, 100L&R, 101T, 108, 109B&T, 110, 111, 112, 113, 116L. 118, 124, 125B,

126L&R, 132–133; Richard Nowitz/APA 9T, 17T, 19B&T, 21B, 23B&T, 25T, 30, 31T, 51B&T, 60T, 74, 88, 98, 99, 107L&R, 115B&T, 116R, 117, 121B&T, 123, 125T, 127; Zoshigaya Missionary Museum 79

Picture Manager: Steven Lawrence

Maps: Steve Ramsey

Series Editor: Jason Mitchell

First Edition 2008

© 2008 Apa Publications GmbH & Co. Verlag KG Singapore Branch, Singapore.

Printed in Singapore by Insight Print Services (Pte) Ltd

Worldwide distribution enquiries:

Apa Publications GmbH & Co. Verlag KG (Singapore Branch) 38 Joo Koon Road, Singapore 628990; tel: (65) 6865 1600; fax: (65) 6861 6438

Distributed in the UK and Ireland by:

GeoCenter International Ltd

Meridian House, Churchill Way West, Basingstoke, Hampshire RG21 6YR; tel: (44

1256) 817 987; fax: (44 1256) 817 988

Distributed in the United States by:

Langenscheidt Publishers, Inc.

36–36 33rd Street 4th Floor, Long Island City, New York 11106; tel: (1 718) 784 0055; fax: (1 718) 784 0640l

Contacting the Editors

We would appreciate it if readers would alert us to errors or outdated information by writing to:

Apa Publications, PO Box 7910, London SE1 1WE, UK; fax: (44 20) 7403 0290; e-mail: insight@apaguide.co.uk

No part of this book may be reproduced, stored in a retrieval system or transmitted in any form or by any means (electronic, mechanical, photocopying, recording or otherwise), without prior written permission of Apa Publications. Brief text quotations with use of photographs are exempted for book review purposes only. Information has been obtained from sources believed to be reliable, but its accuracy and completeness, and the opinions based thereon, are not guaranteed.

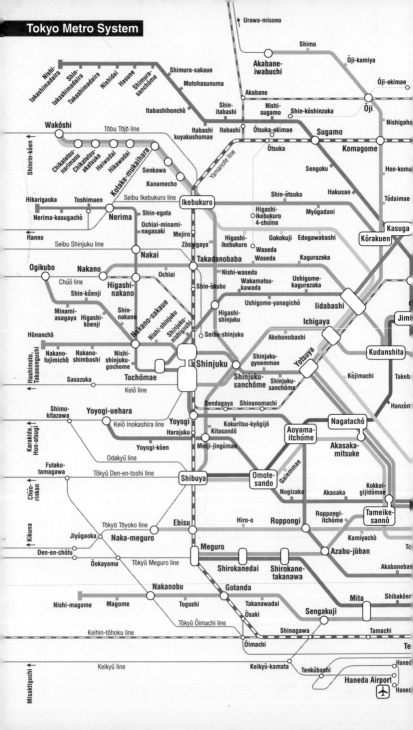

Tokyo Metro System